Illustration of Grayson's Theorem: A front propagating with speed equal to curvature must collapse smoothly to a point

This book is an introduction to level set methods, which are powerful numerical techniques for analyzing and computing interface motion in a host of settings. They rely on a fundamental shift in how one views moving boundaries, rethinking the natural geometric Lagrangian perspective and exchanging it for an Eulerian, initial value partial differential equation perspective. The resulting numerical techniques can be used to track three-dimensional complex fronts that can develop sharp corners and change topology as they evolve.

The book begins with an introduction to the dynamics of moving curves and surfaces. Next, efficient computational techniques for approximating viscosity solutions to partial differential equations are developed, using the numerical technology from hyperbolic conservation laws. This builds the framework for both general level set methods for arbitrary moving fronts, and fast marching techniques for solving special cases arising from stationary Hamilton-Jacobi equations. A large collection of applications are given, including examples from physics, chemistry, fluid mechanics, combustion, image processing, material science, fabrication of microelectronic components, computer vision, and control theory.

This book will be a useful resource for mathematicians, applied scientists, practicing engineers, computer graphic artists, and anyone interested in the evolution of boundaries and interfaces.

CAMBRIDGE MONOGRAPHS ON
APPLIED AND COMPUTATIONAL
MATHEMATICS

Series Editors
P. G. CIARLET, A. ISERLES, R. V. KOHN, M. H. WRIGHT

3 Level Set Methods:

**Evolving interfaces in geometry,
fluid mechanics, computer vision,
and materials science**

The Cambridge Monographs on Applied and Computational Mathematics reflects the crucial role of mathematical and computational techniques in contemporary science. The series publishes expositions on all aspects of applicable and numerical mathematics, with an emphasis on new developments in this fast-moving area of research.

State-of-the-art methods and algorithms as well as modern mathematical descriptions of physical and mechanical ideas are presented in a manner suited to graduate research students and professionals alike. Sound pedagogical presentation is a prerequisite. It is intended that books in the series will serve to inform a new generation of researchers.

Also in this series:

Level Set Methods

Evolving interfaces in geometry, fluid mechanics, computer vision, and materials science

J. A. Sethian

University of California, Berkeley

CAMBRIDGE
UNIVERSITY PRESS

Published by the Press Syndicate of the University of Cambridge
The Pitt Building, Trumpington Street, Cambridge CB2 1RP
40 West 20th Street, New York, NY 10011-4211, USA
10 Stamford Road, Oakleigh, Melbourne 3166, Australia

First Published 1996

Printed in the United States of America

Library of Congress Catalog-in-Publication Data available

A catalog record for this book is available from the British Library

ISBN 0-521-57202-9 Hardback

Contents

List of Illustrations

Acknowledgements

The beginning of this work on level set methods can be found in the author's dissertation on the theory and numerics of propagating interfaces, under the direction of Alexandre Chorin at the University of California at Berkeley. The work continued through a National Science Foundation Postdoctoral Fellowship at the Lawrence Berkeley National Laboratory (LBNL) and the Courant Institute of Mathematical Sciences. I am grateful for all of this support.

The time-dependent level set formulation of these ideas on interface motion was co-authored with S. J. Osher, with whom I have had a thoroughly enjoyable collaboration, and was supported in part by the Applied Mathematical Sciences section of the Department of Energy through the Mathematics Department at LBNL, and by NSF awards through the University of California at Berkeley Mathematics Department. Since the introduction of this technique, there have been many contributors and practitioners. An early application of these techniques, due to D. Chopp, concerns minimal surfaces and includes the genesis of ideas about narrow banding and complex boundary conditions. The work on level set methods for crystal growth and dendritic solidification is joint with J. Strain, and capitalizes on his boundary integral formulation of the equations of motion. The realization that level set techniques can be applied to shape recovery is due to R Malladi. The application of these techniques to image processing began with the work of L. Alvarez, J. M. Morel, and P. L. Lions, and the work of S. Osher and L. Rudin; the work on image processing presented here relies heavily on those contributions. The application of the techniques to problems in combustion and fluid interfaces discussed within is joint work with C. Rhee, J. Zhu and L. Talbot, and the work on adaptive mesh refinement relies on the work of B. Milne. On the theoretical side, the work of C. Evans, J.

Spruck, Y. Chen, Y. Giga, and S. Goto has been instrumental in analyzing and applying the level set approach to problems in geometric evolution.

The fast marching formulation of the level set method presented here was greatly enchanced by the contributions of D. Adalsteinsson and R. Malladi. The application of level set techniques to problems in etching and deposition is joint work with D. Adalsteinsson. The analysis of non-convex Hamiltonians in certain applications benefitted from the contributions of O. Hald. The work on fast marching methods for geodesics is joint with R. Kimmel. In the development of the application of level set techniques to particular areas, the author is grateful for the insights and contributions of O. Hald, R. Kimmel, P. Leon, J. Rey, and K. Toh.

Many other people have contributed to the current state-of-the-art of level set methods, including B. Bence, E. Fatemi, E. Harabetian, B. Merriman, P. Smereka, and M. Sussman. Their work has advanced both the theory and practice of level set methods, particularly in the important areas of fluid interfaces and multiple junctions. I would like to thank W. Coughran for suggesting the application of level set methods to semiconductor simulations, A. Neureuther for many helpful discussions on etching and deposition, B. Knight for encouragement in the application of level set methods to fluid interface problems, C. Ritchie and G. Chiang for their insightful suggestions about shape recovery in medical imaging, T. Baker for helpful conversations about grid generation, L. Gray for suggesting the application of level set methods to material sintering, and C. Evans for his valuable comments on the initial manuscript. I also wish to thank students in Math 273 during fall 1995 for their insightful comments, critical reviewing, and careful suggestions.

At the risk of repetition, I owe a tremendous debt to the talents of D. Adalsteinsson, D. Chopp, R. Kimmel, R. Malladi, B. Milne and J. Zhu; they are the driving force behind much of the work presented here.

Finally, I would like to thank Alan Harvey of Cambridge University Press for his thoughtful suggestions and enthusiasm for this project. His calm hand and unfailing humor have made this a pleasure, and his guidance, wise counsel, and wisdom were invaluable.

Berkeley, California 1996.

Introduction

Propagating interfaces occur in a wide variety of settings, and include ocean waves, burning flames, and material boundaries. Less obvious boundaries are equally important, and include shapes against backgrounds, hand-written characters, and iso-intensity contours in images.

The goal of this book is to unify these ideas and to provide a general framework for modeling the evolution of boundaries. The aim is to provide computational techniques for tracking moving interfaces, and to give some hint of the flavor and breadth of applications. The work includes examples from physics, chemistry, fluid mechanics, combustion, image processing, material science, fabrication of microelectronic components, computer vision, control theory, and seismology. The intended audience is mathematicians, applied scientists, practicing engineers, computer graphic artists, and anyone interested in the evolution of boundaries and interfaces.

Our perspective comes from a large and rapidly growing body of work on level set methods, which are techniques for understanding, analyzing, and computing interface motion in a host of settings. At their core, they rely on a shift in how one views moving boundaries; rethinking the Lagrangian geometric perspective and exchanging it for an Eulerian, initial value partial differential equation. Several advantages result from this new view of propagating interfaces:

- First, from a theoretical/mathematical point of view, some complexities of front motion are illuminated, in particular, the role of singularities, weak solutions, shock formation, entropy conditions, and topological change in the evolving interface.
- Second, from a numerical perspective, natural and accurate ways of computing delicate quantities emerge, including the ability to build

high order advection schemes, compute local curvature in two and three dimensions, track sharp corners and cusps, and handle subtle topological changes of merger and breakage.

- Third, from an implementation point of view, since the approach is based on an initial value partial differential equation, robust schemes result from numerical parameters set at the beginning of the computation. The error is thus controlled by

  (i) The order of the numerical method,
  (ii) The grid spacing Δh,
  (iii) The time step Δt.

- Fourth, computational adaptivity, both in meshing and in computational labor, is possible, as is a clear path to parallelism.
- Fifth, in the case of monotonically advancing fronts under certain speed laws, fast methods based on merging narrow band techniques and sorting algorithms can be devised.

This book surveys what we hope is an illustrative subset of past and current applications of the level set method. We assume that the reader is not necessarily an expert in some of the details required to develop these schemes, and aim to include the necessary theory and details to provide implementation guidelines.

Outline

This book is divided into four parts. Part I focuses on the theoretical aspects of front propagation and on the formulation of the level set methodology. Part II concentrates on numerical and implementation aspects of level set methods. Part III is devoted to viscosity solutions of Hamilton–Jacobi equations and fast marching methods for static Hamilton–Jacobi equations, and Part IV surveys some application areas.

In **Part I**, Chapter 1 begins with a general statement of the problem of a moving interface, and discusses the mathematical theory of curve/surface motion, including the growth/decay of total variation, singularity development, entropy conditions, weak solutions, and shocks in the dynamics of moving fronts. This leads to both the time-dependent level set algorithm and the static Hamilton–Jacobi formulation, which are presented in Chapter 2.

Part II presents numerical aspects of the time-dependent level set formulation; this material has been developed in a collection of papers that are referred to within. Chapter 3 begins with an overview of traditional methods for tracking interfaces, including string methods and cell methods, and makes a first attempt at solving the level set equation. The failure of this first attempt stems from the relationship between front propagation and hyperbolic conservation laws, and is the subject of Chapter 4.

Chapters 5, 6, and 7 present the algorithms, numerical/theoretical analysis, and implementation details of level set methods. Putting implementation issues first, Chapter 5 provides detailed descriptions of the algorithms used to approximate the level set equations. Chapter 6 covers some implementation details, including fast methods, adaptive mesh refinement, and parallel implementations. Finally, Chapter 7 surveys some recent extensions of the level set method, including versions for masking, multiple regions, and triple points.

Part III is devoted to viscosity solutions of Hamilton–Jacobi equations and a class of fast marching methods for computing solutions to static Hamilton–Jacobi equations. Under certain propagation rules, a front can be recast in this stationary framework. Chapter 8 begins with theory of viscosity solutions of Hamilton–Jacobi equations, and sketches the underlying mathematical analysis behind the algorithms. Chapter 9 begins with a discussion of upwind, heapsort-based schemes for rapidly solving the Eikonal equation, and follows with the construction of approximation schemes for general static Hamilton–Jacobi equations.

Part IV focuses on applications of both the time-dependent level set method and the fast marching level method to a large collection of problems. Here, the intent is to touch on some problems that have been modeled using level set methods, both to show the breadth of possible applications and to serve as guideposts for further applications. Chapter 10 begins with some pure geometry problems, including curve/surface shrinkage, the existence of self-similar surfaces, and sintering. Chapter 11 extends this work and shows how level set techniques can be used in grid generation, giving many examples of how these techniques can be used to generate body-fitted logical rectangular grids around complex bodies in two and three dimensions. Chapter 12 moves to image processing, and views images as collections of iso-intensity contours; by constructing a suitable speed law, these contours can be allowed to propagate in a way that both removes noise and enhances desired regions.

Chapter 13 continues with the construction of minimal surfaces, which is naturally performed by viewing a minimal surface as a constrained front, evolving under mean curvature until a final steady-state is achieved.

Chapter 14 considers physical interface problems in which the front is driven both by local effects and by underlying fluid mechanical/transport terms; the applications include flame propagation in turbulent combustion, crystal growth and dendritic solidification, and two-phase flow problems. Chapter 15 focuses on medical imaging, and discusses the transformation of level set techniques into versions of active contours that, when driven by gradients in the image field, extract desired shapes from images.

In Chapter 16, applications of the fast marching level set approach are given, including problems in shape-offsetting, lithography development, shape-from-shading, paths on networks, geodesics on surfaces, seismic travel times, and robotic navigation under constraints; applications based on both the Eikonal equation and more complex static Hamilton–Jacobi equations are considered.. Finally, in Chapter 17, attention is turned to etching and deposition in the microfabrication of semi-conductor components.

By no means is this an exhaustive review of the work that exists on level methods. A large body of work has been reluctantly skipped in the effort to keep this book of reasonable length. The interested reader is referred to a wide range of simulations developed using this methodology; references will be given throughout the text. The goal of this book is to provide windows into these techniques as guides for further interface studies.

The author can be reached at sethian@math.berkeley.edu; a web page may be found at http://math.berkeley.edu/~sethian/level_set.html.

Part I
Equations of Motion for Moving Interfaces

Part I presents some theoretical analysis of propagating interfaces. The goal in this section is to analyze stability and smoothness of solutions as a function of initial shapes and speed functions, and to discuss Lagrangian and Eulerian formulations of the equations of motion.

1

Theory of Front Evolution

Outline: *We formulate the equations of motion of a propagating curve, study its stability, and show that corners (singularities in the curvature) can develop as the front evolves. We then show that these corners are analogous to shocks in the solutions of hyperbolic conservation laws, and that a solution can be naturally constructed beyond the appearance of these corners by exploiting the notion of an entropy-satisfying weak solution.*

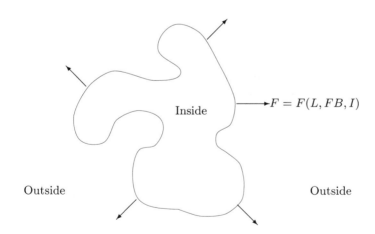

Fig. 1.1. Curve propagating with speed F in normal direction

Consider a boundary, either a curve in two dimensions or a surface in three dimensions, separating one region from another. Imagine that this curve/surface moves in a direction normal to itself (where the normal direction is oriented with respect to an inside and an outside) with a known speed function F. The goal is to track the motion of this interface as it evolves. We are concerned only with the motion of the interface in its normal direction; throughout, we shall ignore motions of the interface in its tangential direction.

The speed function F, which may depend on many factors, can be written as:

$$F = F(L, G, I), \tag{1.1}$$

where

- $L=$ *Local properties* are those determined by local geometric information, such as curvature and normal direction.
- $G=$ *Global properties of the front* are those that depend on the shape and position of the front. For example, the speed might depend on integrals along the front and/or associated differential equations. As a particular case, if the interface is a source of heat that affects diffusion on either side of the interface, and a jump in the diffusion in turn influences the motion of the interface, then this would be characterized as front-based argument.
- $I=$ *Independent properties* are those that are independent of the shape of the front, such as an underlying fluid velocity that passively transports the front.

Much of the challenge in interface problems comes from producing an adequate model for the speed function F; this is a separate issue independent of the goal of an accurate scheme for advancing the interface based on the model for F. In this chapter, it is assumed that the speed function F is known. The goal of Part IV is to formulate good models for F for a collection of applications.

Given F and the position of an interface, the object is to track the evolution of the interface. The first focus is to develop the necessary theory to understand the interplay between the speed function F and the shape of the interface. For ease of discussion, we turn to the simplest case of a closed curve propagating in the plane.

1.1 Fundamental formulation

Let γ be a simple, smooth, closed initial curve in R^2, and let $\gamma(t)$ be the one-parameter family of curves generated by moving $\gamma(t)$ along its normal vector field with speed F. Here, F is the given scalar function.

Thus $\vec{n} \cdot \vec{x}_t = F$, where $\vec{x}$ is the position vector of the curve, t is time, and $\vec{n}$ is the unit normal to the curve.

A natural approach is to consider a parameterized form of the equations. In this discussion, we further restrict ourselves and imagine that the speed function F depends only on the local curvature κ of the curve, that is, $F = F(\kappa)$.[1] Let the position vector $\vec{x}(s, t)$ parameterize γ at time t, where $0 \leq s \leq S$, and assume periodic boundary conditions $\vec{x}(0, t) = \vec{x}(S, t)$. The curve is parameterized so that the interior is on the left in the direction of increasing s (see Figure 1.2). Let $\vec{n}(s, t)$ be

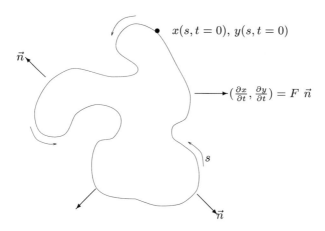

Fig. 1.2. Parameterized view of propagating curve

the parameterization of the outward normal and $\kappa(s, t)$ be the parameterization of the curvature. The equations of motion can then be written in terms of individual components $\vec{x} = (x, y)$ as

$$x_t = F\left[\frac{y_{ss}x_s - x_{ss}y_s}{(x_s^2 + y_s^2)^{3/2}}\right]\left(\frac{y_s}{(x_s^2 + y_s^2)^{1/2}}\right),$$

$$y_t = -F\left[\frac{y_{ss}x_s - x_{ss}y_s}{(x_s^2 + y_s^2)^{3/2}}\right]\left(\frac{x_s}{(x_s^2 + y_s^2)^{1/2}}\right),$$

(1.2)

where we have used the parameterized expression $\kappa = \frac{y_{ss}x_s - x_{ss}y_s}{(x_s^2 + y_s^2)^{3/2}}$ for the curvature inside the speed function $F(\kappa)$. This is a "Lagrangian" representation because the range of $(x(s, t), y(s, t))$ describes the moving front.

---

[1] Curvature is a vector that points in the direction normal to the curve; since we are always taking the speed function in the normal direction, we shall abuse notation and write, for example, $F = -\kappa$.

1.2 Total variation: Stability and the growth of oscillations

What happens to oscillations in the initial curve as it moves? We summarize the argument in Sethian [170] showing that the decay of oscillations depends only on the sign of F_κ at $\kappa = 0$. The metric $g(s, t)$, which measures the "stretch" of the parameterization, is given by $g(s, t) = (x_s^2 + y_s^2)^{1/2}$. Define the total oscillation (also known as the total variation) of the front

$$Var(t) = \int_0^S |\kappa(s, t)| g(s, t) ds. \tag{1.3}$$

Without the absolute value sign around the curvature, this evaluates to 2π; the absolute value sign means that $Var(t)$ measures the amount of "wrinkling". Our goal is to find out if this wrinkling increases or decreases as the front evolves; two possible flows are shown in Figure 1.3.

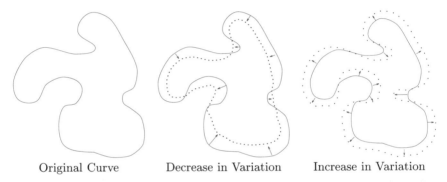

Original Curve   Decrease in Variation   Increase in Variation

Fig. 1.3. Change in variation $Var(t)$

Differentiation of both the curvature and the metric with respect to time, together with substitution from equation (1.2) produces[2] the corresponding evolution equations for the metric and curvature, namely

$$\kappa_t = -g^{-1}(F_s g^{-1})_s - \kappa^2 F \tag{1.4}$$

$$g_t = g\kappa F. \tag{1.5}$$

(Here, g^{-1} is $1/g$, not the inverse.) Now, suppose we have a non-convex initial curve moving with speed $F(\kappa)$, and suppose the moving curve stays smooth. Evaluation of the time change of the total variation in the solution yields the following [170];

---

[2] With some work!

Theorem Consider a front moving along its normal vector field with speed $F(\kappa)$, as in equation (1.2). Assume that the initial curve $\gamma(0)$ is simple, smooth, and non-convex, so that $\kappa(s,0)$ changes sign. Assume that F is twice differentiable, and that $\kappa(s,t)$ is twice differentiable for $0 \leq s \leq S$ and $0 \leq t \leq T$. Then, for $0 \leq t \leq T$,

- if $F_\kappa \leq 0$ ($F_\kappa \geq 0$) wherever $\kappa = 0$, then

$$\frac{dVar(t)}{dt} \leq 0 \quad \left(\frac{dVar(t)}{dt} \geq 0 \right). \qquad (1.6)$$

- if $F_\kappa < 0$ ($F_\kappa > 0$) and $\kappa_s \neq 0$ wherever $\kappa = 0$, then

$$\frac{dVar(t)}{dt} < 0 \quad \left(\frac{dVar(t)}{dt} > 0 \right). \qquad (1.7)$$

Remarks:
The proposition states that if $F_\kappa < 0$ wherever $\kappa = 0$, then the total variation decreases as the front moves and the front "smooths out", that is, the energy of the front dissipates. The front is assumed to remain smooth in the interval $0 \leq t \leq T$ (the curvature is assumed to be twice differentiable); in the next section, we discuss what happens if the front ceases to be smooth and develops a corner. In the special case that $\gamma(t)$ is convex for all t, Proposition 1 is trivial, since $Var(t) = \int_0^S \kappa g ds = 2\pi$.

Proof of Proposition:
The argument breaks the integral up into sections where the curvature changes sign. The differentiation of the total variation with respect to time can then be passed to each section of the curve, and using the expressions for the time derivative of both the metric and the curvature, and noting the change in sign of the curvature κ from one section to the next, the decay or growth in the total variation can be evaluated. A full proof may be found in [170].

Two important cases can easily be checked. A speed function $F(\kappa) = 1 - \epsilon\kappa$ for $\epsilon > 0$ has derivative $F_\kappa = -\epsilon$, and hence the total variation decays. Conversely, a speed function of the form $F(\kappa) = 1 + \epsilon\kappa$ yields a positive speed derivative, and hence oscillations grow. We shall see that the sign of the curvature term in this case corresponds to the backwards heat equation, and hence must be unstable.

1.3 The role of entropy conditions and weak solutions

The above theorem assumes that the front stays smooth. In all but the simplest flows, this smoothness is soon lost. For example, consider the periodic initial cosine curve

$$\gamma(0) = (-s, [1 + \cos 2\pi s]/2) \tag{1.8}$$

propagating with speed $F(\kappa) = 1$. (The parameterization is chosen so that the inside is on the left as we move in the direction of increasing s.) The exact solution to this problem at time t may be constructed by advancing each point of the front in its normal direction a distance t. In terms of our parameterization of the front, the solution is given by

$$x(s, t) = \frac{y_s(s, t = 0)}{(x_s^2(s, t = 0) + y_s^2(s, t = 0))^{1/2}} \; t + x(s, t = 0), \tag{1.9}$$

$$y(s, t) = \frac{-x_s(s, t = 0)}{(x_s^2(s, t = 0) + y_s^2(s, t = 0))^{1/2}} \; t + y(s, t = 0). \tag{1.10}$$

As can be seen in Figure 1.4, the front develops a sharp corner in finite time. Once this corner develops, the normal is ambiguously defined, and it is not clear how to continue the evolution. Thus, beyond the formation of the discontinuity in the derivative, we will need a *weak solution*, so called because the solution weakly satisfies the definition of differentiability.[3]

How can a solution be continued beyond the formation of the singularity in the curvature corresponding to the corner in the front? A reasonable answer depends on the nature of the interface under discussion. If the interface is viewed as a geometric curve evolving under the prescribed speed function, then one possible weak solution is the "swallowtail" solution formed by letting the front pass through itself; this solution is in Figure 1.4(a). This solution is in fact the one given by equations (1.9) and (1.10); the lack of differentiability at the center point does not destroy the solution, since the exact solution is written only in terms of the initial data.

---

[3] A solution is said to be a "weak solution" of a differential equation if it satisfies an integral formulation of the equation. The advantage to such a formulation is that it may not require the same degree of differentiability of a potential solution, and thus may allow more general solutions. As an example, consider the one-dimensional wave equation $u_t = u_x$. A solution to this equation must be differentiable in both x and t. However, if we integrate both sides of the equation with respect to x over the interval $[a, b]$, we then obtain $\frac{d}{dt} \int u \, dx = u(b) - u(a)$, which does not require that the solution be differentiable in space. Weak solutions will be discussed in more detail in Chapter 4.

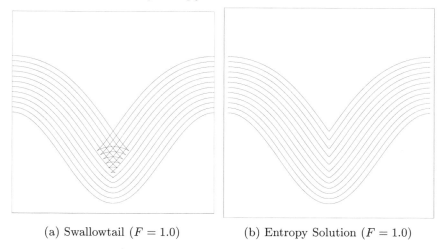

(a) Swallowtail ($F = 1.0$)   (b) Entropy Solution ($F = 1.0$)

Fig. 1.4. Cosine curve propagating with unit speed

However, suppose the moving curve is regarded as an interface separating two regions. From a geometrical argument, the front at time t should consist of only the set of all points located a distance t from the initial curve. (This is known as the Huyghen's principle construction; see [170].) Roughly speaking, we want to remove the "tail" from the "swallowtail". Figure 1.4(b) shows this alternate weak solution. Another way to characterize this weak solution is through the following "*entropy condition*" posed by Sethian [167, 170]: If the front is viewed as a burning flame, then *once a particle is burnt it stays burnt.* Careful adherence to this stipulation produces the Huyghen's principle construction.

What does this "entropy condition" have to do with the notion of "entropy"? While the answer will be made more precise in Chapter 4, an intuitive answer is as follows. Entropy refers to the organization of information. In general terms, an entropy condition is one that says that no new information can be created during the evolution of the problem. Furthermore, the example shows that once the entropy condition is invoked, some information about the initial data is lost. Indeed, the entropy condition "once a particle is burnt, it stays burnt" means that once a corner has developed, the solution is no longer reversible. The problem cannot be run "backwards" in time; if we try to do so, the initial data will not be retrieved. Thus, some information about the solution is forever lost.

As further illustration, consider the case of a V-shaped front propa-

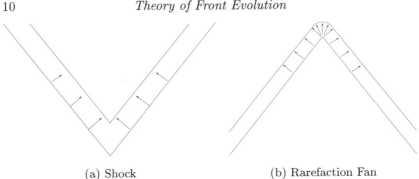

(a) Shock   (b) Rarefaction Fan

Fig. 1.5. Front propagating with unit normal speed

gating normal to itself with unit speed ($F = 1$). In Figure 1.5(a), the
point of the front is downwards; as the front moves inwards with unit
speed, a "shock" propagates upwards as the front pinches off, and an
entropy condition is required to select the correct solution to stop the
solution from being multiple-valued. Conversely, in Figure 1.5(b), the
point of the front is upwards; in this case the unit normal speed results
in a circular fan that connects the left state with slope $+1$ to the right
state, which has slope -1.

It is important to summarize a key point in the above discussion.
The choice of weak solution given by our entropy condition [4] rests on
the perspective that the front separates two regions, and the assumption
that one is interested in tracking the progress of one region into the other.
Considerable confusion about the level set perspective, to be discussed
below, has resulted from a misunderstanding of the basic assumption
inherent in this model.

1.4 Effects of curvature: The viscous limit and the link to hyperbolic conservation laws

Now, consider a speed function of the form $F = 1 - \epsilon\kappa$, where ϵ is
a constant. The modifying effects of the term $\epsilon\kappa$ are profound, and in
fact pave the way towards constructing accurate numerical schemes that
adhere to the correct entropy condition.

Following Sethian [170], the curvature evolution equation given by

---

[4] Strictly speaking, this notion of an entropy condition will have meaning only for
a propagating graph; a more precise formulation will be given in Chapter 8. We
shall be somewhat loose with our use of the word "entropy" until then.

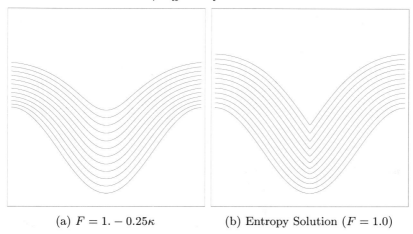

(a) $F = 1. - 0.25\kappa$ (b) Entropy Solution ($F = 1.0$)

Fig. 1.6. Entropy solution is the limit of viscous solutions

equation (1.4) can be rewritten as

$$\kappa_t = \epsilon\kappa_{\alpha\alpha} + \epsilon\kappa^3 - \kappa^2, \tag{1.11}$$

where the second derivative of the curvature κ is taken with respect to arclength α. This is a reaction-diffusion equation; the drive toward singularities due to the reaction term ($\epsilon\kappa^3 - \kappa^2$) is balanced by the smoothing effect of the diffusion term ($\epsilon\kappa_{\alpha\alpha}$). Indeed, with $\epsilon = 0$, whose solution was given above, we have a pure reaction equation $\kappa_t = -\kappa^2$, and the developing corner can be seen in the exact solution $\kappa(s, t) = \kappa(s, 0)/(1 + t\kappa(s, 0))$. This is singular in finite t if the initial curvature is anywhere negative.

Consider again the cosine front given in equation (1.8) and the speed function $F(\kappa) = 1 - \epsilon\kappa$, $\epsilon > 0$. As the front moves, the trough at $s = n + 1/2$ is sharpened by the negative reaction term (because $\kappa < 0$ at such points) and smoothed by the positive diffusion term (see Figure 1.6(a)). For $\epsilon > 0$, it can be shown (see [170, 144]) that the moving front stays C^∞. The entropy solution to this problem when $F = 1$ is shown in Figure 1.6(b).

The central observation, key to the level set approach, is the following link:

Consider the above propagating cosine curve and the two solutions:

- $X^\epsilon_{\text{curvature}}(t)$, *obtained by evolving the initial front with* $F_\epsilon = 1 - \epsilon\kappa$,
- $X_{\text{constant}}(t)$, *obtained with speed function* $F = 1$ *and the entropy condition.*

Then, at any time T,

$$\lim_{\epsilon \to 0} X^\epsilon_{\text{curvature}}(T) = X_{\text{constant}}(T). \qquad (1.12)$$

Thus, the limit of motion with curvature, known as the "viscous limit", is the entropy solution for the constant speed case.

Why is this known as the viscous limit; in fact, what does this have to do with viscosity? To see why viscosity is an appropriate name, we turn to the link between propagating fronts and hyperbolic conservation laws. The following material, taken from [170], is presented in considerably more depth in Chapter 4; the ideas are presented here as motivation.

An equation of the form

$$u_t + [G(u)]_x = 0 \qquad (1.13)$$

is known as a hyperbolic conservation law. A simple example is Burger's equation, given by

$$u_t + uu_x = 0, \qquad (1.14)$$

which describes the motion of a compressible fluid in one dimension. The solution to this equation can develop discontinuities, known as "shocks", where the fluid undergoes a sudden expansion or compression. These shocks (for example, a sonic boom) can arise from arbitrarily smooth initial data; they are a function of the equation itself. Fluid viscosity appears as a diffusive term on the right-hand side, namely,

$$u_t + uu_x = \epsilon u_{xx}, \qquad (1.15)$$

and this second derivative acts like a smoothing term and stops the development of such shocks; it can be shown that for $\epsilon > 0$, the solution must remain smooth for all time.

What does this have to do with our propagating front equation? Consider the initial front given by the graph of $f(x)$, with f and f' periodic on $[0, 1]$, and suppose that the propagating front remains a function for all time. Let ψ be the height of the propagating function at time t, thus $\psi(x, 0) = f(x)$. The tangent at (x, ψ) is $(1, \psi_x)$. Referring to Figure 1.7,

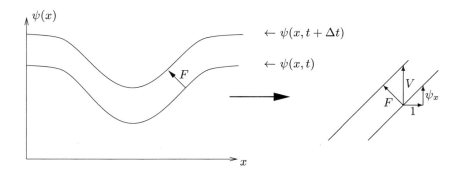

Fig. 1.7. Variables for propagating graph

the change in height V in a unit time is related to the speed F in the tangent direction by

$$\frac{V}{F} = \frac{(1 + \psi_x^2)^{1/2}}{1}, \tag{1.16}$$

and thus the equation of motion becomes

$$\psi_t = F(1 + \psi_x^2)^{1/2}. \tag{1.17}$$

Using the speed function $F(\kappa) = 1 - \epsilon\kappa$ and the formula $\kappa = -\psi_{xx}/(1 + \psi_x^2)^{3/2}$ yields

$$\psi_t - (1 + \psi_x^2)^{1/2} = \epsilon\frac{\psi_{xx}}{1 + \psi_x^2}. \tag{1.18}$$

This is a partial differential equation with a first order time and space derivative on the left side, and a second order term on the right. Differentiating both sides of this equation yields an evolution equation for the slope $u = d\psi/dx$ of the propagating front, namely,

$$u_t + [-(1 + u^2)^{1/2}]_x = \epsilon\left[\frac{u_x}{1 + u^2}\right]_x. \tag{1.19}$$

Thus, as shown in Sethian [171], the derivative of the curvature-modified equation for the changing height ψ looks like some form of a viscous hyperbolic conservation law with $G(u) = (1 + u^2)^{1/2}$ for the propagating slope u. Hyperbolic conservation laws of the above form have been studied in considerable detail; in fact, our entropy condition is equivalent to the one for propagating shocks in hyperbolic conservation laws. To recap, the role of curvature for a propagating graph is analogous to the role of viscosity in the hyperbolic conservation law of the evolution of its slope. Our next goal will be to explain and exploit the theory and technology of numerical solutions of hyperbolic conservation laws to devise accurate numerical schemes to solve the equation of motion for propagating fronts.

However, the discussion so far is limited by the fact that the equation of motion given by equation (1.17) refers only to fronts that remain graphs as they move. The above ideas must be extended to include propagating fronts that are not easily written as functions. This is the basis for the time-dependent level set method introduced by Osher and Sethian [144].

2

The Level Set Formulation

Outline: *We derive two level set formulations of the equations of motion, and discuss the advantages of this Eulerian perspective.*

2.1 Formulation

Given a closed $(N-1)$-dimensional hypersurface $\Gamma(t=0)$, we now produce an *Eulerian* formulation for the motion of the hypersurface $\Gamma(t)$ propagating along its normal direction with speed F, where F can be a function of arguments such as the curvature, normal direction, etc. The main idea of the level set methodology is to embed this propagating interface as the zero level set of a higher dimensional function ϕ. Define ϕ as follows. Let $\phi(x, t=0)$, where x is a point in R^N, be defined by

$$\phi(x, t=0) = \pm d, \qquad (2.1)$$

where d is the distance from x to $\Gamma(t=0)$, and the plus (minus) sign is chosen if the point x is outside (inside) the initial hypersurface $\Gamma(t=0)$. Thus, we have an initial function $\phi(x, t=0) : R^N \to R$ with the property that

$$\Gamma(t=0) = [x|\phi(x, t=0) = 0]. \qquad (2.2)$$

The goal is to produce an equation for the evolving function $\phi(x, t)$ that contains the embedded motion of $\Gamma(t)$ as the level set $\phi = 0$. To do so, let $x(t)$ be the path of a point on the propagating front. That is, $x(t=0)$ is a point on the initial front $\Gamma(t=0)$, and $x_t \cdot n = F(x(t))$ with the vector x_t normal to the front at $x(t)$. The stipulation that the zero level set of the evolving function ϕ always match the propagating hypersurface means that

$$\phi(x(t), t) = 0. \qquad (2.3)$$

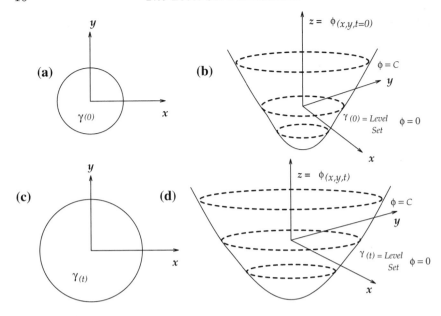

Fig. 2.1. Propagating circle

By the chain rule,

$$\phi_t + \nabla\phi(x(t), t) \cdot x'(t) = 0. \tag{2.4}$$

Since F supplies the speed in the outward normal direction, then $x'(t) \cdot n = F$ where $n = \nabla\phi/|\nabla\phi|$ and this yields an evolution equation for ϕ, namely,

$$\phi_t + F|\nabla\phi| = 0, \tag{2.5}$$

$$\text{given} \quad \phi(x, t = 0). \tag{2.6}$$

This is the level set equation introduced by Osher and Sethian [144]. For certain forms of the speed function F, one obtains a standard Hamilton–Jacobi equation.

To help illustrate these ideas, Figure 2.1 (taken from [175]), shows the outward propagation of an initial curve and the accompanying motion of the level set function ϕ.

In Figure 2.1(a), an initial circle is shown, together with the circle at a later time in Figure 2.1(c). Figure 2.1(b) shows the associated initial position of the level set function ϕ, and Figure 2.1(d) shows this function at a later time. We refer to this as an *Eulerian formulation* because the underlying coordinate system remains fixed.

2.2 Aspects of the level set formulation

There are several desirable aspects of this Eulerian Hamilton–Jacobi formulation.

- First, the evolving function $\phi(x,t)$ always remains a function as long as F is smooth. However, the level surface $\phi = 0$, and hence the propagating hypersurface $\Gamma(t)$, may change topology, break, merge, and form sharp corners as the function ϕ evolves.
- Second, because $\phi(x,t)$ remains a function as it evolves, numerical simulations may be developed using a discrete grid in the domain of x and substitution of finite difference approximations for the spatial and temporal derivatives. For example, using a uniform mesh of spacing h, with grid nodes (i,j), and employing the standard notation that ϕ_{ij}^n is the approximation to the solution $\phi(ih, jh, n\Delta t)$, where Δt is the time step, one might write

$$\frac{\phi_{ij}^{n+1} - \phi_{ij}^n}{\Delta t} + (F)|\nabla_{ij}\phi_{ij}^n| = 0. \tag{2.7}$$

Here, a forward difference scheme in time has been used, and $|\nabla_{ij}\phi_{ij}^n|$ represents some appropriate finite difference operator for the spatial derivative. Thus, an explicit finite difference approach is possible. The construction of correct entropy-satisfying approximations to the difference operator is the subject of Part II.

- Third, intrinsic geometric properties of the front are easily determined from the level function ϕ. For example, at any point of the front, the normal vector is given by

$$\vec{n} = \frac{\nabla \phi}{|\nabla \phi|}, \tag{2.8}$$

and the curvature of each level set is easily obtained from the divergence of the unit normal vector to the front, i.e.,

$$\kappa = \nabla \cdot \frac{\nabla \phi}{|\nabla \phi|} = \frac{\phi_{xx}\phi_y^2 - 2\phi_x\phi_y\phi_{xy} + \phi_{yy}\phi_x^2}{(\phi_x^2 + \phi_y^2)^{3/2}}. \tag{2.9}$$

- Finally, there are no significant changes required to follow fronts in three space dimensions. By extending the array structures and gradient operator, propagating surfaces are easily handled.

To illustrate, consider once again the problem of a front propagating with speed $F(\kappa) = 1 - \epsilon\kappa$. Figure 2.2 shows two cases of a propagating initial triple sine curve. For ϵ small (Figure 2.2(a)), the troughs sharpen up. For ϵ large (Figure 2.2(b)), parts of the boundary with high values of positive curvature initially move downwards, and concave parts of the front move quickly up.

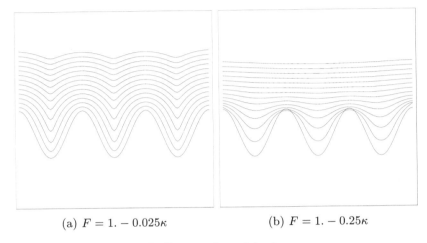

(a) $F = 1. - 0.025\kappa$ (b) $F = 1. - 0.25\kappa$

Fig. 2.2. Propagating triple sine curve

To summarize the discussion so far:

(i) A front propagating at a constant speed can form corners as it evolves; at such points, the front is no longer differentiable and a weak solution must be constructed to continue the solution.

(ii) The correct weak solution, motivated by viewing the front as an evolving interface separating two regions, comes by means of an entropy condition.

(iii) A front propagating at a speed that depends on its curvature does not form corners and stays smooth for all time. Furthermore, as the dependence on curvature vanishes, the limit of this motion is the entropy-satisfying solution obtained for the constant speed case.

(iv) If the propagating front remains a graph as it moves, there is a direct link between the equation of motion and one-dimensional hyperbolic conservation laws. The role of curvature in a propagating front is analogous to the role of viscosity in the equations of viscous compressible fluid flow.

(v) By embedding the motion of a hypersurface as the zero level set of a higher dimensional function, an initial value partial differential equation can be obtained that extends the above to include arbitrary curves and surfaces moving in two and three space dimensions.

2.3 Theoretical aspects of the level set formulation

While methods for numerically approximating moving fronts have received much attention, the theoretical analysis of moving curves and surfaces has been a subject of considerable importance in its own right. The work of Gage [72], Gage and Hamilton [73], and Grayson [78], discussed later in this book, provided some groundbreaking analysis of flow of curves under the curvature, leading to the beautiful result that a closed curve shrinking under its curvature collapses smoothly to a point.

Using a very different approach, Brakke [26] applied varifold theory to the problem of a hypersurface moving under its curvature, and in doing so provided a wide-ranging perspective for these problems, including cases in which the results were not necessarily smooth.

Since its introduction, there has been considerable theoretical analysis of the Eulerian level set view of interface motion and its relation to other perspectives on front propagation. The flame/entropy model from [167] served as the basis for theoretical analysis by Barles [15]. The embedding of the front as a higher dimensional function meant that some of the issues of topological change and corner formation, as discussed above, could be studied in a more natural manner. Furthermore, the transformation of a geometry problem into an initial value partial differential equation meant that the considerable technology available in that area, including regularity of solutions, viscous solutions of Hamilton–Jacobi equations, and tools for analyzing existence and uniqueness, could be applied in this geometrical setting.

Using the above level set approach, Evans and Spruck [64, 65, 66, 67] and Chen, Giga, Goto, and Ishii [40, 75, 76] performed detailed analysis of curvature flow in a series of papers. They exploited much of the work on viscosity solutions of partial differential equations developed over the past 15 years (see Lions [116]), which itself was inspired by the corresponding work applied to hyperbolic conservation laws. These papers examined the regularity of curvature flow equations, pathological cases, and the link between the level set perspective and the varifold approach of Brakke. These papers opened up a series of investigations into further issues; we also refer the interested reader to Evans, Soner, and Souganidis [63], and Ilmanen [90, 91].

2.4 A stationary level set formulation

In the above level set equation

$$\phi_t + F|\nabla\phi| = 0 \tag{2.10}$$

the position of the front is given by the zero level set of ϕ at a time t. Suppose attention is restricted to the particular case of a front propagating with a speed F that is either always positive or always negative. In this case, the level set formulation can be converted from a time-dependent partial differential equation to a stationary one in which time has disappeared. We now describe a stationary level set formulation which is at the core of the fast marching method discussed later.

Imagine the two-dimensional case in which the interface is a propagating curve, and suppose we graph the evolving zero level set above the xy plane. That is, let $T(x, y)$ be the time at which the curve crosses the point (x, y). The surface $T(x, y)$ then satisfies the equation

$$|\nabla T|F = 1. \tag{2.11}$$

In Figure 2.3, we show a circular front expanding with unit speed, together with the surface $T(x, y)$. Equation (2.11) simply says that the

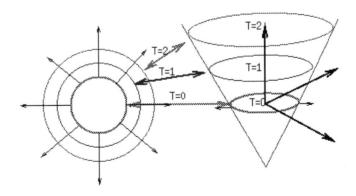

Fig. 2.3. Plot of stationary level set surface $T(x, y)$

gradient of arrival time surface is inversely proportional to the speed of the front. This is a Hamilton–Jacobi equation, and the recasting of a front motion problem into a stationary one is common in a variety of applications; see [68, 69]. If the speed function F depends only on position, we get the well-known Eikonal equation. If the speed function is always positive[1] then the crossing time surface $T(x, y)$ is single-valued.

To summarize,

- In the time-dependent level set equation, the position of the front Γ at time t is given by the zero level set of ϕ at time t; that is $\Gamma(t) = \{(x, y)|\phi(x, y, t) = 0\}$.
- In the stationary level set equation, the position of the front Γ is given by the level set of value t of the function $T(x, y)$; that is $\Gamma(t) = \{(x, y)|T(x, y) = t\}$.

That is, we wish to solve

Level Set Formulation   **Stationary Formulation**

$$\phi_t + F|\nabla\phi| = 0 \qquad\qquad |\nabla T|F = 1$$
$$\text{Front} = \Gamma(t) = \{(x, y)|\phi(x, y, t) = 0\} \quad \text{Front} = \Gamma(t) = \{(x, y)|T(x, y) = t\}$$
$$\text{Applies for arbitrary } F \qquad\qquad \text{Requires } F > 0$$

$$(2.12)$$

Both cases require an "entropy-satisfying" approximation to the gradient term. In this next section, we discuss appropriate approximations for this term, leading to schemes for both the time-dependent and stationary level set formulations. The goal is to develop the necessary theory and numerics to accurately approximate the two initial value partial differential equations.

---

[1] Or, conversely, always negative.

Part II

Approximation Schemes for Level Set Methods

In this part, we discuss the numerical approximation of the level set equation for tracking evolving interfaces and develop basic algorithms and underlying details.

3

Traditional Techniques for Tracking Interfaces

Outline: *Before focusing on the level set equation itself, we consider other numerical methods for tracking interfaces. We then make a first attempt at solving the level set equation using a central difference scheme, and show why this fails to capture the correct weak solution.*

3.1 Marker/string methods

A standard approach to modeling moving fronts comes from discretizing the Lagrangian form of the equations of motion given in equation (1.2). In this technique, the parameterization is discretized into a set of marker particles whose position at any time is used to reconstruct the front. This approach is known under a variety of names, including marker particle techniques, string methods, and nodal methods. In two dimensions, the front may be reconstructed as line segments; in three dimensions, triangles might be chosen.

This approach can be illustrated through a straightforward scheme that constructs a simple difference approximation to the Lagrangian equations of motion. Divide the parameterization interval $[0, S]$ into M equal intervals of size Δs, yielding $M + 1$ mesh points $s_i = i\Delta s$, $i = 0, \ldots, M$, as shown in Figure 3.1. Divide time into equal intervals of length Δt. The image of each mesh point $i\Delta s$ at each time step $n\Delta t$ is a marker point (x_i^n, y_i^n) on the moving front. The goal is a *numerical algorithm* that produces new values (x_i^{n+1}, y_i^{n+1}) from the previous positions; we follow the discussion in [170].

First, approximate parameter derivatives at each marker point by using neighboring mesh points. Central difference approximations based

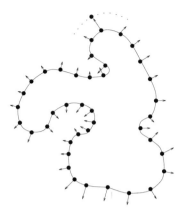

Fig. 3.1. Discrete parameterization of curve

on Taylor series (see Chapter 4) yield

$$\frac{dx_i^n}{ds} \approx \frac{x_{i+1}^n - x_{i-1}^n}{2\Delta s}, \qquad \frac{dy_i^n}{ds} \approx \frac{y_{i+1}^n - y_{i-1}^n}{2\Delta s}, \tag{3.1}$$

$$\frac{d^2 x_i^n}{ds^2} \approx \frac{x_{i+1}^n - 2x_i^n + x_{i-1}^n}{\Delta s^2}, \qquad \frac{d^2 y_i^n}{ds^2} \approx \frac{y_{i+1}^n - 2y_i^n + y_{i-1}^n}{\Delta s^2}. \tag{3.2}$$

Similarly, time derivatives may be replaced by the forward difference approximations

$$\frac{dx_i^n}{dt} \approx \frac{x_i^{n+1} - x_i^n}{\Delta t}, \qquad \frac{dy_i^n}{dt} \approx \frac{y_i^{n+1} - y_i^n}{\Delta t}. \tag{3.3}$$

Substitution of these approximations into the equations of motion given by equation (1.2) produces the scheme

$$(x_i^{n+1}, y_i^{n+1}) = (x_i^n, y_i^n) + \Delta t \ F(\kappa_i^n) \ \frac{(y_{i+1}^n - y_{i-1}^n, -(x_{i+1}^n - x_{i-1}^n))}{((x_{i+1}^n - x_{i-1}^n)^2 + (y_{i+1}^n - y_{i-1}^n)^2)^{1/2}}, \tag{3.4}$$

where

$$\kappa_i^n = 4 \frac{(y_{i+1}^n - 2y_i^n + y_{i-1}^n)(x_{i+1}^n - x_{i-1}^n) - (x_{i+1}^n - 2x_i^n + x_{i-1}^n)(y_{i+1}^n - y_{i-1}^n)}{((x_{i+1}^n - x_{i-1}^n)^2 + (y_{i+1}^n - y_{i-1}^n)^2)^{3/2}}. \tag{3.5}$$

Using the periodicity of the curve, this is a complete recipe for updating the positions of the particles from one time step to the next.

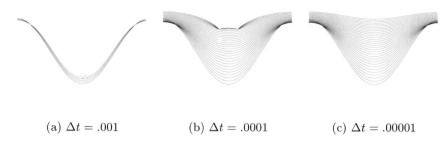

(a) $\Delta t = .001$ (b) $\Delta t = .0001$ (c) $\Delta t = .00001$

Fig. 3.2. Marker particle solution to $F = 1 - .25\kappa$

Observe that the fixed discretization interval Δs has dropped out of the above expression. Consequently, as marker particles come together, quotients on the right-hand side of equation (3.4) approach zero over zero, yielding a very sensitive calculation. The computed curvature can change drastically from one particle to the next because of small and unavoidable errors in the positions.

This unstable growth of small errors is seen in a marker particle scheme to follow the initial cosine curve propagating with speed $1 - \epsilon\kappa$, $\epsilon = .25$. Since $\epsilon > 0$, the exact solution is always smooth, and the entropy condition is not required. Fifty marker points are used, together with a time step of $\Delta t = 0.001$. Although the propagating front begins to sharpen as expected (see Figure 3.2(a)), oscillations soon develop, which grow uncontrollably. These oscillations result from a feedback cycle: (1) small errors in approximate marker positions produce (2) local variations in the computed derivatives leading to (3) variation in the computed particle velocities causing (4) uneven advancement of markers, which yields (5) larger errors in approximate marker positions. Within a few time steps, the small oscillations in the curvature have grown wildly and the computed solution becomes unbounded. Figure 3.2(a) shows the calculation until the computer program stops running.

Suppose we try to increase accuracy by using a smaller time step. Figure 3.2(b) and Figure 3.2(c) show calculations with $\Delta t = .0001$ and $\Delta t = .00001$, respectively. With time step $\Delta t = .0001$, once again, the solution becomes unstable, and the smooth decay of the trough is not seen. Only in the finest case of a time step of $\Delta t = .00001$ is the solution acceptable. This is because for any $\epsilon > 0$, there is a bound on the minimum distance between particles, and thus a small enough time step does exist to ensure stability. However, note that with a smaller value of ϵ, the marker trajectories come closer together, and a smaller time step is required for stability. As an example, with value of $\epsilon = .1$ (a large value, when one considers the role of curvature to be similar to that of surface tension), the time step required for stability is $\Delta t = .000005$! This is absurdly small for any practical calculation.

What can be done? Typically, there are three remedies:

- "Smooth" the speed function so that the marker points stay far enough apart to allow a reasonable time step.
- Redistribute marker particles according to arclength (or a related quantity) every few time steps so that they stay far enough apart.
- Invent some filtering technique to remove noise (oscillations) in the particle positions as they develop.

While all three techniques are used in practice, none are appealing. They all boil down to the same thing; they alter the equations of motion in non-obvious ways. Significant amounts of smoothing may be required to ensure a practical time step. Thus, one has chosen to sacrifice the most interesting propagation characteristics, such as front sharpening and curvature singularities, simply in order to keep the calculation alive. similarly, calculation of arclength adds a smoothing term to the speed function and is difficult to analyze. The computed solution may be far from the desired one; in the worst case, time and effort are spent solving an unrelated problem.

The situation is even bleaker in the limiting case $\epsilon = 0$. As discussed above, a solution forms a sharp corner, and an entropy condition must be invoked to produce a reasonable weak solution beyond the formation of the singularity. However, a marker particle approach does not "know" about the necessary entropy condition, because it attempts to track a Lagrangian formulation in which the swallowtail solution given in Figure 1.4(a) is the correct weak solution. In Figure 3.3 we show a marker particle solution that incorporates the swallowtail solution.

No time step, no matter how small, can correctly produce a scheme that incorporates our entropy condition from [167]. In fact, in this case the equations for the markers themselves reduce to a linearly unstable hyperbolic system; see [144]. From an algorithmic point of view, markers must somehow be eliminated from the discretization as information (total variation) is removed. This corresponds to deleting the "tail" from the swallowtail as discussed earlier; in some arenas, this procedure is called "de-looping". While there have been reasonable procedures for

Fig. 3.3. Marker particle solution to swallowtail under $F = 1$

doing so in two dimensions [85], de-looping in three dimensions is not for the fainthearted, and such codes can break down in complex situations.

The above problems with marker particle/Lagrangian methods refer to stability and local singularity problems. Topological changes in the moving front are also problematic. Consider two separate regions of substance growing in a plane. Suppose these patches merge and the boundary becomes a single curve. It is difficult to produce a systematic way of removing those markers that no longer sit on the actual boundary. The bookkeeping of removing, redistributing, and connecting markers is complex, and an arduous task for higher dimensional interface problems.

To summarize, Lagrangian approximations provide numerical schemes based on a parameterized description of the moving front. They can be highly accurate for small-scale motions of interfaces because of their adaptive nature. However, under complex motions of the interface, they can suffer from instability and topological limitations because they follow a local representation of the front, rather than a global one that takes into account the proper entropy conditions and weak solutions.

3.2 Volume-of-fluid techniques

A significantly different approach to front motion is provided by volume-of-fluid techniques, introduced by Noh and Woodward [140] and based instead on an Eulerian view. Since their introduction, they have appeared in a variety of forms and been re-introduced under many names, such as the "cell method" and the "method of partial fractions".

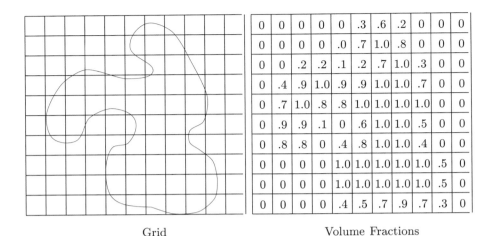

Grid		Volume Fractions								

0	0	0	0	0	.3	.6	.2	0	0	0
0	0	0	0	.0	.7	1.0	.8	0	0	0
0	0	.2	.2	.1	.2	.7	1.0	.3	0	0
0	.4	.9	1.0	.9	.9	1.0	1.0	.7	0	0
0	.7	1.0	.8	.8	1.0	1.0	1.0	1.0	0	0
0	.9	.9	.1	0	.6	1.0	1.0	.5	0	0
0	.8	.8	0	.4	.8	1.0	1.0	.4	0	0
0	0	0	0	1.0	1.0	1.0	1.0	1.0	.5	0
0	0	0	0	1.0	1.0	1.0	1.0	1.0	.5	0
0	0	0	0	.4	.5	.7	.9	.7	.3	0

Fig. 3.4. Volume-of-fluid method

The basic idea (see Figure 3.4) is as follows. Imagine a fixed grid on the computational domain, and assign values to each grid cell based on the fraction of that cell containing material inside the interface. Given a closed curve, we assign a value of unity to those cells completely inside this curve, a cell value of zero to those completely outside, and a fraction between 0 and 1 to cells that straddle the interface, based on the amount of the cell inside the circle.

The idea, then, is to rely solely on these "cell fractions", shown in Figure 3.4, to characterize the interface location. Approximation techniques are then used to reconstruct the front from these cell fractions. The original Noh and Woodward algorithm was known as "SLIC", for "Simple Line Interface Calculation", and reconstructed the front as either a vertical or a horizontal line.

In order to evolve the interface, the idea is to update the cell fractions on this fixed grid to reflect the progress of the front. To do so, suppose that we wish to advect the front passively under the transport velocity $\vec{u}$ (here, this is not a speed normal to the front but merely a transport term). Noh and Woodward provide a methodology in which the value in each cell is updated under this transport velocity in each coordinate direction by locally reconstructing the front and then exchanging material in neighboring cells under this motion. After completing coordinate sweeps, one has produced new cell fractions at the next time step cor-

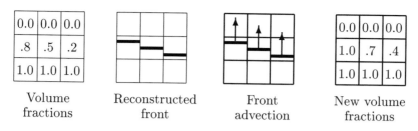

0.0	0.0	0.0
.8	.5	.2
1.0	1.0	1.0

Volume fractions

Reconstructed front

Front advection

0.0	0.0	0.0
1.0	.7	.4
1.0	1.0	1.0

New volume fractions

Fig. 3.5. Reconstruction and advection of volume fractions

responding to the updated front. In Figure ??, we show the advection of an interface under a simple vertical velocity field $\vec{u} = (0, 1)$.

Since its introduction, many elaborate reconstruction techniques have been developed over the years to include pitched slopes and curved surfaces; see Chorin [47], Hirt and Nichols [86], and Lafaurie, Nardone, Scardovelli, Zaleski, and Zanetti [107]. The accompanying accuracy depends on the sophistication of the reconstruction and the "advection sweeps" which advance the material. Some of the most elaborate and accurate versions of these schemes to date are due to Puckett [152].

The original SLIC algorithm was designed for transport under an advection velocity field in a given direction that depended on the location of the front, but not the local shape/orientation of the front. A valuable extension to volume-of-fluid techniques was developed by Chorin [47], who provided a way of applying these methods to a speed function given in a direction normal to the front. As we have seen in Part I, under such motion corners and cusps can occur, and an entropy condition must be invoked to provide the correct weak solution beyond the occurrence of singularities. Chorin did so by relying on a Huyghen's principle construction, which considers each spot on the front as a point source; the envelope of the influence of these sources gives the new position of the front. By advancing the front in enough directions to approximate this point source, this construction satisfies our entropy condition and provides the correct weak solution. This version of SLIC was used in a collection of flame propagation/combustion calculations; see Chorin [47], Ghoniem, Chorin, and Oppenheim [74], and Sethian [169].

It is the Eulerian nature of volume-of-fluid techniques that allows them to avoid many of the time step and topological change problems that plague marker particle methods. As such, they can be quite useful. However, there are some drawbacks:

- Such techniques are inaccurate; a large number of cells are often required to obtain reasonable results, owing to the difficult task of approximating fronts through the volume fractions.
- Evolution under complex speed functions is problematic. There are often significant grid effects (that is, one can discern from the results the underlying orientation of the grid). These problems become worse in the presence of directional velocity fields, such as those under non-convex laws and sharp anisotropy.
- Calculation of intrinsic geometric properties of the front, such as curvature and normal direction, may be inaccurate.
- Considerable work may be required to develop higher order versions of such schemes; in higher dimensions, accurate calculations of mean and Gaussian curvature, especially at saddle points, are difficult to perform.

Nonetheless, such schemes can be powerful, and we refer the interested reader to Puckett [152].

3.3 A first attempt at constructing an approximation to the gradient

We now turn to the level set equation itself, and attempt to construct a numerical approximation. Recall that the goal is to solve the level set equation given in equation (2.5) by

$$\phi_t + F|\nabla \phi| = 0, \tag{3.6}$$

$$\phi(x, t = 0) \quad \text{given.} \tag{3.7}$$

The marker particle method discretizes the front. The volume-of-fluid (VOF) method divides the domain space into cells that contain fractions of material. The level set method divides the domain into grid points that hold approximations to the values of the level set function ϕ. Thus, the grid values give the height of a surface above the domain, and slicing this surface by the xy plane extracts the zero level set corresponding to the front.

Another way to look at this is to say that each grid point contains the value of the level set function at that point. Thus, there is an entire family of contours, only one of which is the zero level set (see Figure 3.6). Rather than move each of the contours in a Lagrangian fashion, one stands at each grid point and updates its value to correspond to the

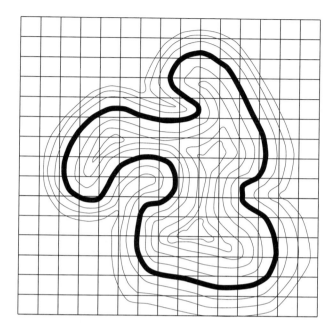

Fig. 3.6. Dark line is zero level set corresponding to front

motion of the surface, thus producing a new contour value at that grid point.

What is a suitable approximation to the level set equation? One possible numerical approach comes from studying the simpler case of an evolving curve whose position can always be described as the graph of a function. The equation of motion for this case was given in equation (1.17) as shown in Figure 1.7, namely,

$$\psi_t = F(1 + \psi_x^2)^{1/2}. \tag{3.8}$$

Just as was done in the Lagrangian case, one might try to approximate the solution by replacing all spatial derivatives with central differences and the time derivative with a forward difference. However, it is easy to see that such an algorithm may not work. Let $F(\kappa) = 1$ and consider the initial value problem

$$\psi_t = (1 + \psi_x^2)^{1/2}, \tag{3.9}$$

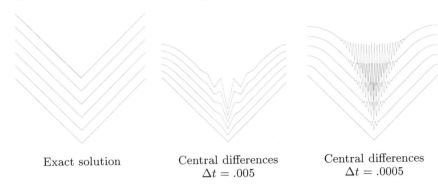

| Exact solution | Central differences
$\Delta t = .005$ | Central differences
$\Delta t = .0005$ |

Fig. 3.7. Central difference approximation to level set equation

$$\psi(x,0) = f(x) = \left\{ \begin{array}{ll} 1/2 - x & x \le 1/2 \\ x - 1/2 & x > 1/2 \end{array} \right\}. \qquad (3.10)$$

The initial front is a "V" formed by rays meeting at $(1/2, 0)$. Invoking the entropy condition, the solution at any time t is the set of all points located a distance t from the initial "V". To construct a central difference numerical scheme, divide the interval $[0, 1]$ into $2M - 1$ points, and form the approximation to the spatial derivative ψ_x in equation (3.9) given by

$$\psi_t \approx= \frac{\psi_i^{n+1} - \psi_i^n}{\Delta t} = \left[1 + \left[\frac{\psi_{i+1}^n - \psi_{i-1}^n}{2\Delta x} \right]^2 \right]^{1/2}. \qquad (3.11)$$

Since $x_M = 1/2$, by symmetry, $\psi_{M+1} = \psi_{M-1}$, thus the right-hand side is 1. However, for all $x \ne 1/2$, ψ_t is correctly calculated to be $\sqrt{2}$, since the graph is linear on either side of the corner and thus the central difference approximation is exact. Note that this has nothing to do with the size of the space step Δx or the time step Δt. *No matter how small we take the numerical parameters, as long as we use an odd number of points the approximation to ψ_t at $x = 1/2$ gets no better.* It is simply due to the way in which the derivative ψ_x is approximated. Figure 3.7 shows results using this scheme, with the time derivative ψ_t replaced by a forward difference scheme.

It is easy to see what has gone wrong. In the exact solution, $\psi_t = \sqrt{2}$ for all $x \ne 1/2$. This should also hold at $x = 1/2$ where the slope is not defined; the Huyghen's construction sets $\psi_t(x = 1/2, t)$ equal to $\lim_{x \to 1/2} \psi_t$. Unfortunately, the central difference approximation chooses a different (and, for our purpose, wrong) limiting solution. It sets the undefined slope ψ_x equal to the average of the left and right slopes. As the calculation progresses, this miscalculation of the slope propagates outwards from the spike as wild oscillations. Eventually, these oscillations cause blowup in the code.

It is clear that more care must be taken in formulating an algorithm. Schemes are required that approximate the gradient term $|\nabla\phi|$ in a way that correctly accounts for the entropy condition. This is the topic of the next chapter.

4

Hyperbolic Conservation Laws

Outline: *The aim of this chapter is to develop numerical schemes for solving the level set equation*

$$\phi_t + F|\nabla\phi| = 0 \tag{4.1}$$

that also satisfy the entropy condition; as we have seen, this must be enforced to select the correct weak solution corresponding to the viscous limit of the associated curvature-driven equation. This chapter is a review of the basics of the technology for hyperbolic conservation laws, and may be skipped if the reader is already acquainted with this material; good reviews may be found in the monograph by Lax [109] and the book by LeVeque [112]. The goal at the end of this chapter is an understanding of basic schemes for approximating a single hyperbolic conservation law. To motivate such schemes, we start with a simple, first order, constant coefficient wave equation.

4.1 The linear wave equation

4.1.1 First order schemes

Consider the one-dimensional wave equation

$$u_t(x,t) + u_x(x,t) = 0 \quad \text{with} \quad u(x,0) = f(x). \tag{4.2}$$

The exact solution to this equation can be given in terms of the initial data, namely $u(x,t) = f(x-t)$, which can be checked by differentiation using the chain rule. This means that the solution u at any point x at time t is the same as the value of the initial data at the point $x-t$ on the x axis. Another way to say this is that the solution u is constant on lines of slope 1 drawn in the x,t plane (see Figure 4.1).

36

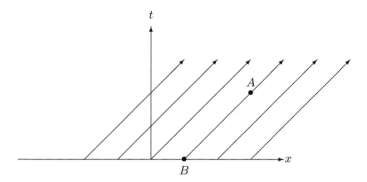

Fig. 4.1. Solution to $u_t = -u_x$ is constant along lines of slope 1

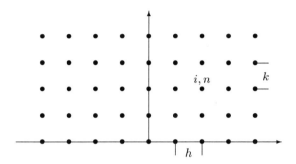

Fig. 4.2. Computational grid

Consider a point A located in the x, t plane (see Figure 4.1). The solution at point A can be found by tracing back along a line with slope 1 to the point B on the initial line; hence we say that the *domain of dependence* of the point A is the point B. Conversely, the *domain of influence* of point B is the set of all points on the line with slope 1 emanating from B. We shall now see that these curves in x, t space, which give rise to domains of dependence and influence and are known as *characteristics*, are important in constructing appropriate numerical schemes.

In order to approximate the equation $u_t + u_x = 0$, we begin by following the standard approach and discretize $x - t$ space into a collection of grid points so that $\Delta x = h$ and $\Delta t = k$. Thus every grid point can be represented by the coordinate pair (i, n) corresponding to the point (ih, nk) (see Figure 4.2).

Consider now the various ways of approximating the equation $u_t +$

$u_x = 0$, which we write as $u_t = -u_x$. We begin with the left side of the equation. The solution u at time $t + \Delta t = t + k$ can be expanded as a Taylor series in time around the point (x,t); thus we have

$$u(x, t + k) = u(x, t) + u_t(x, t)k + O(k^2), \tag{4.3}$$

where the expression $O(k^2)$ includes all terms of order k^2 or higher. Rearranging the above, we can then write the time derivative at the point (x, t) as

$$u_t = \frac{u(x, t + k) - u(x, t)}{k} + O(k). \tag{4.4}$$

This is known as a *forward difference* operator for the time variable, because we have used a Taylor series ahead in time to approximate u_t. Define the notation

$$D^{+t}u \equiv \frac{u(x, t + k) - u(x, t)}{k}. \tag{4.5}$$

We can then rewrite equation (4.4) as

$$u_t = D^{+t}u + O(k). \tag{4.6}$$

What about the spatial derivative u_x? Define the operators

$$\begin{aligned} D^{+x}u &\equiv \tfrac{u(x+h,t)-u(x,t)}{h}, \\ D^{-x}u &\equiv \tfrac{u(x,t)-u(x-h,t)}{h}, \\ D^{0x}u &\equiv \tfrac{u(x+h,t)-u(x-h,t)}{2h}. \end{aligned} \tag{4.7}$$

Forward, backward, or centered Taylor series expansions in x for the value u around the point (x, t) can be constructed to produce the following approximations:

$$u_x = D^{+x}u + O(h), \quad u_x = D^{-x}u + O(h), \quad u_x = D^{0x}u + O(h^2). \tag{4.8}$$

Although the last is a more accurate approximation, we will see in a later section that accuracy is not the only concern. Nonetheless, the above leads to three distinct schemes for computing the solution to the equation $u_t = -u_x$. Let u_i^n be the computed solution at time nk at the point ih. Then, dropping the error terms, we have

(i) *Forward Scheme:* $u_i^{n+1} = u_i^n - kD^{+x}u_i^n$.
(ii) *Backward Scheme:* $u_i^{n+1} = u_i^n - kD^{-x}u_i^n$.
(iii) *Centered Scheme:* $u_i^{n+1} = u_i^n - kD^{0x}u_i^n$.

Which scheme is better? The answer lies in the previous discussion about domains of dependence and characteristics. Recall that the solution u is constant along lines of slope 1 in the $x - t$ plane; this means that information is propagating from the left to the right. Consider now the three difference operators:

- D^{+x}: to compute the new value at i, uses information at i and $i + 1$; hence information for the solution propagates from right to left.
- D^{-x}: to compute the new value at i, uses information at i and $i - 1$; hence information for the solution propagates from left to right.
- D^{0x}: to compute the new value at i, uses information at $i + 1$ and $i - 1$; hence information for the solution propagates from both sides.

From this discussion alone, we can dismiss the forward difference scheme from consideration. The backward scheme is referred to as an *upwind scheme*, because it uses values upwind of the direction of information propagation; clearly, this is highly desirable. Another way to say this is that *"The numerical domain of dependence should contain the mathematical domain of dependence".*

Thus, the backward difference scheme correctly respects the "upwind" nature of the differential equation, and sends information in the direction that correctly matches the differential equation.[1]

4.1.2 Higher order schemes for the linear wave

Can we construct a scheme of higher order space accuracy by trying to knock off more terms in the Taylor series? Using Taylor series and the equation $u_t = -u_x$, we have that

$$u(x, t+k) = u + ku_t + \frac{k^2}{2}u_{tt} + O(k^3) = u - ku_x + \frac{k^2}{2}u_{xx} + O(k^3). \quad (4.9)$$

---

[1] At issue here is the "stability" of a scheme, that is, what it does to small errors in the initial data. A more precise way to analyze the stability is through a "Fourier stability analysis", which is performed by considering a set of discrete grid data as wave numbers of the discrete Fourier transform of some periodic function. Then the differential operators in the scheme are equivalent to algebraic operations on the data, and an "amplification factor" can be derived that shows how energy in a particular wave number (that is, data at a particular grid point) is amplified from one time step to the next. Stability is examined by finding those values for the time step and space step such that the amplification factor is less than unity; if such a condition is satisfied, then small errors in the solution cannot grow uncontrollably.

Thus, this suggests the scheme

$$u_i^{n+1} = u_i^n - kD^{0x}u_i^n + \frac{k^2}{2}D^{+x-x}u_i^n. \qquad (4.10)$$

(Here, the notation $D^{+x-x}u_i^n$ is the centered approximation to the second derivative given by $D^{+x-x}u \equiv \frac{u(x+h,t)-2u(x,t)+u(x-h,t)}{h^2}$.) This scheme is known as *Lax–Wendroff*, and is second order.

The last term in the Lax–Wendroff looks like a diffusion term. In fact, it can be thought of as replacing the solution to the first order wave equation $u_t = -u_x$ with the solution to the advection-diffusion equation

$$u_t = -u_x + \frac{k}{2}u_{xx}, \qquad (4.11)$$

where the size of the smoothing second derivative term depends on the time step. This, in fact, is very closely related to the discussion in Chapter 1; a second order smoothing term can dissipate oscillations in the solution, and as the numerical method is refined, the scheme converges to the correct solution to the original problem.

Why wouldn't one always use a higher order scheme? If the solution is smooth for all time, then the additional accuracy offered by a higher order scheme may be worth it. However, in the presence of sharp corners, which are often a natural part of front propagation, preserving corners may be important, and higher order schemes can smooth them out. In order to build schemes that handle corners correctly, we need to focus on schemes that can treat such sharp discontinuities.

4.2 The non-linear wave equation

4.2.1 Discontinuous solutions and shocks

Let's expand the above discussion and examine the wave equation with a non-constant speed. Consider an equation of the form

$$u_t + a(x)u_x = 0, \qquad (4.12)$$

in which the propagation speed depends on a known function $a(x)$ of the position. We can build variations of the above upwind schemes that select the correct direction of the "upwinding" depending on the sign of a. For example, the following scheme, which will in fact suggest some of our later schemes for the non-linear case, chooses the correct direction of the upwinding so that the difference scheme always includes the mathematical domain of dependence:

$$u_i^{n+1} = u_i^n - \Delta t[\max(0, a_i)D^{-x}u_i^n + \min(0, a_i)D^{+x}u_i^n], \qquad (4.13)$$

where here the notation a_i means $a(ih)$. Note how the above scheme works: when the propagation speed a is positive (as it was in our constant coefficient case), information travels from left to right and the backward difference operator is selected; when the wave speed a is negative, the forward difference operator is selected.

However, what about the fully non-linear equation, namely,

$$u_t + uu_x = 0, \qquad (4.14)$$

in which the propagation speed depends on the value of u itself? We first observe that the solution u is still constant along lines that leave the initial line $t = 0$ in x, t space; however, the straight lines are no longer parallel. To see that this is true, consider a particle moving through the xt plane whose position x at any time t is parameterized by s. Then, by the chain rule,

$$\frac{du(x(s), t(s))}{ds} = u_x \frac{dx}{ds} + u_t \frac{dt}{ds} = \frac{dt}{ds}\left[u_t + \frac{dx}{dt}u_x\right]. \qquad (4.15)$$

Now, suppose the trajectory of the particle is set so that $\frac{dx}{dt} = u$; then the right-hand side is zero by the differential equation, and thus $\frac{du}{ds} = 0$. Thus, u is constant along the characteristics, which means that the slope does not change, which means that the characteristics are straight lines.

As an example, consider the above non-linear equation and initial data given by

$$u(x, 0) = \left\{ \begin{array}{ll} 1 & x \leq 0 \\ 1 - x & 0 < x < 1 \\ 0 & x \geq 1 \end{array} \right\}. \qquad (4.16)$$

For this data, the characteristics are straight lines along which the solution u is constant and hence transported; they are shown in Figure 4.3.

At some finite time t_1, the characteristics collide. Each colliding characteristic leaves with slope $\frac{1}{u}$ and carries its own value of u from the initial line. Beyond the collision time it is not clear how to carry the solution ahead uniquely in time. Along the line that marks the collision, known as a shock, the solution discontinuously jumps from the left state (which corresponds to a u value of 1, as seen from the initial data) to the right state of 0.

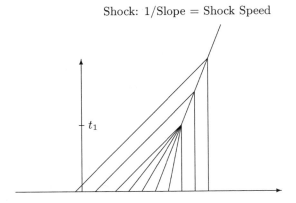

Fig. 4.3. Converging characteristics: Formation of shocks

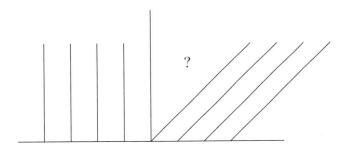

Fig. 4.4. Diverging characteristics: A gap in the solution

If the problem is reversed, the issue is equally unclear. Consider now the same equation with initial data

$$u(x,0) = \left\{ \begin{array}{ll} 0 & x < 0 \\ 1 & x \geq 0 \end{array} \right\}. \tag{4.17}$$

Again, the characteristics are straight lines transporting the solution; the solution is graphed in Figure 4.4.

The empty gap containing the question mark is called a "rarefaction zone" because of its connection with fluid mechanics; the solution must somehow expand from $u = 0$ on the left to $u = 1$ on the right to fill in the rarefied area. What is the proper way to build the solution in the empty gap? One can think of at least two solutions.

One option is to put in a shock, as shown in Figure 4.5.

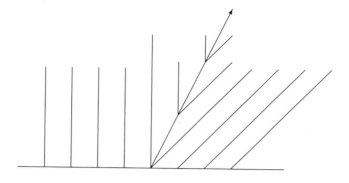

Fig. 4.5. Rarefaction shock

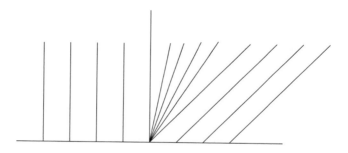

Fig. 4.6. Rarefaction fan

An alternative is to connect the two states by means of a fan, as in Figure 4.6. Which solution is correct? In order to answer that question, consider an associated *viscous non-linear wave equation*

$$u_t + uu_x = \epsilon u_{xx}. \tag{4.18}$$

This is the same non-linear wave equation, with a second derivative added to the right-hand side. This viscous second derivative smooths out sharp corners as they develop, since it acts like the heat equation $u_t = \epsilon u_{xx}$. Thus, the solution stays smooth for all time; see Lax [109] and Chorin and Marsden [49]. We thus *choose* our solution to the non-linear wave equation with zero viscosity to be the one obtained as the limit of the solution to the viscous non-linear equation as the viscosity coefficient ϵ vanishes. Such a solution, which is the vanishing limit of solutions to viscous equations, is known as an *entropy solution*. The word "entropy" here means that the information is not created as the problem unfolds. In terms of our drawings, it means that characteristics flow *into* shocks (Figure 4.3), rather than emanate from them (Figure 4.5). Thus, our goal is to build numerical schemes for the non-linear equation that satisfy this entropy condition.

Before doing so, it is instructive to recall the initial V shapes of Figure 1.5 propagating with constant speed. In the case of an inward pointing corner (that is, the slope on the left was negative and that on the right was positive), a corner formed in the propagating curve, and a shock formed where the normals collided. In the case of an outward pointing corner, where the signs of the slopes were switched, a fan developed as the front moved outwards. Both solutions are limiting solutions of the equation for a front propagating with curvature-dependent speed $(1-\epsilon\kappa)$ as the curvature coefficient ϵ vanishes. This is analogous to the above discussion and is the fundamental reason why we are led to analyzing schemes for shocks and hyperbolic equations.

4.2.2 Weak solutions, flux condition, and approximation schemes

The goal in this section is to design numerical schemes that correctly extend solutions beyond when they are no longer differentiable (known as "weak solutions"). We would like to do so in a way that is physically reasonable and adheres to the entropy condition.

Consider the general form of our first order non-linear hyperbolic equation, that is,

$$u_t + [G(u)]_x = 0. \tag{4.19}$$

If $G(u) = u$, this gives the linear constant coefficient case; if $G(u) = u^2/2$, this gives the non-linear equation $u_t + uu_x = 0$. Integration of both sides of the equation produces

$$
\begin{aligned}
0 &= \int_a^b (u_t + [G(u)]_x)dx \\
&= \int_a^b u_t dx + \int_a^b [G(u)]_x dx \\
&= \frac{d}{dt}\int_a^b u dx + G(u(b,t)) - G(u(a,t)). \tag{4.20}
\end{aligned}
$$

Thus,

$$\frac{d}{dt} \int_a^b u \, dx = G(u(a,t)) - G(u(b,t)). \qquad (4.21)$$

This leads to a physical interpretation of the hyperbolic conservation law given in equation (4.19): the change in the amount of u between a and b is equal to the flux $G(u)$ flowing into the interval. $G(u)$ is referred to as the *flux* function (see Figure 4.7).[2]

We say that u is *conserved* under equation (4.21), since there is a balance between the change of u in the interval $[a, b]$ and the flux of material into the interval. The reason we have re-written equation (4.19) in the conservative form of equation (4.21) is that the latter does not assume that the solution is differentiable with respect to x. Thus, the solution class of equations has been markedly broadened.

Equation (4.19) allows us to compute the speed of the shock in Figure 4.3 as follows. Pick three points x_1, x_*, and x_2 such that at time t the shock is at $(x_*(t), t)$ and $x_1(t) < x_*(t) < x_2(t)$. Let u_1 be the constant initial state on the left of the shock and u_2 be the constant initial state on the right of the shock. Then the shock speed $S = \frac{dx_*}{dt}$ can be found by the following:

$$
\begin{aligned}
\frac{d}{dt} \int_{x_1}^{x_2} u(x,t)dx &= \frac{d}{dt}\left[\int_{x_1}^{x_*(t)} u(x,t)dx + \int_{x_*(t)}^{x_2(t)} u(x,t)dx\right] \\
&= \frac{d}{dt}\left[\int_{x_1}^{x_*(t)} u_1 dx + \int_{x_*(t)}^{x_2} u_2 dx\right] \\
&= \frac{d}{dt}\left[(x_*(t) - x_1)u_1 + (x_2 - x_*(t))u_2\right] \\
&= u_1\frac{dx_*}{dt} - u_2\frac{dx_*}{dt} \\
&= (u_1 - u_2)S. \qquad (4.22)
\end{aligned}
$$

Thus, using the conservation form, we have the *Rankine–Hugoniot* condition for the shock speed, given by

$$S = \frac{G(u_2) - G(u_1)}{u_2 - u_1}. \qquad (4.23)$$

The plan is to construct weak solutions to the conservation form of

---

[2] Typically, everyone uses F for flux instead of G, but we have reserved F for the speed function of propagating interfaces in our level set equation, and it's too late now.

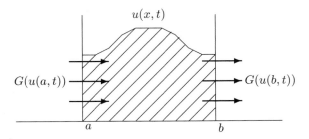

Fig. 4.7. Flux G of substance u into interval $[a, b]$

equation (4.21) of the hyperbolic conservation law that are viscous limits of the equations. This will lead to schemes that satisfy the conservation form of the equation, choose the correct entropy condition by yielding the limit of the viscous equation as the viscosity goes to zero, and stay as smooth away from discontinuities where the solution itself is smooth.

4.2.2.1 The method of artificial viscosity

One straightforward approach is to approximate numerically the viscous version of the equation, that is, to solve the equation

$$u_t + [G(u)]_x = \epsilon u_{xx}, \tag{4.24}$$

using a scheme that performs upwinding in the proper direction and relies on the viscosity term to keep things smooth. Thus, recalling our scheme (equation (4.13)) that picks out the correct direction of the upwinding, for the equation $u_t + uu_x = \epsilon u_{xx}$ we have the scheme

$$u_i^{n+1} = u_i^n - \Delta t[\max(0, u_i)D^{-x}u_i^n + \min(0, u_i)D^{+x}u_i^n + \epsilon D^{-x}D^{+x}u_i^n]. \tag{4.25}$$

While this can work, it is not great, mostly because the amount of required artificial diffusion (a large value for ϵ) causes significant rounding at sharp corners. Nonetheless, it has a long history and is still in use today. As one might guess, many variants exist, mostly those that attempt somehow to detect and invoke smoothing where needed.

4.2.2.2 Less diffusive schemes: Lax–Friedrichs

From a practical point of view, a desirable scheme reduces oscillations and confines shocks to a few grid points (that is, doesn't smear things out). Certainly the above method of artificial viscosity reduces oscillations; our goal now is to limit smearing.

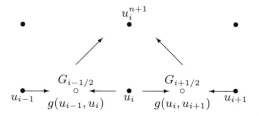

Fig. 4.8. Update of u through numerical flux function g

A further advancement in schemes comes from carefully constructing a method that respects the conservation form of the equation. Consider again the conservation law

$$u_t + [G(u)]_x = 0, \tag{4.26}$$

any solution of which also satisfies an integral form of the equation given by

$$\frac{d}{dt} \int_a^b u \, dx = G(u(a,t)) - G(u(b,t)). \tag{4.27}$$

A discrete version of the above leads to the following definition: a scheme is said to be in *conservation form* if there exists a "numerical flux function" $g(u_{i-1}, u_i)$ $(g(u_i, u_{i+1}))$ which can approximate $G_{i-1/2}$ $(G_{i+1/2})$ (see Figure 4.8), such that

$$\frac{u_i^{n+1} - u_i^n}{\Delta t} = -\frac{G_{i+1/2} - G_{i-1/2}}{\Delta x}. \tag{4.28}$$

This definition is natural; any scheme must at least approximate the hyperbolic conservation law, subject to the consistency requirement $g(u, u) = G(u)$. Thus, any scheme that can be put into conservation form gives a weak solution. But how does one guarantee that the scheme picks out the correct entropy-satisfying weak solution? One answer lies in a further restriction. Consider a scheme W that takes three arguments, the value of u at $i - 1$, i, and $i + 1$, and hands back the value of u at i at the next time step. A 3-point finite difference scheme of the form $u_i^{n+1} = W(u_{i-1}^n, u_i^n, u_{i+1}^n)$ is said to be *monotone* if W is a non-decreasing function of all its arguments. The main fact can now be stated, which we will not prove (see Sod [186] and LeVeque [112]):

A conservative, monotone scheme produces a solution that satisfies the entropy condition. Thus, we need only check monotonicity and conservation form to verify that a scheme gives the correct entropy condition.

This means that to construct a viable scheme, we need only make sure that it is in conservation form and is a monotone increasing function of its arguments. One such simple scheme, called the *Lax–Friedrichs method*, is built from central difference approximations and is given by

$$u_i^{n+1} = \frac{1}{2}[u_{i-1}^n + u_{i+1}^n] - \frac{\lambda}{2}[G_{i+1} - G_{i-1}], \qquad (4.29)$$

where $\lambda = \Delta t/\Delta x$. It is straightforward to check that this scheme is monotone if $\frac{dG}{du}\lambda < 1$ and that it can be put into conservation form by means of the numerical flux function

$$g_{LF}(u_1, u_2) = -\frac{\Delta x}{2\Delta t}(u_2 - u_1) + \frac{1}{2}[G(u_2) + G(u_1)]. \qquad (4.30)$$

This is a straightforward way of approximating the solution to the general hyperbolic equation. There are other such schemes of this general type, including the Lax–Wendroff method and Fromm's method.

4.2.2.3 Even less diffusive schemes:
Exact and approximate Riemann solvers

The advantage of a Lax–Friedrichs scheme is that one need know almost nothing about the structure of the flux function G; a drawback is that it still introduces considerable diffusion into the solution. In other words, sharp discontinuities are smoothed over a large number of grid cells, and hence fronts do not stay sharp. In cases where one knows more about the structure of the flux function G, more can be done. In this section, we focus on schemes that keep sharp corners (and hence fronts) very sharp and limit smearing to only a few grid cells. We will apply them when the flux G is convex, that is, when $d^2G/du^2 > 0$. Thus, our first job is to make sure that the flux function G is convex.[3]

Given a convex flux function $G(u)$, we want to devise a numerical scheme to solve $u_t + [G(u)]_x = 0$. A fundamental idea, due to Godunov (see [109, 112, 186]), is to take the initial data $\{u_i^n\}$, $i = 1, \ldots, N$, and construct an exact solution at time step $n+1$ by solving a *local Riemann problem* for each interval. At any time n, stand over each interval at the intermediate grid point $i - 1/2$ and consider the local problem given by

[3] Things work for non-convex flux functions, with some modification.

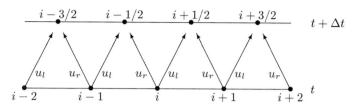

Fig. 4.9. Setup of local Riemann problem

the solution to the hyperbolic problem with initial data:

$$u(x,0) = \left\{ \begin{array}{ll} u_{\text{left}} = u^n_{i-1} & x < 0 \\ u_{\text{right}} = u^n_{i} & x \geq 0 \end{array} \right\}. \tag{4.31}$$

The exact solution can be constructed by means of the wave pictures shown previously; we use either a shock with shock speed given by the Rankine–Hugoniot condition or a rarefaction in the case of an expansion wave. The exact solution of each interval's individual Riemann problem is known at time step $n+1$, and all of them can then be patched together (see Figure 4.9). There are many ways to do this patching; Godunov constructed a method that averages the solution over staggered intervals and uses that to construct a discrete solution at grid points i at time $n+1$.

Since the invention of this approach, a vast array of flux functions g have been developed that solve either exactly or approximately the local Riemann problem to construct the solution at the next time step. The philosophy is always the same: first, make sure that the conservation form of the equation is preserved; second, make sure that enough of the exact solution is taken so that the entropy condition is satisfied; and third, try to give smooth (highly accurate) answers away from the discontinuities. We refer the reader to an excellent discussion of these issues in Colella and Puckett [51], whose discussion we now follow.

One of the easiest such approximate numerical fluxes is the Engquist–Osher scheme [61], which is particularly convenient in the case of problems that arise in front propagation. This flux is given by

$$g_{EO}(u_1, u_2) = G(u_1) + \int_{u_1}^{u_2} \min\left(\frac{dG}{du}, 0\right) du. \tag{4.32}$$

To see why this is a good scheme, let's examine what it does. Recall

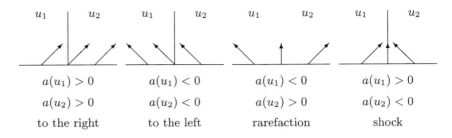

Fig. 4.10. Possible solutions to local Riemann problem

that

$$u_t + [G(u)]_x = 0, \tag{4.33}$$

and assume $G(u)$ is convex, hence $\frac{d^2 G}{du^2} > 0$. Performing the differentiation produces

$$u_t + \frac{dG}{du} u_x = 0. \tag{4.34}$$

Thus, $\frac{dG}{du} = a(u)$ is the "speed of propagation". Standing in the middle of an interval with a grid point on the left with value u_1 and one on the right with value u_2, we consider all of the cases (see Figure 4.10).

(i) $a(u_1), a(u_2) > 0$: Then the wave should simply move to the right; indeed, since the integrand is zero, $g_{EO}(u_1, u_2) = G(u_1)$.

(ii) $a(u_1), a(u_2) < 0$: Then the wave should simply move to the left; since the integrand is then $\frac{dG}{du}$, integration by the Fundamental Theorem of Calculus produces $g_{EO}(u_1, u_2) = G(u_2)$.

(iii) $a(u_1) < 0, a(u_2) > 0$: Then a rarefaction develops, since the speed on the left is negative and those characteristics go to the left, while the speed on the right is positive and hence those characteristics go to the right. The scheme then picks the inverse image of zero, thus $g_{EO}(u_1, u_2) = G(a^{-1}(0))$.

(iv) $a(u_1) > 0, a(u_2) < 0$: Here, a shock must develop, since the speed on the left is positive and hence those characteristics move to the right, while the speed on the right is negative and hence those characteristics move to the left. The exact solution from the local Riemann problem depends on the shock speed S; if $S > 0$, then the left value $G(u_1)$ is the answer, while if $S < 0$, then the right value $G(u_2)$ is the answer.

In all except the shock case, this scheme yields the right solution. Let's look more closely at what happens in the shock case (4). The exact solution is either $G(u_1)$ or $G(u_2)$, depending on the sign of the wave speed S, which comes from the Rankine–Hugoniot condition. However, the scheme gives

$$
\begin{aligned}
g_{EO}(u_1, u_2) &= G(u_1) + \int_{u_1}^{u_2} \min\left(\frac{dG}{du}, 0\right) du \\
&= G(u_1) + \int_{u_1}^{a^{-1}(0)} \min\left(\frac{dG}{du}, 0\right) du + \int_{a^{-1}(0)}^{u_2} \min\left(\frac{dG}{du}, 0\right) du
\end{aligned}
$$

Now the first integral is zero, since the wave speed is positive from u_1 on the left until $a^{-1}(0)$. Thus the solution given by the scheme is

$$
g_{EO}(u_1, u_2) = G(u_1) + G(u_2) - G(a^{-1}(0)). \tag{4.35}
$$

Thus, this scheme is more diffusive than the exact solution, which means that discontinuities are somewhat smoothed. Fortunately, the characteristics help sharpen things up again, so that the scheme has only a little diffusion. In the specific case of the non-linear wave equation $u_t + [u^2]_x = 0$ one can directly write down the scheme introduced in [144] as

$$
g(u_1, u_2) = (\max(u_1, 0)^2 + \min(u_2, 0)^2). \tag{4.36}
$$

Thus, all the four cases are nicely selected; three of them give the exact solution, and the fourth case adds a little diffusion to the exact solution. For additional schemes, see LeVeque [112], Sod [186], and Colella and Puckett [51].

Now that we have a suitable (that is, entropy-satisfying with relatively little diffusion) difference scheme, we can now return to the level set equation itself.

5

Approximating the Level Set Equation

Outline: *Using the previous schemes for a single hyperbolic conservation law, we build first and second order schemes for the level set equation itself; including algorithms for multi-dimensions and non-convex Hamiltonians.*

Recall the level set equation

$$\phi_t + F|\nabla\phi| = 0, \tag{5.1}$$

which can be rewritten in a little more generality as

$$\phi_t + H(\phi_x, \phi_y, \phi_z) = 0. \tag{5.2}$$

The function H is known as the "Hamiltonian", where, for our current problem, we have the Hamiltonian

$$H(u, v, w) = F\sqrt{u^2 + v^2 + w^2}. \tag{5.3}$$

Let's focus on the one-dimensional version, that is, $\phi_t + H(\phi_x) = 0$, where $H(u) = \sqrt{u^2}$. From the previous chapter, given the equation

$$u_t + [G(u)]_x = 0, \tag{5.4}$$

numerical fluxes g can be constructed that accurately approximate this equation through the expression

$$\frac{u_i^{n+1} - u_i^n}{\Delta t} = -\frac{g(u_i^n, u_{i+1}^n) - g(u_{i-1}^n, u_i^n)}{\Delta x}. \tag{5.5}$$

Let's look a little more carefully at this expression in terms of the computational grid shown in Figure 4.8(a). The value of G at the point $(i - 1/2)\Delta x$ (called $G_{i-1/2}$) is approximated by the numerical flux function g as

$$G_{i-1/2} \approx g(u_{i-1}^n, u_i^n). \tag{5.6}$$

Similarly, at the point $i + 1/2$,

$$G_{i+1/2} \approx g(u_i^n, u_{i+1}^n). \tag{5.7}$$

Then from Figure 4.8, the right-hand side of equation (5.5) is just the central difference operator applied to the numerical flux function g. As the grid size goes to zero, consistency requires that $g(u, u) = G(u)$.

This is enough to build a scheme for the level set equation. Letting $u = \phi_x$, we can write

$$\phi_t + H(u) = 0. \tag{5.8}$$

In terms of the computational grid in Figure 5.1, construction of ϕ_i^{n+1} requires ϕ_i^n as well as a value for $H(u_i^n)$. Fortunately, an approximate value for $H(u_i^n)$ is *exactly* what is given by the numerical flux function, thus we have

$$H(u_i^n) \approx g(u_{i-1/2}, u_{i+1/2}). \tag{5.9}$$

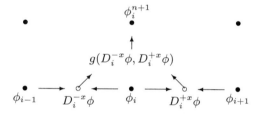

Fig. 5.1. Update of ϕ through numerical Hamiltonian

All that remains is to construct values for u in the middle of our computational cells. Since $u = \phi_x$, forward and backward difference approximations in ϕ can be used to construct those values. Thus (see Figure 5.1), we have

$$\phi_i^{n+1} = \phi_i^n - \Delta t \, g\left(\frac{\phi_i^n - \phi_{i-1}^n}{\Delta x}, \frac{\phi_{i+1}^n - \phi_i^n}{\Delta x}\right), \tag{5.10}$$

where g is one of the numerical flux functions and, again, we have substituted forward and backward difference operators on ϕ for the values of u at the left and right states.

In the specific case of a one-dimensional level set equation, that is,

$H(u) = \sqrt{u^2}$, we can simply apply the scheme given in Chapter 4 and, for speed $F = 1$, write

$$\phi_i^{n+1} = \phi_i^n - \Delta t \, (\max(D_i^{-x}, 0)^2 + \min(D_i^{+x}, 0)^2)^{1/2}. \tag{5.11}$$

This is the level set scheme given in [144]. (Here, we are using a slightly different shorthand notation; for example, D_i^{-x} means $D_i^{-x}\phi$.) As long as the Hamiltonian is symmetric in each of the space dimensions, the above can be replicated simply in each space variable to construct schemes for two- and three-dimensional front propagation problems.

In general, we adopt the following philosophy:

(i) If the Hamiltonian "H" is convex, then we use the level set flux function presented in [144] and described below.

(ii) If the Hamiltonian "H" is non-convex, then we use a variant on the Lax–Friedrichs scheme described below.

It is important to point out that far more sophisticated schemes exist than the ones presented here. In the applications of these schemes to hyperbolic problems and shock dynamics, high order resolution schemes are often necessary, because differentiation of the numerical flux function g leads to additional smearing. However, in our case, because we are solving $\phi_t + H(u) = 0$ rather than $u_t + [H(u)]_x$, the differentiation is not required. For almost all practical purposes, the first and second order schemes presented below are adequate. Complete details of these schemes for advancing the level set equation under convex and non-convex Hamiltonians are given below.

Before constructing the general schemes, let's return to the example of the propagating curve. In Section 3.3, a central difference approximation was used to track the propagation of a simple V moving with speed $F = 1$, and this scheme failed. Figure 5.2 shows the application of the upwind scheme given in equation (5.11). The exact answer is shown, together with two simulations. The first uses the entropy-satisfying scheme with only 20 points (Figure 5.2(b)), the second (Figure 5.2(c)) with 100 points. In the first approximation, the entropy condition is satisfied, but the corner is somewhat smoothed due to the small number of points used. In the more refined calculation, the corner remains sharp, and the exact solution is very closely approximated.

(a) Exact Solution   (b) Scheme with 20 Points   (c) Scheme with 100 Points

Fig. 5.2. Upwind, entropy-satisfying approximations to the level set equation

5.1 First and second order schemes for convex speed functions

Given a convex speed function F (that is, a speed function F such that the resulting Hamiltonian $H = F|\nabla\phi|$ is convex), the equation

$$\phi_t + H(\phi_x, \phi_y, \phi_z) = 0, \tag{5.12}$$

can be approximated by

$$\phi_i^{n+1} = \phi_i^n - \Delta t\, g \left(\frac{\phi_{ijk}^n - \phi_{i-1,j,k}^n}{\Delta x}, \frac{\phi_{i+1,j,k}^n - \phi_{i,j,k}^n}{\Delta x}, \right.$$
$$\frac{\phi_{ijk}^n - \phi_{i,j-1,k}^n}{\Delta y}, \frac{\phi_{i,j+1,k}^n - \phi_{i,j,k}^n}{\Delta y},$$
$$\left. \frac{\phi_{ijk}^n - \phi_{i,j,k-1}^n}{\Delta z}, \frac{\phi_{i,j,k+1}^n - \phi_{i,j,k}^n}{\Delta z} \right). \tag{5.13}$$

A multi-dimensional version [144] of the level set scheme is then

$$g_{LS}(u_1, u_2, v_1, v_2, w_1, w_2) = [\, \max(u_1, 0)^2 + \min(u_2, 0)^2 + \tag{5.14}$$
$$\max(v_1, 0)^2 + \min(v_2, 0)^2 +$$
$$\max(w_1, 0)^2 + \min(w_2, 0)^2\,]^{1/2}.$$

Thus we have

(i) *First order space convex:*

$$\phi_{ijk}^{n+1} = \phi_{ijk}^n - \Delta t[\max(F_{ijk}, 0)\nabla^+ + \min(F_{ijk}, 0)\nabla^-], \tag{5.15}$$

where

$$\nabla^+ = [\, \max(D_{ijk}^{-x}, 0)^2 + \min(D_{ijk}^{+x}, 0)^2 +$$

$$\max(D_{ijk}^{-y},0)^2 + \min(D_{ijk}^{+y},0)^2 + \\ \max(D_{ijk}^{-z},0)^2 + \min(D_{ijk}^{+z},0)^2]^{1/2} \tag{5.16}$$

$$\nabla^- = [\max(D_{ijk}^{+x},0)^2 + \min(D_{ijk}^{-x},0)^2 + \\ \max(D_{ijk}^{+y},0)^2 + \min(D_{ijk}^{-y},0)^2 + \\ \max(D_{ijk}^{+z},0)^2 + \min(D_{ijk}^{-z},0)^2]^{1/2}. \tag{5.17}$$

Here, we have used a short-hand notation in which $D^{+x}\phi_i^n$ is written as D_i^{+x}, etc.

(ii) *Second order space convex:*

The above schemes can be extended to higher order. The basic trick is to build a switch that turns itself off whenever a shock is detected; otherwise, it will use a higher order approximation to the left and right values by means of a higher order polynomial using an ENO construction, see Harten et al. [83]. These details will not be presented; see [83, 144]. The scheme is the same as the above, however this time ∇^+ and ∇^- are given by

$$\nabla^+ = [\max(A,0)^2 + \min(B,0)^2 + \\ \max(C,0)^2 + \min(D,0)^2 + \\ \max(E,0)^2 + \min(F,0)^2]^{1/2} \tag{5.18}$$

$$\nabla^- = [\max(B,0)^2 + \min(A,0)^2 + \\ \max(D,0)^2 + \min(C,0)^2 + \\ \max(F,0)^2 + \min(E,0)^2]^{1/2}, \tag{5.19}$$

where

$$A = D_{ijk}^{-x} + \frac{\Delta x}{2} m(D_{ijk}^{-x-x}, D_{ijk}^{+x-x}) \tag{5.20}$$

$$B = D_{ijk}^{+x} - \frac{\Delta x}{2} m(D_{ijk}^{+x+x}, D_{ijk}^{+x-x}) \tag{5.21}$$

$$C = D_{ijk}^{-y} + \frac{\Delta y}{2} m(D_{ijk}^{-y-y}, D_{ijk}^{+y-y}) \tag{5.22}$$

$$D = D_{ijk}^{+y} - \frac{\Delta y}{2} m(D_{ijk}^{+y+y}, D_{ijk}^{+y-y}) \tag{5.23}$$

$$E = D_{ijk}^{-z} + \frac{\Delta z}{2} m(D_{ijk}^{-z-z}, D_{ijk}^{+z-z}) \tag{5.24}$$

$$F = D_{ijk}^{+z} - \frac{\Delta z}{2} m(D_{ijk}^{+z+z}, D_{ijk}^{+z-z}), \qquad (5.25)$$

and the switch function is given by

$$m(x, y) = \left\{ \begin{array}{c} \left\{ \begin{array}{cc} x & if \; |x| \le |y| \\ y & if \; |x| > |y| \end{array} \right\} \;\; xy \ge 0 \\ 0 \qquad\qquad xy < 0 \end{array} \right\}. \qquad (5.26)$$

5.2 Schemes for non-convex speed functions

Given a non-convex speed function F (that is, a speed function F such that the resulting Hamiltonian $H = F|\nabla\phi|$ is non-convex)[1], a set of schemes were introduced in Shu and Osher [145]. One straightforward such scheme results from replacing the Hamiltonian $F|\nabla\phi|$ with the Lax–Friedrichs numerical flux function. The equation

$$\phi_t + H(\phi_x, \phi_y, \phi_z) = 0 \qquad (5.27)$$

is then approximated by

$$\phi_i^{n+1} = \phi_i^n - \Delta t \, g \left(\frac{\phi_{ijk}^n - \phi_{i-1,j,k}^n}{\Delta x}, \frac{\phi_{i+1,j,k}^n - \phi_{i,j,k}^n}{\Delta x}, \right.$$
$$\frac{\phi_{ijk}^n - \phi_{i,j-1,k}^n}{\Delta y}, \frac{\phi_{i,j+1,k}^n - \phi_{i,j,k}^n}{\Delta y},$$
$$\left. \frac{\phi_{ijk}^n - \phi_{i,j,k-1}^n}{\Delta z}, \frac{\phi_{i,j,k+1}^n - \phi_{i,j,k}^n}{\Delta z} \right). \qquad (5.28)$$

A multi-dimensional version of the Lax–Friedrichs numerical flux function is then given by

$$g_{LF}(u_1, u_2, v_1, v_2, w_1, w_2) = -\frac{\Delta x}{2\Delta t}(u_2 - u_1) + \frac{1}{2}[H(u_2) + H(u_1)] (5.29)$$
$$-\frac{\Delta y}{2\Delta t}(v_2 - v_1) + \frac{1}{2}[H(v_2) + H(v_1)]$$
$$-\frac{\Delta z}{2\Delta t}(w_2 - w_1) + \frac{1}{2}[H(w_2) + H(w_1)]$$

to obtain the following schemes:

---

[1] In N-dimensions, if H is smooth, then H is convex if $\frac{\partial^2 H(u)}{\partial p_i p_j} \ge 0$, where $P = (p_1, \ldots, p_N)$. Alternatively, H is convex if $H(\lambda p + (1-\lambda)q) \le H(p) + (1-\lambda)H(q)$ for all $0 \le \lambda \le 1$, $p, q \in R^n$.

(i) First order space non-convex:

$$\phi_{ijk}^{n+1} = \phi_{ijk}^n - \Delta t \left[H \left(\frac{D_{ijk}^{-x} + D_{ijk}^{+x}}{2}, \frac{D_{ijk}^{-y} + D_{ijk}^{+y}}{2}, \frac{D_{ijk}^{-z} + D_{ijk}^{+z}}{2} \right) \right. \tag{5.3}$$

$$\left. - \frac{1}{2}\alpha_u(D_{ijk}^{+x} - D_{ijk}^{-x}) - \frac{1}{2}\alpha_v(D_{ijk}^{+y} - D_{ijk}^{-y}) - \frac{1}{2}\alpha_w(D_{ijk}^{+z} - D_{ijk}^{-z}) \right.$$

where α_u (α_v, α_w) is a bound on the partial derivative of the Hamiltonian with respect to the first (second, third) argument, and the non-convex Hamiltonian is a user-defined input function.

(ii) Second order space non-convex:

$$\phi_{ijk}^{n+1} = \phi_{ijk}^n - \Delta t [H(\frac{A+B}{2}, \frac{C+D}{2}, \frac{E+F}{2}) \tag{5.31}$$

$$- \frac{1}{2}\alpha_u(B - A) - \frac{1}{2}\alpha_v(D - C) - \frac{1}{2}\alpha_w(F - E)]$$

where A, B, C, D, E, and F are defined as above. For details, see Shu and Osher [145], as well as Adalsteinsson and Sethian [2, 3, 4].

5.3 Approximations to curvature and normals

As discussed above, one advantage of the level set formulation is that geometric properties of the propagating interface, such as curvature and normal direction, are easily calculated. For example, consider the case of a curve propagating in the plane. The expression for the curvature of the zero level set assigned to the interface itself (as well as all other level sets) is given by

$$\kappa = \nabla \cdot \frac{\nabla \phi}{|\nabla \phi|} = \frac{\phi_{xx}\phi_y^2 - 2\phi_y\phi_x\phi_{xy} + \phi_{yy}\phi_x^2}{(\phi_x^2 + \phi_y^2)^{3/2}}. \tag{5.32}$$

In the case of a surface propagating in three space dimensions, one has many choices for the curvature of the front, including the mean curvature κ_M and the Gaussian curvature κ_G. Both may be conveniently expressed in terms of the level set function ϕ as

$$\kappa_M = \nabla \cdot \frac{\nabla \phi}{|\nabla \phi|} = \frac{\left\{ \begin{array}{c} (\phi_{yy} + \phi_{zz})\phi_x^2 + (\phi_{xx} + \phi_{zz})\phi_y^2 + (\phi_{xx} + \phi_{yy})\phi_z^2 \\ - 2\phi_x\phi_y\phi_{xy} - 2\phi_x\phi_z\phi_{xz} - 2\phi_y\phi_z\phi_{yz} \end{array} \right\}}{(\phi_x^2 + \phi_y^2 + \phi_z^2)^{3/2}} \tag{5.33}$$

$$\kappa_G = \frac{\left\{\begin{array}{c} \phi_x^2(\phi_{yy}\phi_{zz} - \phi_{yz}^2) + \phi_y^2(\phi_{xx}\phi_{zz} - \phi_{xz}^2) + \phi_z^2(\phi_{xx}\phi_{yy} - \phi_{xy}^2) \\ + 2[\phi_x\phi_y(\phi_{xz}\phi_{yz} - \phi_{xy}\phi_{zz}) + \phi_y\phi_z(\phi_{xy}\phi_{xz} - \phi_{yz}\phi_{xx}) \\ + \phi_x\phi_z(\phi_{xy}\phi_{yz} - \phi_{xz}\phi_{yy}) \end{array}\right\}}{(\phi_z^2 + \phi_y^2 + \phi_x^2)^2}.$$

(5.34)

Construction of the normal itself can require a more sophisticated scheme than simply building the difference approximation to $\nabla\phi$. This is because the normal can undergo a jump at corners. This suggests the following technique, introduced in Sethian and Strain [182]. First, the one-sided difference approximations to the unit normal in each possible direction are formed. All four limiting normals are then averaged to produce the approximate normal at the corner. Thus, the normal n_{ij} is formed by first letting

$$n_{ij}^* \equiv \frac{\phi_x, \phi_y}{(\phi_x^2 + \phi_y^2)^{1/2}}$$

(5.35)

$$= \frac{(D_{ij}^{+x}, D_{ij}^{+y})}{[(D_{ij}^{+x})^2 + (D_{ij}^{+y})^2]^{1/2}} + \frac{(D_{ij}^{-x}, D_{ij}^{+y})}{[(D_{ij}^{-x})^2 + (D_{ij}^{+y})^2]^{1/2}}$$

$$+ \frac{(D_{ij}^{+x}, D_{ij}^{-y})}{[(D_{ij}^{+x})^2 + (D_{ij}^{-y})^2]^{1/2}} + \frac{(D_{ij}^{-x}, D_{ij}^{-y})}{[(D_{ij}^{-x})^2 + (D_{ij}^{-y})^2]^{1/2}}$$

(5.36)

and then normalizing so that $n_{ij} \equiv n_{ij}^*/|n_{ij}^*|$. If any of the one-sided approximations to $|\nabla\phi|$ is zero, that term is not considered and the weights are adjusted accordingly.

5.4 Initialization

The level set approach requires an initial function $\phi(x, t = 0)$ with the property that the zero level set of that initial function corresponds to the position of the initial front. A straightforward[2] technique is to compute the signed-distance function from each grid point to the initial front that is matched to the zero level set. As a practical rule, accuracy is required only near the initial front itself, and a discrete value based on grid distances can suffice far away.

---

[2] And expensive.

5.5 Boundary conditions

The use of a finite computational grid requires boundary conditions. If the speed function F causes the front to expand (such as in the case $F = 1$), upwind schemes will naturally default to outward-flowing one-sided differences at the boundary of the domain, and there will be no need for particular attention to boundary conditions. However, in most cases the speed function will cause more complex motion, and in such cases we have usually chosen periodic boundary conditions. These are implemented by creating an extra layer of ghost cells around the domain whose values are simply direct copies of the ϕ values along the actual boundaries. By limiting the given difference schemes to grid points actually on and inside the boundary, the value of ϕ is correctly updated with mirror reflection boundary conditions. At the end of each time step, the new values on the boundary are copied to the ghost cells.

5.6 Putting it all together

As an example, imagine that we are given an initial closed curve that is moving under three simultaneous motions. First, it is expanding with a constant speed F_0 in its normal direction. Second, it is collapsing with speed proportional to its curvature. Third, it is being passively advected by an underlying velocity field $\vec{U}(x, y, t)$ whose direction and strength depend on position and time, but not on the front itself. This entire motion can then be written in terms of the speed function as follows:

$$F = F_{\text{prop}} + F_{\text{curv}} + F_{\text{adv}}, \tag{5.37}$$

where $F_{\text{prop}} = F_0$ is the propagation expansion speed, $F_{\text{curv}} = -\epsilon\kappa$ is the dependence of the speed on the curvature, and $F_{\text{adv}} = \vec{U}(x, y, t) \cdot \vec{n}$ is the advection speed, where $\vec{n}$ is the normal to the front.

Rather than simply plug this speed function into the schemes, it is a better idea to rearrange terms a bit. Since the normal is given by $\vec{n} = \nabla\phi/|\nabla\phi|$, the level set equation may be re-written as

$$\phi_t + F_0|\nabla\phi| + \vec{U}(x, y, t) \cdot \nabla\phi = \epsilon\kappa|\nabla\phi|. \tag{5.38}$$

The first term on the left (after the time derivative) describes motion in the normal direction to the front, and must be approximated through the entropy-satisfying schemes discussed above. The second term on the left corresponds to pure passive advection. This term may be approximated through simple upwind schemes. That is, we check the sign of each component of $\vec{U}$ and construct one-sided upwind differences in the appropriate direction. As discussed earlier, the term on the right, which depends on the curvature, is a parabolic contribution to the equation of motion, and hence the use of an upwind scheme, designed for a hyperbolic advection term, is inappropriate. Loosely speaking, this term is like a non-linear heat equation, and information propagates in both directions. Consequently, in terms of our numerical scheme, the most straightforward approach is to use central difference approximations to each of the derivatives in the expression on the right-hand side. For the sake of completeness, we write the complete first order convex scheme to approximate equation (5.38) as

$$
\phi_{ij}^{n+1} = \phi_{ij}^n + \Delta t \begin{bmatrix} -[\max(F_{0ij},0)\nabla^+ + \min(F_{0ij},0)\nabla^-] \\[2mm] -\left\{ \begin{array}{l} [\max(u_{ij}^n,0)D_{ij}^{-x} + \min(u_{ij}^n,0)D_{ij}^{+x} \\ + \max(v_{ij}^n,0)D_{ij}^{-y} + \min(v_{ij}^n,0)D_{ij}^{+y}] \end{array} \right\} \\[2mm] +[\epsilon\, K_{i,j}^n (D_{ij}^{0x\,2} + D_{ij}^{0y\,2})^{1/2}] \end{bmatrix}
$$

(5.39)

where $\vec{U} = (u,v)$, and $K_{i,j}^n$ is the central difference approximation to the curvature expression given in equation (5.32).

6

A Hierarchy of Fast Level Set Methods

Outline: *The level set method presented above is a relatively straightforward version that may be easily programmed. However it is not particularly fast, nor does it make efficient use of computational resources. In this chapter, we consider more sophisticated versions of the basic scheme.*

6.1 Parallel algorithms

The straightforward approach presented above is to solve the initial value partial differential equation for the level set function ϕ in the entire computational domain. We call this a "full matrix approach", since one is updating *all* the level sets, not just the zero level set corresponding to the front itself. The advantage of this approach is that the data structures and operations are extremely clear, and it is a good starting point for building level set codes.

There are a variety of circumstances in which this approach is desirable. If, in fact, all the level sets are themselves important (such as in problems encountered in image processing discussed in a later section), then computation over the entire domain is required. In this case, one simple speedup is obtained through a parallel computation. Since each grid point is updated by a nearest neighbor stencil using only grid points on each side, this technique almost falls under the classification of "embarrassingly parallel". A parallel version of the level set method was developed in Sethian [172] for the Connection Machine CM-2 and CM-5. In the CM-2, nodes are arranged in a hypercube fashion; in the CM-5, nodes are arranged in a fat-tree. The code was written in global CMFortran, and at each grid point CSHIFT operators were used to update the level set function. A time-explicit second order space method

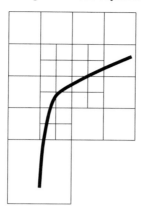

Fig. 6.1. Cell hierarchy

was used to update the level set equation. Output was controlled by linking the level set evolution to a parallel volume rendering routine, with associated display through access to a parallel frame buffer. As expected, the operation count per time step reduces to $O(1)$, since in most cases the full grid can be placed into physical memory. Thus, most applications of updating propagating interfaces according to given speed functions transpire as real-time movies, the main limitation being the speed of display.

6.2 Adaptive mesh refinement

One version of an efficient level set method comes from pursuing an adaptive mesh refinement strategy. This is the approach taken by Milne in [136], motivated by the adaptive mesh refinement work in Berger and Colella [19]. Adaptivity may be desired in regions where level curves develop high curvature or where speed functions change rapidly; if the zero level curve identified with a front is the object of interest, then the mesh can be adaptively refined around its location. To illustrate this approach, Figure 6.1 shows mesh cells that are hierarchically refined in response to a parent–child relationship around a large curvature in the zero level set of ϕ. Calculations are performed on both the fine grids and the coarse grids, and grid cell boundaries always lie along xyz coordinate lines and patches do not overlap; no attempt was made to align the refined cells with the front.

The data structures for the adaptive mesh refinement are fairly

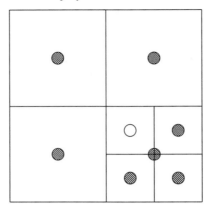

Fig. 6.2. Grid values at boundary between refinement levels

straightforward. However, considerable care must be taken at the interfaces between coarse and fine cells; in particular, the update strategy for ϕ at so-called "hanging nodes" is subtle. These are nodes at the boundary between two levels of refinement that do not have the full set of nearest neighbors required to update ϕ. To illustrate, Figure 6.2 shows a two-dimensional adaptive mesh; the goal is to determine an accurate update strategy for the hanging node marked ∘.

The strategy laid out by Milne for updating ϕ at such points is as follows. Consider the archetypical speed function $F(\kappa) = 1 - \epsilon\kappa$.

- The advection term 1 leads to a hyperbolic equation; here, straightforward interpolation of the updated values of ϕ from the coarse cell grid is used to produce the new value of ϕ at ∘. More sophisticated technology is not required, since we are modeling the update according to the numerical flux function g, not the derivative of the numerical flux function as required for hyperbolic conservation laws.

- In the case of the curvature term $-\epsilon\kappa$, the situation is not so straightforward, since this corresponds to a parabolic term that cannot be approximated through simple interpolation. Milne showed that straightforward interpolation from updated values on the coarse grid to the fine grid provides poor answers; if this procedure is employed, the boundary between the two levels of refinement acts as a source of noise, and significant error is generated at the boundary. In fact, such an approach tested against the simple heat equation using a coarse/fine mesh produces more error in the computed solution than would be produced using a coarse mesh everywhere. Instead, Milne devises the

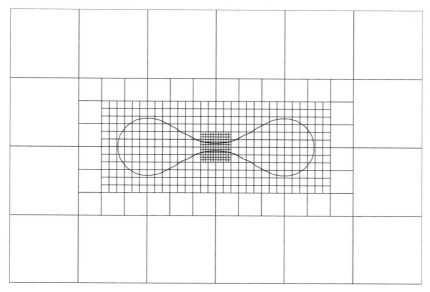

Fig. 6.3. Two-dimensional slice of adaptive mesh for propagating surface

following technique. Values from both the coarse and refined grid around the hanging node are used to construct a least squares solution for ϕ before the update. This solution surface is then formally differentiated to produce the various first and second derivatives in each component direction. These values are then used to produce the update value for ϕ similar to all other nodes.

As illustration, in Figure 6.3, we show a two-dimensional slice of a fully three-dimensional adaptive mesh calculation of a surface collapsing under its mean curvature. As is discussed in a later section, the dumbbell neck pinches off under such a configuration, because one principal axis of curvature is very large and positive.

6.3 Narrow banding and fast methods

There are several disadvantages with the "full-matrix" approach given above if one is only interested in a specific front.

- *Speed:* Performing calculations over the entire computational domain requires $O(N^2)$ operations in two dimensions, and $O(N^3)$ operations in three dimensions, where N is the number of grid points along a side.

As an alternative, an efficient modification is to perform work only in a neighborhood of the zero level set; this is known as the *narrow band approach*. In this case, the operation count in three dimensions drops to $O(kN^2)$, where k is the number of cells in the narrow band, a significant cost reduction.

- *Calculating Extension Variables*: As outlined above, the level set approach requires the extension of the speed function F in equation (2.5) to *all* of space; this then updates all of the level sets, not simply the zero level set on which the speed function is naturally defined. Recall that three types of arguments may influence the front speed F: local, global, and independent. Some of these variables may have meaning only on the front itself, and it may be both difficult and awkward to design a speed function that extrapolates the velocity away from the zero level set in a smooth fashion. Thus, another advantage of the narrow band approach is that this extension need only be done to points lying in the narrow band, as opposed to all points in the computational domain.

- The full-matrix approach requires a time step that satisfies a CFL condition with regard to the maximum velocity over the entire domain, not simply in response to the speed of the front itself. In a narrow band implementation, the time step can be adaptively chosen in response to the maximum velocity field only within the narrow band. This is advantageous when the front speed changes substantially as it moves (such as in curvature flow). In such problems, the CFL restriction for the velocity field for *all* the level sets may be much more stringent than the one for those sets within the narrow band.

The above "narrow band method" was introduced in Chopp [41], used in recovering shapes from images in Malladi, Sethian and Vemuri [120], and analyzed extensively by Adalsteinsson and Sethian in [1]. The idea is straightforward, and can be best understood by means of two figures.

Figure 6.4 shows the placement of a narrow band around the familiar initial front. The entire two-dimensional grid of data is stored in a square array. A one-dimensional object is then used to keep track of the points in this array (dark grid points in Figure 6.4 are located in a narrow band around the front of a user-defined width) (see Figure 6.5). Only the values of ϕ at such points within the tube are updated. Values of ϕ at grid points on the boundary of the narrow band are frozen. When the front moves near the edge of the tube boundary, the calculation is stopped, and a new tube is built with the zero level set

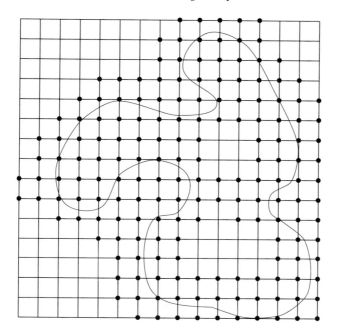

Fig. 6.4. Dark grid points are members of narrow band

interface boundary at the center. This rebuilding process is known as "re-initialization".

Thus, the narrow band method consists of the following loop:

- Tag "Alive" points in narrow band.
- Build "Land Mines" to indicate near edge.
- Initialize "Far Away" points outside (inside) narrow band with large positive (negative) values.
- Solve level set equation until land mine hit.
- Rebuild, loop.

Use of narrow bands leads to level set front advancement algorithms that are computationally equivalent in terms of complexity to traditional marker methods and cell techniques, while maintaining the advantages of topological merger, accuracy, and easy extension to multi-dimensions. Typically, the speed associated with the narrow band method is about ten times faster on a 160×160 grid than the full matrix method. Such a speed-up is substantial; in three-dimensional simulations, it can make the difference between computationally intensive problems and those

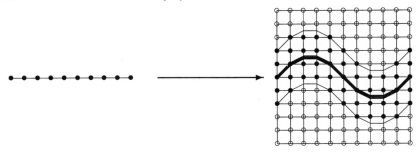

Fig. 6.5. Pointer array tags interior and boundary band points

that can be done with relative ease. Details on the accuracy, typical tube sizes, and number of times a tube must be rebuilt may be found in Adalsteinsson and Sethian [1].

This narrow banding technique requires rebuilding and re-initializing a new narrow band around the location of the front. Several ways to perform this re-initialization are described below.

6.3.1 Re-initialization techniques, direct evaluation, iteration, Huyghen's flowing

6.3.1.1 Direct evaluation

A straightforward re-initialization technique to rebuild the band is to first find the zero level set by using a contour plotter and then recalculate the signed-distance from each grid point to this zero level set. This technique can be used to ensure that the level set function stays well-behaved. However, it has two drawbacks. First, one must find the front itself; in two dimensions one can use a contour plotter, in three dimensions, some version of Lorenson and Cline's [117] voxel scheme is possible. Nonetheless, finding the front is something that the level set scheme tries to avoid at all costs, since it introduces considerable complication to the technique. Second, such an approach is expensive; for example, in two dimensions a representation of the front as N segments will require N evaluations to find the distance to each of N^2 grid points. This is an $O(N^3)$ calculation; more expensive than updating the level set function ϕ over the entire grid N times!

6.3.1.2 Iteration

An alternative to this was given by Sussman, Smereka, and Osher [193], based on an observation of Morel. Its virtue is that one need not find the zero level set to re-initialize the level set function. Consider the partial differential equation

$$\phi_t = sign(\phi)(1 - |\nabla\phi|), \tag{6.1}$$

where $sign(\phi)$ gives the sign of ϕ. Given any initial data for ϕ, solving the above equation to steady-state provides a new value for ϕ with the property that $|\nabla\phi| = 1$, since convergence occurs when the right-hand side is zero. The sign function controls the flow of information in the above; if ϕ is negative, information flows one way and if ϕ is positive, then information flows the other way. The net effect is to "straighten out" the level sets on either side of the zero level set and produce a ϕ function with $|\nabla\phi| = 1$ corresponding to the signed-distance function. Thus, their approach is to stop the level set calculation periodically and solve the above until convergence; if done often enough, the initial guess is often close to the signed-distance function and few iterations are required. One potential disadvantage of the above scheme is the relative crudeness of the switch function based on checking the sign of the level set equation; considerable motion of the zero level set can occur during the re-initialization, since the sign function does not do an accurate job of using information about the exact location of the front. A hybrid method combining a volume-of-fluid approach and a level set method for this problem may be found in [24].

6.3.1.3 Dynamic allocation of points in narrow band

Another approach is to dynamically add grid points to the narrow band as it moves. Thus, points whose ϕ values dip below a certain negative level are removed, while neighbors are added around those that dip below a certain positive value. When new grid points are added, they must be given appropriate ϕ values. This is accomplished by re-initializing every time step, usually by the above iterative technique, to return to the signed-distance function. Thus, new grid points are added, the ϕ function in the entire narrow band is re-initialized, and the calculation is advanced one time step.

6.3.1.4 Huyghen's principle flowing

An alternative technique, described in Sethian [176], is based on the idea of computing crossing times as discussed in [175], and is related to the ideas given by Kimmel and Bruckstein [99]. Consider a particular value for the level set function $\phi_{\text{initial}}(x, t)$. The goal is to produce a new level set function $\phi(x, t)$ with the zero level set unchanged and that corresponds to the signed-distance function around that zero level set. This new function may be built as follows. With speed function $F = 1$, flow the level set function both forwards and backwards in time and calculate crossing times (that is when ϕ changes sign) at each grid point. These crossing times (both positive and negative) are equal to the signed-distance function by Huyghen's principle. This approach has the advantage that one knows how long one must run the problem forward and backward to re-initialize grid points a given distance from the front, since one is using a speed function of unity. One can perform this iteration using a high order scheme to produce accurate values for the crossing times.

This idea of computing crossing times is equivalent to converting the level set evolution problem into the stationary problem that was discussed earlier. In this converted state, we can develop an ultra-fast level set scheme for the particular case of solving the level set equation for speed function $F = F(x, y, z)$, where F is always either positive or negative. This is discussed in Part III.

7

Extensions to the Basic Method

Outline: *Since their introduction, the capabilities and applicability of level set methods have been considerably refined and extended. In this chapter, we discuss a few of those extensions that have proven to be useful in a variety of applications, including internal boundary conditions, sub-grid resolution, and the motion of multiple interfaces and triple points.*

7.1 Masking and sources

Consider the problem of a front propagating with a speed F and subject to the constraint that the evolving interface cannot enter into a region Ω in the domain. This region Ω is referred to as a "mask", since it inhibits all motion. There are several solutions to this problem, depending on the degree of accuracy required.

The simplest solution is to set the speed function F equal to zero for all grid points inside Ω. The location of all points inside Ω can be determined before any calculation is carried out. This technique assures that the front stops within one grid cell of the mask. Figure 7.1 shows a plane front propagating upwards with speed $F = 1$ in the upwards direction, with a rectangular block in the center of the domain serving as a mask. In Figure 7.1(a), the speed function is reset to zero inside the mask region, and as the front propagates upwards it is stopped in the vicinity of the mask and is forced to bend around it.

The calculations in Figure 7.1(a) are performed on a very crude 13×13 mesh in order to accentuate a problem with this approach, which is that the front can be guaranteed to stop only within one grid cell of the obstacle itself. This is because the level set method constructs an interpolated speed between grid points, and hence by setting the speed

71

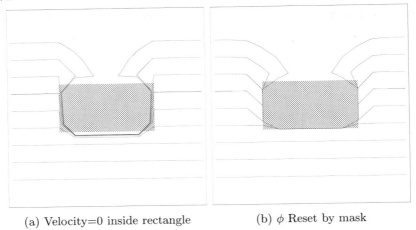

(a) Velocity=0 inside rectangle   (b) ϕ Reset by mask

Fig. 7.1. Front propagating upwards around masking block: 13×13 grid

function to zero on and in the mask, the front slows down before it actually reaches the mask. Note that since this means one grid cell *normal* to the mask's boundary, a considerable amount of error can result.

A different fix, which eliminates much of this problem, comes from an alternate view; see Sethian [180]. Given a mask area Ω, construct the signed-distance function ϕ^{Ω} by taking the positive distance if inside Ω and the negative distance if outside (note that this is an opposite sign choice from the one we typically use). Then we limit motion into the masked region, not by modifying the speed function, but instead by resetting the evolving level set function. Let $\phi^{(*)}$ be the value produced by advancing the level set ϕ^n one time step. Then let

$$\phi^{n+1} = \max(\phi^*, \phi^{\Omega}). \tag{7.1}$$

This resets the level set function so that penetration is not possible; of course, this is accurate only to the order of the grid. Results using this scheme are shown in Figure 7.1(b). Again, we have used a very coarse grid to accentuate the differences.

If we consider now the opposite problem, in which a region Ω acts as a source, the solution is equally straightforward, and given by $\phi^{n+1} = \min(\phi^*, -\phi^{\Omega})$; this is the technique used in [154].

7.2 Discontinuous speed functions and sub-grid resolution

Suppose the above problem is generalized and one wants to solve an interface propagation problem in which there is a discontinuous speed function. For example, one may want to track the propagation of an interface through materials in which propagation rate changes quite sharply. As an example, consider again the evolution of the upwards propagating front, but this time the rectangular block slows the speed to $1/2$. (That is, $F = 1$ outside Ω and $F = 0.5$ inside and on Ω.) The standard level set method will interpolate between these two speeds, and the results obtained will depend on the placement of the underlying grid; substantial variation in results will occur depending on whether a grid line lies directly on, below, or above the bottom edge of the rectangular block.

In order to solve this problem accurately, some sub-grid information about the speed function is needed to correctly construct the speed function for those cells that lie only partially within Ω. Such a technique can be devised, motivated by the idea of the volume-of-fluid methods discussed earlier. Given a region Ω, before any calculation proceeds we construct the cell fraction $\mathrm{Vol}_{ij}^{\Omega}$, which is a number between 0 and 1 for those cells that have at least one grid point in Ω and one outside Ω. This cell fraction corresponds to the amount of Ω material in the cell. These values are stored, and a list is kept of such boundary cells. Then proceed with the level set calculation, letting F be given by its value in the corresponding region. However, we modify the speed function for those cells that are marked as boundary cells. At the beginning of the time step, compute the volume fraction Vol_{ij}^{ϕ} for the zero level set in each cell; this may be done approximately without explicitly finding the zero level set through a least squares fit. This value is then compared with the stored value $\mathrm{Vol}_{ij}^{\Omega}$, and the speed function is modified accordingly.

7.3 Multiple interfaces

As initially designed in [144], the level set technique applies to problems in which there is a clear distinction between an "inside" and "outside". This is because the interface is assigned the zero level value between the two regions. Extensions to multiple (more than two) interfaces have been made in some specific cases. In the case in which interfaces are passively transported and behave nicely, one may be able to use only one level set function and judiciously assign different values at the interfaces. For

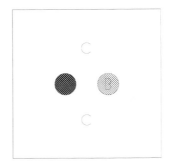

Fig. 7.2. Regions A and B expand into region C

example, the zero level set may correspond to the boundary between two regions A and B, with the level set value 10 corresponding to the interface between two regions B and C. If A and C never touch, then this technique may be used to follow the interfaces in some cases.

However, in the more general case involving the emergence and motion of triple points, a different approach is required, since many different situations can occur (see, for example, Bronsard and Wetton [29] and Taylor and Cahn [194]). Consider the following canonical example, as illustrated in Figure 7.2. Regions A and B are both circular disks growing into region C with speed unity in the direction normal to each interface. At some point, the interfaces will touch and meet at a triple point, where a clear notion of "inside" and "outside" cannot be assigned in a consistent manner.

A solution lies in recasting the interface motion as the motion of one level set function for each material. In some sense, this is what was done in the re-ignition idea given in [154], where the front was a flame that propagated downstream under a fluid flow. This front was re-ignited at each time step at a flame holder point by taking the minimum of the advancing flame and its original configuration around the flame holder, thus ensuring that the maximum burned fluid is achieved. We now discuss a technique, presented in [177, 176], which works in some cases.

In general, imagine N separate regions and a full set of all possible pairwise speed functions F_{IJ} that describe the propagation speed of region I into region J: F is taken as zero if region I cannot penetrate J. The idea is to advance each interface to obtain a trial value for each interface with respect to motion into every other region, and then combine the trial values in such a way as to obtain the maximum possible motion of the interface.

In general, then, proceed as follows. Given a region I, obtain $N - 1$ trial level set functions ϕ^*_{IJ} by moving the region I into each possible region J, J = 1, N (J≠I) with speed F_{IJ}. During the motion of region I into region J, assume that all other regions are impenetrable, that is, use the masking rule given by equation (7.1). We then test the penetrability of region J itself, leaving the value of ϕ^*_{IJ} unchanged if $F_{IJ} \neq 0$, else modifying it with the maximum of itself and $-\phi^*_{IJ}$. Finally, to allow region I to evolve as much as possible, we take the minimum over all possible motions to obtain the new position; this is the re-ignition idea described earlier. Complete details of the approach may be found in Sethian [176].

Three examples are shown to illustrate this approach. Given regions A, B, and C, the *influence matrix* describes the interaction of the various regions with each other. The interaction of each region with itself is left blank. The interaction of any pair of regions must be zero in one of the two interactions.

In Figure 7.3, regions A and B expand with unit speed into region C, but cannot penetrate each other. They advance and meet; the boundary between the two becomes a vertical straight line.

Next, we consider a problem with different evolution rates. In Figure 7.4, region A grows with speed 1 into region C (and region C grows with speed 0 into region A), and region B grows with speed 2 into region C. Once they come into contact, region A dominates region B with speed 3, thus region B grows through C and then is "eaten up" by the advancing region A. Note what happens; region A advances with speed 3 to the edge of region B, which is advancing only with speed 1 into region C. However, region A cannot pass region B, because *its* speed into region C is slower than that of region B.

Finally, in Figure 7.5 the motion of a triple point between regions A, B, and C is shown. Assume that region A penetrates B with speed 1, B penetrates C with speed 1, and C penetrates A with speed 1. The exact solution is given by a spiral with no limiting tangent angle as the triple point is approached. The triple point does not move; instead, the regions spiral around it. In Figure 7.5, results are shown from a calculation on a 98 × 98 grid. Starting from the initial configuration, the regions spiral around each other, with the leading tip of each spiral controlled by the grid size. In other words, we are unable to resolve spirals tighter than the grid size, and hence that controls the fine scale description of the motion. However, we note that the triple point remains fixed.

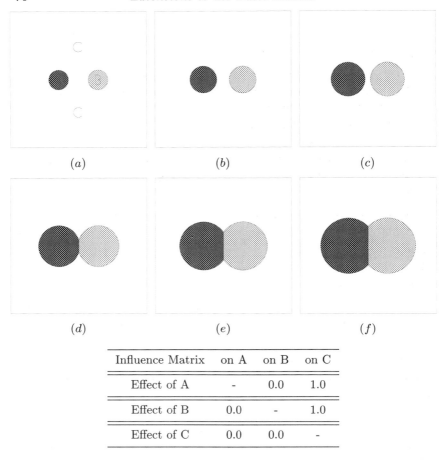

(a)   (b)   (c)

(d)   (e)   (f)

Influence Matrix	on A	on B	on C
Effect of A	-	0.0	1.0
Effect of B	0.0	-	1.0
Effect of C	0.0	0.0	-

Fig. 7.3. A and B move into C with speed 1, stop at each other

A series of additional calculations using this approach may be found in [177].

7.4 Triple points

The true motion of multiple interfaces and multiple junctions is highly complex; some of the most elaborate level set schemes are due to Bence, Merriman, and Osher [134]. As illustration, consider now the case of a triple point motion in which the speed of each interface is driven by curvature, which may correspond to surface tension. Imagine a triple point, in which each of the three regions is attempting to move according

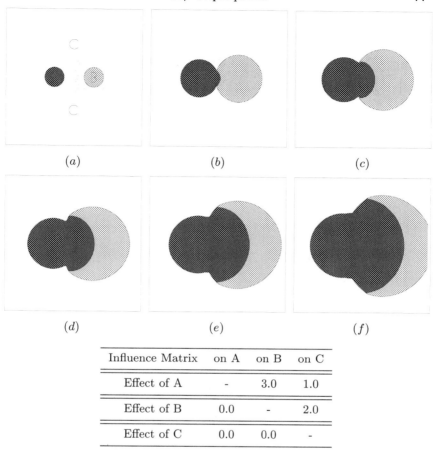

(a)   (b)   (c)

(d)   (e)   (f)

Influence Matrix	on A	on B	on C
Effect of A	-	3.0	1.0
Effect of B	0.0	-	2.0
Effect of C	0.0	0.0	-

Fig. 7.4. A into C with speed 1, A into B with speed 3, B into C with speed 2

to its own curvature. In Figure 7.6(a), we show an initial configuration on the left and a final state in Figure 7.6(b) on the right, which consists of the three lines meeting in equal angles of 120 degrees.

If one attempts to apply the level set method for multiple interfaces described in the previous sections, a difficulty occurs because each level function attempts to move away from the others, creating a gap. In Figure 7.6(c), we show this gap developing when a level set technique is applied to the final state.

Two different level set type algorithms were introduced in Merriman, Bence, and Osher [134] to tackle this problem. The first can be viewed

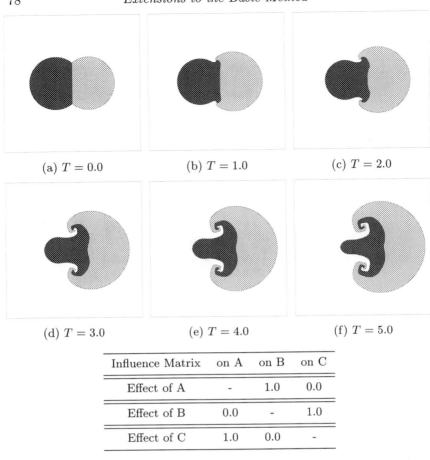

(a) $T = 0.0$ (b) $T = 1.0$ (c) $T = 2.0$

(d) $T = 3.0$ (e) $T = 4.0$ (f) $T = 5.0$

Influence Matrix	on A	on B	on C
Effect of A	-	1.0	0.0
Effect of B	0.0	-	1.0
Effect of C	1.0	0.0	-

Fig. 7.5. Spiraling triple point: 98×98 grid

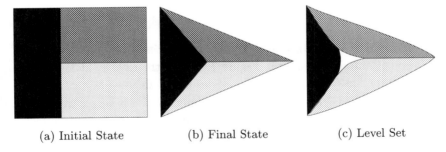

(a) Initial State   (b) Final State   (c) Level Set

Fig. 7.6. Evolution of triple point under curvature

as a "fix" to the above problem; the second is a wholly different level set approach.

To begin, the problem with the above calculation is that the various level sets pull apart. The level set functions are reset to hold the triple point in place; that is,

$$\phi_i = \phi_i - \max_{i \neq j} \phi_j. \tag{7.2}$$

This keeps the triple point in place, however, the cost is that the level set functions can develop spontaneous zero crossings later in time. A remedy is to re-initialize all the level sets using any of the re-initialization techniques described in the previous chapter. With those two added steps in the algorithm, level set methods can handle some problems concerning triple points.

A considerably different approach works by applying a reaction-diffusion type equation to a characteristic function assigned to each region, which is one inside the region and zero outside. This algorithm works by exploiting the link between curvature flow and a diffusion equation, along the lines of the material discussed earlier. The basic idea is that a diffusion term is applied, and then a sharpening term is executed that sharpens up the solution. The net effect is to evolve the boundary line under curvature. For additional work on curvature flow and the limit of related partial differential equations, see [28, 29, 77, 159].

7.5 Building extension velocity fields

What happens when the speed of the moving front has meaning only on the front itself? This is a common occurrence in areas such as combustion, material science, and fluid mechanics, in which the philosophy of embedding the front as the zero level set of a family of contours can be problematic. In fact, the most difficult part of level set methods is this "extension" problem, and will be a central focus of Part IV.

Recall the division of arguments in the speed function F given in equation (1.1). Local arguments are those that depend on geometric quantities of the front, such as curvature and normal vector, and have a clear meaning for all the level sets. Independent variables are equally straightforward, since their contribution to the speed makes no reference to particular information from the front itself.

The troublesome variables are the so-called "global" variables, which can arise from solving differential equations on either side of the interface. Four possible ways to extend a velocity from the front to the grid points are:

(i) At each grid point, find the closest point on the front, and use the speed function at that point. This was the technique used in [120], and may be done efficiently in many cases by tracing backwards along the gradient given by $\nabla \phi$.

(ii) Evaluate the speed function off the front using an equation that has meaning only on the front itself. This is the technique used in the crystal growth/dendritic solidification calculations employed in [182], where a boundary integral is evaluated both on and off the front.

(iii) Develop an evaluation technique that assigns artificial speeds to the level set going through any particular grid point. For example, in the etching/deposition simulations of [2, 3, 4], visibility of the zero level set must be evaluated away from the front itself.

(iv) Smear the influence of the front. In the combustion calculations of [154] and the fluid dynamics calculations of [39, 193, 208], the influence of the front is mollified to neighboring grid points, which contribute terms to an appropriate equation. The solution to this equation then naturally gives a speed function for all the level sets.

We shall discuss numerous extension velocities in Part IV. First, however, we turn to some theoretical considerations, which lead to fast marching methods for the stationary formulation of the level set equation.

Part III

Viscosity Solutions, Hamilton–Jacobi Equations, and Fast Marching Level Set Methods

In this part, we focus on Hamilton–Jacobi equations, beginning with the formal definition of a viscosity solution. We then introduce a class of new fast marching methods for the static Hamilton–Jacobi equation, which arises in the case of a monotonically advancing front, and discuss appropriate approximation schemes.

8

Viscosity Solutions and Hamilton–Jacobi Equations

Outline: *We present the formal definition of a viscosity solution to the level set equation based on its behavior at extrema. This turns out to be a more appropriate way of characterizing the correct weak solution; using this definition, one then proves that the viscosity solution is the limit of smooth solutions as the smoothing term goes to zero.*

Our presentation of level set methods has taken an algorithmic approach. That is, we have been motivated by presenting an intuitive feel for the mechanism linking moving fronts and hyperbolic conservation laws. We have taken this approach for two reasons. First, as we have seen, the notion of what happens when a corner develops in an evolving one-dimensional curve neatly parallels the development of shocks and rarefaction fans in the conservation law for evolving slope. Second, the rich wealth of numerical schemes from hyperbolic schemes is what gives rise to the array of level set algorithms just presented.

Formally, however, this link cannot be extended in higher dimensions. Recall that in the one-dimensional case of a graph propagating with speed F in its normal direction, equation (1.17) gave the change in the height of the function ψ as

$$\psi_t = F(1 + \psi_x^2)^{1/2}. \tag{8.1}$$

Differentiating both sides of this equation yielded an evolution equation for the slope $u = d\psi/dx$ of the propagating front, namely,

$$u_t + [-(1 + u^2)^{1/2}]_x = \epsilon \left[\frac{u_x}{1 + u^2}\right]_x, \tag{8.2}$$

which is a viscous hyperbolic conservation law with $G(u) = (1 + u^2)^{1/2}$ for the propagating slope u.

In contrast, imagine a level set equation that embeds a one-dimensional curve in the higher dimensional level set function ϕ as

$$\phi_t + F(\phi_x^2 + \phi_y^2)^{1/2} = 0. \tag{8.3}$$

If we try letting $u = \phi_x$ and $v = \phi_y$, and differentiate both sides with respect to x and y, we get a pair of equations for u and v. These are linked by the equality of mixed partials, in which $u_y = v_x$. Thus, unlike our one-dimensional case, we cannot simply take the theory of viscous solutions and entropy conditions for hyperbolic conservation laws and "integrate it upwards".

Instead, a better approach is to work *directly* with the level set equation, and add a viscous right-hand side. Once again, the solution to this equation is smooth for all time, and the limit as the viscosity term goes to zero produces the appropriate weak solution. Since the notion of an "entropy solution" is intimately linked with hyperbolic conservation laws, the appropriate weak solution that permits corners is instead referred to as a "viscosity solution". In fact, the preferred construction of such viscosity solutions proceeds along a different line: a definition of a viscosity solution is given that is then shown to be equivalent to the classical (smooth) solution where the solution is smooth, and, under certain restrictions, equal to the limit as the viscous smoothing term vanishes. Thus, rather than define the viscosity solution as the limit of the smooth solutions, an alternate definition is given which is then *proved* to be this limit. These are the ideas of viscosity solutions of Hamilton–Jacobi equations, introduced by Crandall and Lions [54]; see also Crandall, Evans and Lions [52] and Crandall, Ishii, and Lions [53]. In the rest of this brief chapter, we make these ideas more precise; for further details, see Evans [62].

8.1 Viscosity solutions of Hamilton–Jacobi equations

Consider the level set equation $\phi_t + F|\nabla\phi| = 0$. If the speed F depends only on position x and first derivatives of ϕ, this is a particular case of the more general Hamilton–Jacobi equation

$$u_t + H(Du, x) = 0, \tag{8.4}$$

where $H = F|\nabla\phi|$. Here, Du represents the partials of u in each variable, for example, u_x and u_y. Assume that the Hamiltonian H is a smooth function of its arguments. We want to admit non-smooth solutions, that is, those that may have corners, similar to the previous desire to admit non-smooth solutions of a hyperbolic conservation law. A natural approach, in parallel with the earlier discussion, is to add a viscosity term, that is,

$$u_t + H(Du, x) = \epsilon \Delta u, \tag{8.5}$$

where ϵ is a positive constant. Then, given a solution u_ϵ to the above, one wants to show that such a solution is smooth, and that its limit as ϵ vanishes gives an appropriate weak solution.

Rather than define the weak solution as a limit of smooth solutions, Crandall, Evans, and Lions [52], reformulating an earlier definition in Crandall and Lions [54], instead define a weak solution as follows:

Definition u is said to be a *viscosity solution* of equation (8.4), if, for all smooth test functions v,

(i) if $u - v$ has a local maximum at a point (x_o, t_o) then

$$v_t(x_o, t_o) + H(Dv(x_o, t_o), x_o)) \leq 0 \tag{8.6}$$

(ii) if $u - v$ has a local minimum at a point (x_o, t_o) then

$$v_t(x_o, t_o) + H(Dv(x_o, t_o), x_o)) \geq 0. \tag{8.7}$$

Note that nowhere in this definition is the viscosity solution u differentiated; everything is done in terms of the test function h. The motivation comes from the usual trick of integration by parts; one uses a smooth test and moves all the derivatives onto the test function in exchange for some boundary conditions.

The above is only a definition; several things need to be checked before it can be viewed as a reasonable solution to the Hamilton–Jacobi equation. In fact, it can be shown that

- *If u is a smooth solution of the Hamilton–Jacobi equation, then it is a viscosity solution.*

In other words, any classical solution that stays smooth for all time satisfies the two inequalities in the above definition.

- *If a viscosity solution u is differentiable at some point, then it satisfies the Hamilton–Jacobi equation there.*

    In other words, where the viscosity solution is smooth, it gives the same answer as the classical solution.

- *The above viscosity solution is unique, given appropriate initial conditions.*

    That is, there is only one viscosity solution satisfying the above definition.

- *The solution produced by taking the limit of the smooth solutions u_ϵ as ϵ goes to zero is a viscosity solution; by uniqueness, this solution must be the one given above.*

We shall prove none of these here; instead, precise statements and proofs may be found in [54, 52, 62]. The salient point is that the viscosity solution is now defined in a way that does not require differentiation, and in fact can then be proven to be the unique viscous limit of the smoothed Hamilton–Jacobi equation.

8.2 Numerical approximations

To summarize, two sets of schemes have been developed in a previous chapter for approximating the solution to our level set equations, depending on whether the Hamiltonian H is convex or non-convex. A considerable body of work exists to show that these schemes, as well as others, converge to the above viscosity solution. In fact, Crandall and Lions [54] analyze an explicit finite difference scheme; see also, for example, Souganidis [187]. Most of these schemes are finite difference expressions that contain some forms of smoothing, often in the spirit of the method of artificial viscosity discussed earlier. Convergent schemes result from the same criteria of monotonicity and consistency.

9

Approximating the Stationary Level Set Formulation
Fast Marching Level Set Methods

Outline: *We introduce a class of fast marching methods for solving the static Hamilton–Jacobi equation; the techniques result from a blend of fast narrow band methods and heapsort algorithms.*

9.1 Foundations

The static Hamilton–Jacobi equation, namely,

$$H(Du, x) = 0, \tag{9.1}$$

comes from removing the time derivative. We have seen that the special case of a monotonically advancing front, that is, a front moving with speed F where F is always positive (or negative), leads to a particular stationary level set equation for the crossing time T given by

$$|\nabla T|F = 1. \tag{9.2}$$

If F is a function of position only, this becomes the well-known Eikonal equation. We refer the interested reader to a large body of literature on this subject, including relevant theory in Barles and Souganidis [17], Crandall, Evans, and Lions [52], Lions [116], and Souganidis [187], and numerical algorithms in Bardi and Falcone [14], Falcone, Giorgi, and Falcone [69], Kimmel [98], and Rouy and Tourin [156].

Let us focus for a moment on the Eikonal equation, namely,

$$|\nabla T|F(x) = 1. \tag{9.3}$$

Thus, the speed does not depend on the orientation of the front (it depends only on *independent variables*, using our earlier terminology).

One way to solve this Eikonal equation is through finite difference operators on a fixed cartesian grid. Following our earlier discussions, an upwind, viscosity-solution approximation to the gradient leads to

$$\max(D_{ij}^{-x}T, 0)^2 + \min(D_{ij}^{+x}T, 0)^2 + \max(D_{ij}^{-y}T, 0)^2 + \min(D_{ij}^{+y}T, 0)^2 = F_{ij}^2.$$

$$(9.4)$$

How does one in fact *solve* for the solution T given by the above scheme? Since equation (9.4) is in essence a quadratic equation for the value at each grid point (assuming the others are held fixed), one can iterate until convergence by solving the equation at each grid point, selecting the largest possible value as the solution in accordance with obtaining the correct viscosity solution; one such scheme was introduced by Rouy and Tourin in [156]; see also Falcone [69, 14]. Typically, one iterates several times through the entire set of grid points until a converged solution is reached.

We now discuss a *fast marching method*, introduced by Sethian in [180] and discussed in detail in [178], that provides an extremely fast method for solving the Eikonal equation. It relies on a marriage between the narrow band methodology and a fast heapsort algorithm, and can be viewed as an extreme one-cell version of our narrow band technique.

9.2 The Eikonal equation and the fast marching method

The key to constructing a fast marching algorithm is the observation that the upwind difference structure of equation (9.4) means that information propagates "one way", that is, from smaller values of T to larger values. Hence, we can "solve" equation (9.4) by building the solution outwards from the smallest T value. The algorithm is made fast by confining the "building zone" to a narrow band around the front. The idea is to sweep the front ahead in an upwind fashion by considering a set of points in narrow band around the existing front, and to march this narrow band forwards, freezing the values of existing points and bringing new ones into the narrow band structure. The key is in the selection of *which* grid point in the narrow band to update. The technique is easiest to explain algorithmically, see Figure 9.1.

To illustrate, consider the Eikonal equation on an $N \times N$ grid on the unit box $[0, 1] \times [0, 1]$ with right-hand side $F_{ij} > 0$; as initial data, let $T = 0$ along the top of the box. Here $(i, j) = (1, 1)$ corresponds to the coordinate $(0, 0)$, while $(i, j) = (N, N)$ corresponds to coordinate $(1, 1)$.

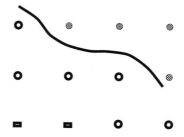

Fig. 9.1. A snapshot from $N \times N$ larger grid, after several iterations of the fast marching algorithm

Algorithm:

(i) Initialize

    (a) (Alive points: gray disks): Let *Alive* be the set of all grid points at which the value of T is zero. In the example, $Alive = \{(i,j) : i \in \{1, .., N\}, j = N\}$.

    (b) (Narrow Band points: black circles): Let *NarrowBand* be the set of all grid points in the narrow band. For this example $NarrowBand = \{(i,j) : i \in \{1, .., N\}, j = N - 1\}$; set $T_{i,N-1} = dy/F_{ij}$.

    (c) (Far Away points: black rectangles): Let *FarAway* be the set of all the rest of the grid points $\{(i,j) : j < N - 1\}$; set $T_{i,j} = \infty$ for all points in *FarAway*.

(ii) Marching forwards

    (a) Begin loop: Let $(i_{\min}, j_{\min})$ be the point in *NarrowBand* with the smallest value for T.

    (b) Add the point $(i_{\min}, j_{\min})$ to *Alive*; remove from *Narrow-Band*.

    (c) Tag as neighbors any points $(i_{\min}-1, j_{\min})$, $(i_{\min}+1, j_{\min})$, $(i_{\min}, j_{\min} - 1)$, $(i_{\min}, j_{\min} + 1)$ that are not *Alive*; if the neighbor is in *FarAway*, remove it from that set and add it to the *NarrowBand* set.

    (d) Recompute the values of u at all neighbors according to equation (9.4), solving the quadratic equation given by our scheme.

    (e) Return to top of loop.

We take periodic boundary conditions where required. Assuming for

	B	
A	T_{old}	C
	D	

Fig. 9.2. Matrix of neighboring values

the moment that it takes no work to determine the member of the narrow band with the smallest value of T, then the total work required to compute the solution at all grid points is $O(N^2)$, where calculation is performed on an $N \times N$ grid.

Why does the above algorithm work? Since the smallest value in the narrow band is selected, its value for T must be correct; other narrow band points or far away points with larger T values cannot affect it. As shown below, the process of recomputing the T values at neighboring points (that have not been previously accepted) cannot yield a value smaller than any of that at any of the accepted points. Thus, the solution can be marched outwards, always selecting the narrow band grid point with minimum trial value for T, and readjusting neighbors. Another way to look at this is that each minimum trial value begins an application of Huyghen's principle, and the expanding wave front touches and updates all others.

9.2.1 *Proof that the technique produces a viable solution*

We now prove that the above construction produces a viable solution to the Eikonal equation. A detailed constructive proof was given in [180, 178], here a more abstract approach is taken that leads to more general schemes. Recall the difference operator

$$\max(D_{ij}^{-x}T, 0)^2 + \min(D_{ij}^{+x}T, 0)^2 + \max(D_{ij}^{-y}T, 0)^2 + \min(D_{ij}^{+y}T, 0)^2 = F_{ij}^2.$$

$$(9.5)$$

and consider the matrix of grid values given in Figure 9.2. Our argument will follow the computation of the new value of T in the center grid point to replace the value of T_{old} based on the neighboring values. Assume, without loss of generality, that the narrow band point with the smallest value is located in the cell marked A[1]. Then T_{old} is greater than or equal to A, since it is available for being updated and was not the smallest such

---

[1] We shall use A to stand for both the value of u and grid point location.

value. We shall show that the recomputation of a new value T_{new} at T_{old} *cannot* yield a value smaller than A; the proof will be by contradiction.

Suppose the value of T_{new} when recomputed under the influence of A is less than A. Then by the structure of the upwind operator in equation (9.4), A does not participate in the value of T_{new} since only neighbors smaller than the new value for T_{new} contribute. This means that the recomputation of T_{new} due to A has no effect, and hence $T_{new} = T_{old}$. But this value is greater than or equal to A, which is a contradiction, hence we are done.

Thus, the selection of the smallest possible member in the narrow band and the use of an upwind scheme guarantees that the construction builds a viable solution.

9.2.2 The min-heap data structure

The key to an efficient version of the above technique lies in a fast way of locating the grid point in the narrow band with the smallest value for T. An efficient scheme to do so is discussed in detail in Adalsteinsson, Kimmel, Malladi and Sethian [5]; here we follow that discussion.

We use a variation on a heap algorithm (see Sedgewick [166]) with back pointers to store the T values. Specifically, we use a min–heap data structure. In an abstract sense, a min-heap is a "complete binary tree" with a property that the value at any given node is less than or equal to the values at its children. In practice, it is more efficient to represent a heap sequentially as an array by storing a node at location k and its children at locations $2k$ and $2k + 1$. From this definition, the parent of a given node at k is located at $k/2$. Therefore, the root which contains the smallest element is stored at location $k = 1$ in the array. Finding the parent or children of a given element are simple array accesses which take $O(1)$ time.

The values of u are stored, together with the indices which give their location in the grid structure. The marching algorithm works by first looking for the smallest element in the *NarrowBand*; this **FindSmallest** operation involves deleting the root and one sweep of **DownHeap** to ensure that the remaining elements satisfy the heap property. The algorithm proceeds by tagging the neighboring points that are not *Alive*. The *FarAway* neighbors are added to the heap using an **Insert** operation and values at the remaining points are updated using equation (9.4). **Insert** works by increasing the heap size by one and trickling the new element upward to its correct location using an **UpHeap** operation. Lastly, to ensure that the updated u values do not violate the heap property, we need to perform an UpHeap operation starting at that location and proceeding up the tree.

The DownHeap and UpHeap operations (in the worst case) carry an element all the way from root to bottom or vice versa. Therefore, this takes $O(\log N)$ time assuming there are N elements in the heap. It is important to note that the heap which is a complete binary tree is always guaranteed to remain balanced. All that remains is the operation of searching for the *Narrow Band* neighbors of the smallest element in the heap. This can be made $O(1)$ in time by maintaining back pointers from the grid to the heap array. Without the back pointers, the above search takes $O(N)$ in the worst case.

As an example, Figure 9.3 shows a typical heap structure and an UpHeap operation after the element at location $(2,7)$ gets updated from 3.1 to 2.0.

Thus, since the total work in changing the value of one element of the heap and bubbling its value upwards is $O(\log N)$, where N is the size of the heap, this produces a total operation count of $N \log N$ for the fast marching method on a grid of total N points.

9.2.3 Initial conditions

The above technique considered a flat initial interface for which trial values at the narrow band points could be easily initialized. Given an arbitrary closed curve or surface as the initial location of the front, one can use the original narrow band level set method to initialize the problem. First, label all grid points as "far away" and assign them T values of ∞. Then, in a very small neighborhood around the interface, construct the signed-distance function from the initial hypersurface Γ. Propagate that surface both forwards and backwards in time until a layer of grid points is crossed in each direction, computing the signed crossing times as in [175]. Then collect the points with negative crossing times as "alive" points with T value equal to the crossing time, and the points with positive crossing times as narrow band points with T value equal to the positive crossing times. Then begin the fast marching algorithm.

A more sophisticated technique for initializing the fast marching method is given in [5].

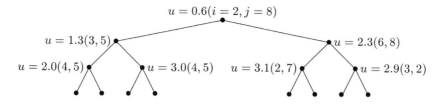

Step 1: Change u value at $(2,7)$

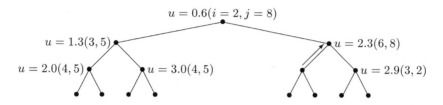

Step 2: New value at $(2,7)$; `UpHeap`

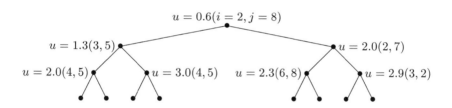

Heap property restored

Fig. 9.3. Heap structure and UpHeap+ operation

9.3 General static Hamilton–Jacobi equations

Suppose we try to extend the above technique to a more general static Hamiltonian–Jacobi equation. Thus, let $u(x)$ be a scalar function from $x = (x_1, \ldots, x_n)$; i.e, $u : R^N \to R$. The goal is to solve the static Hamilton–Jacobi equation

$$H(Du, x) = 0 \tag{9.6}$$

where Du is represents the derivatives in each of the component variables $u_{x_1}, \ldots, u_{x_N}$. As initial conditions, assume that u is known on a subset Ω of R^N (without loss of generality, assume that $u = 0$ on Ω).

In [5], the fast marching technique was extended to handle this more general class. Assume that H is convex. Suppose we approximate the Hamiltonian by a difference operator of the form

$$H_{ij}(u_{ij}, u_{i-1,j}, u_{i+1,j}, u_{i,j-1}, u_{i,j+1}, x_{ij}) = 0. \qquad (9.7)$$

Here, a two-dimensional problem is considered with a stencil consisting of the four neighboring values. (Operators with larger stencils and more space dimensions are allowed.) Now,

• Solve for u_{ij} using the scheme $H_{ij} = 0$, holding the neighboring values fixed. Let A be the subset of the neighboring values that contribute to u_{ij}. Suppose u_{ij} is greater than or equal to all the values in the subset A (this is just the upwind property that we demonstrated for our Eikonal approximation).

Then, under these conditions, our fast marching method can be used to systematically produce the solution.

Of course, construction of such a scheme may not be straightforward, and some work may be required to devise a scheme that satisfies the above requirement (while, of course, remaining consistent and producing the viscosity solution in the sense of the previous chapter). However, if such a scheme can be generated, the fast marching algorithm can be used. General schemes for a variety of static Hamilton–Jacobi equations are given in Chapter 16.

We note that a straightforward application of the above is in re-initializing the front. Here, we simply compute the arrival time function T for a front moving forwards and one moving backwards; this then gives the signed-distance function, producing an extremely fast initialization procedure for the narrow band method.

9.4 Some clarifying comments

Both the time-dependent level set method and the stationary formulation require careful construction of upwind, entropy-satisfying schemes, and make use of the dynamics and geometry of front propagation analyzed in [170]. However, we note that the time-dependent level set method advances the front *simultaneously*, while the stationary scheme constructs "scaffolding" to build the time solution surface T one grid point at a time. This means that the time at which the surface crosses a grid point (that is, its T value) is found before nearby values are determined. As such, there is *no* notion of a time step in the stationary method; one is simply constructing the stationary surface in an upwind fashion.

This means that if one is attempting to solve a problem in which the the speed of a front depends on the current position of the front (such as in the case of visibility), or on subtle orientations in the front (such as in sputter yield problems), it is not clear how to use the stationary method, since the front is being constructed one grid point at a time.

To summarize,

- The fast marching method is convenient for problems in which the front speed depends on independent variables, such as in the Eikonal equation, and applies only if the speed function does not change sign. In the case of more general static Hamilton–Jacobi equations, appropriate schemes must be developed.
- The time-dependent level set method is designed for more delicate speed functions, and can accurately track fronts evolving under highly complex arguments.

In the next part, we discuss a variety of applications which employ both the time-dependent level set method and the fast marching method for monotonically advancing fronts.

Part IV

Applications

In this part, we present a series of applications of both the time-dependent level set methodology and the fast marching algorithm for propagating interfaces. The intent is to indicate the range of problems that may be framed in this perspective.

10

Geometry

Curve/Surface Shrinkage and Self-Similar Surfaces

Outline: *We begin with the application of level set methods to problems in the geometric evolution of curves and surfaces. The motion here depends only on local geometric properties such as normal direction and curvature; nonetheless, this is a rich area.*

10.1 Statement of problem

Given a hypersurface in R^n propagating with some speed $F(\kappa)$, previously we have considered speed functions of the form $F(\kappa) = 1 - \epsilon\kappa$, where κ is the curvature. We now focus on a special speed function, namely $F = -\kappa$, where κ is the curvature (at least in two dimensions; other forms for the curvature are required in higher dimensions).

Why does one care about such a speed function? One answer is that this motion corresponds to a geometric version of the heat equation. Substituting the speed function into the level set equation (2.5) we have

$$\phi_t = \nabla \cdot \frac{\nabla\phi}{|\nabla\phi|}|\nabla\phi|, \qquad (10.1)$$

where we have substituted $\nabla \cdot \frac{\nabla\phi}{|\nabla\phi|}$ for the curvature κ. Thus motion under curvature resembles a non-linear heat equation; large oscillations are immediately smoothed out, and long-term solutions result from dissipation of information about the initial state.

Another reason, as we shall see in later sections, is that motion by curvature plays an important role in many applications. Because it corresponds to a diffusion-like term, it can be used to relax and reshape boundaries, account for surface tension in flexible membranes, and act as a viscous term in physical phenomena.

Thus, as a precursor to a collection of problems, we investigate motion of an interface under its own curvature. We would like to study four questions:

(i) What happens to a simple closed curve moving under its curvature?

(ii) What happens to a hypersurface in higher dimensions?

(iii) Are there self-similar structures under this motion, that is, hypersurfaces that do not change shape as they evolve?

(iv) What happens to curves moving under higher derivatives of curvature?

The answer to the first question about the evolution of a simple closed curve moving under its curvature was definitively answered through the remarkable work of Gage and Grayson. First, Gage [72, 73] showed that any convex curve moving under such a motion remains convex and must shrink to a point. Grayson [78] followed this work with the beautiful result that *all* simple closed curves must shrink to a round point, regardless of their initial shape.

What about the second question? The first point to note is that a variety of different curvatures for hypersurfaces in R^3 and higher are possible, such as mean curvature, Gaussian curvature, etc. Focussing on mean curvature. Huisken [88] has shown that convex shapes shrink to spheres as they collapse, analogous to the result of Gage. However, Grayson [79] showed that non-convex shapes may in fact *not* shrink to a sphere and provided the counterexample of the dumbbell. A narrow handle of a dumbbell may have such a high inner radius that the mean curvature of the saddle point at the neck may still be positive, and hence the neck will pinch off. A study of motion under Gauss curvature may be found in [142].

Next, what about self-similar shapes? In two dimensions, it is clear that a circle collapsing under its own curvature remains a circle; this can be seen by integrating the ordinary differential equation for the changing radius. In three dimensions, a sphere is self-similar under mean curvature flow, since its curvature is always constant. Are there other shapes?

Finally, what about flow under speeds that depend on derivatives of the curvature? Are there similar results?

10.2 Equations of motion

The transformation of these questions to a level set framework is particularly straightforward. The level set equation (10.1) is solved everywhere, and each level set moves under its own curvature. Thus, the problem we "care" about is embedded in an entire family of such problems, each of which proceeds according to the prescribed motion.

10.3 Results

We begin with a calculation designed to illustrate Grayson's theorem. In Figure 10.1, an odd-shaped initial curve is viewed as the zero level set of a function defined in all of R^2. Here, for illustration, black corresponds to $\phi < 0$, while white corresponds to $\phi > 0$, thus the zero level set is the boundary between the two. As the level curves flow under curvature, the ensuing motion carries each to a circle that then disappears. In the evolution of the front, one clearly sees that the large oscillations disappear quickly, and then as the front becomes circular, motion slows, and the front eventually disappears.

Next, Grayson's counterexample of the collapse of a dumbbell in three dimensions under its mean curvature is computed. In Figure 10.2, taken from Sethian [173], the two-dimensional cross-section of the motion of a dumbbell collapsing under its mean curvature is shown at various times. Because the principal radius of curvature around the neck is so large, it dominates the negative value of the other principal radius, and the handle shrinks inwards and disappears.

This result shows that a simply connected surface propagating under its mean curvature in three dimensions can break into two separate surfaces as it evolves. In fact, a different choice of initial surface shows that the front can go from a single surface to *five* separate surfaces before each collapses to a sphere and disappears. Figure 10.3, taken from Chopp and Sethian [43], shows two connected dumbbells. As the intersection point collapses, the necks break off and leave a remaining "pillow"-like region behind. This pillow region collapses as well, and eventually all five regions disappear.

Finally, what about the existence of self-similar surfaces that remain morphologically unchanged as they evolve under curvature? As mentioned above, a sphere is obviously one such shape. To find another one, imagine a torus-shaped object. If the torus is fat, then the inside will pinch off and become sphere-like; the shape will then continue to evolve

Fig. 10.1. $F(\kappa) = -\kappa$

and collapse to a point. On the other hand, if the initial shape is closer to a thin ring, the ring will collapse down and disappear all at once. This suggests the existence of an intermediate shape between the two that exactly balances these two competing pulls so that the shape stays the same as the object collapses. In fact, Angenent [10] was the first to prove the existence of a self-similar torus that preserves this balance.

Are there other self-similar shapes? Here, we describe an algorithm due to Chopp that yields a collection of such surfaces. The following discussion is taken from Chopp [42]; we refer the interested reader to that work.

In order to produce self-similar shapes, we need two things. First, since hypersurfaces get smaller as they move under their curvature, a mechanism is needed to "rescale" their motion so that the evolution can

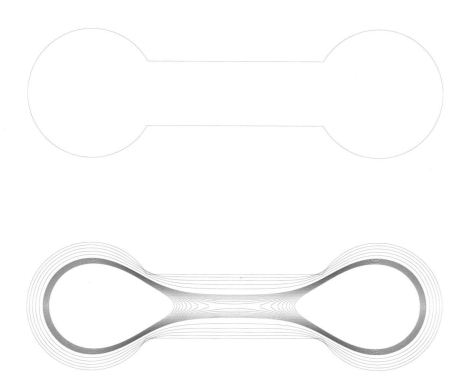

Fig. 10.2. Cross-section of dumbbell evolution. Top: initial shape; Bottom: evolution

be continued towards a possible self-similar shape. And second, a way of testing self-similarity is required.

Chopp first constructs an evolution equation associated with rescaling as follows; here, we follow his arguments. Begin with the level set equation for mean curvature flow, given by

$$\phi_t = \kappa |\nabla \phi|. \tag{10.2}$$

Then define a new function ψ as

$$\psi(x,t) = \phi(\sigma(t)x, t)/\sigma^2(t) - L(t), \tag{10.3}$$

where $\sigma(t)$ acts as a stretching function and $L(t)$ will be used to pick

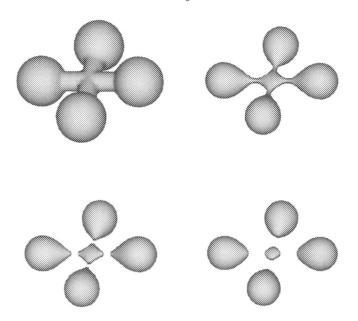

Fig. 10.3. Collapse of two-handled dumbbell

out the level set corresponding to the front of interest. Differentiating
equation (10.3) with respect to t and combining with equation (10.2)
produces a new partial differential equation for ψ given by

$$\psi_t = \frac{\sigma'(t)}{\sigma(t)} \left(x \cdot \nabla\psi - 2(\psi + L(t))\right) + \kappa_\psi ||\nabla\psi|| - L'(t), \qquad (10.4)$$

where κ_ψ is the mean curvature of the level set surface of ψ through the
point (x,t).

The functions $\sigma(t)$ and $L(t)$ are determined dynamically as time evolves.
The stretching function $\sigma(t)$ is chosen so that the zero level set of ψ has
constant volume for all t. Assuming that the interior of a surface is given
by $\phi(x,t) < 0$, then let

$$V(t) = \int_{\{x:\phi(x,t)\leq 0\}} dV.$$

Then

$$\sigma(t) = \left(\frac{V(t)}{V(0)}\right)^{1/3}$$

so that

$$\frac{\sigma'(t)}{\sigma(t)} = \frac{V'(t)}{3V(t)}.$$

Note that the functional $V'(t)/3V(t)$ is independent of scale. This scale-independent functional can be evaluated using ψ instead of ϕ. It is approximated numerically by assuming $\tilde{\phi}(x,t) = \psi(x,t)$, and then letting $\tilde{\phi}(x,t)$ flow by mean curvature alone (i.e., σ remains fixed) to $\tilde{\phi}(x,t+\Delta t)$. The change of volume can be used to compute $V'(t)/3V(t)$.

The level function $L(t)$ is determined by using a predetermined functional $\rho(\ell,t)$ that depends solely on the geometry of the level surface $\phi(x,t) = \ell$. In the case of the torus, ρ measures a ratio of the inner radius of the torus to the thickness of the cross-section of the torus. In this way, $\rho \to 0$ if the torus evolves towards a sphere, and $\rho \to +\infty$ if the torus evolves towards a thin ring. Furthermore, a self-similar torus would necessarily have $\frac{\partial \rho}{\partial t} = 0$, because the geometric ratio should remain constant. The level function $L(t)$ is then defined by the equation $\frac{\partial \rho}{\partial t}(L(t),t) = 0$. In this context, the self-similar solution is the limiting surface $L(t)$ level set of $\psi(x,t)$. For details, see [42].

How does one check that the surfaces so obtained are indeed self-similar? Here, one can use a simple condition given by Huisken [89] that is sufficient for self-similarity. Suppose that Γ_0 is a 2-manifold such that for each point $x \in \Gamma_0$,

$$\kappa(x) = (2T)^{-1/2}x \cdot n, \tag{10.5}$$

where n is the unit normal to Γ_0 at x and T is some constant. Define $\Gamma_t = (2(T-t))^{1/2}\Gamma_0$. Then

$$\left(\frac{d}{dt}\Gamma_t\right)^{\perp} = \frac{-1}{(2(T-t))^{1/2}}\kappa_0 \cdot n = -\kappa n. \tag{10.6}$$

Therefore, Γ_t is equivalent to curvature flow with initial surface Γ_0 and hence Γ_0 must be a self-similar solution. The constant T is the time to singularity for the surface Γ_0. This test can be implemented numerically in a fairly straightforward manner.

Using the above technique, Chopp has identified a series of self-similar surfaces. One family of surfaces are constructed as follows. Begin with a sphere, and drill holes in each of the three coordinate directions; thus one can think of each hole as exiting the face of a cube, producing a surface of genus five. As this surface evolves under mean curvature flow, the holes expand and contort. The final shape, shown in Figure 10.4(a), is numerically self-similar.

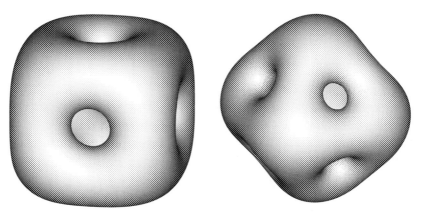

(a) Self-Similar Cube with Holes　　　(b) Self-Similar Octahedron with Holes

Fig. 10.4. Self-similar shapes

This construction continues through Chopp's observation that "every regular polyhedron with holes will produce a corresponding self-similar solution for mean curvature flow"; see [42]. Figure 10.4(b) shows another surface, produced by starting with a sphere with six cylinders drilled into it through the diagonals; this is equivalent to an octahedron, and yields a surface of genus seven. This construction of higher and higher order regular polyhedra yields a family of self-similar surfaces.

The above technique produces one class of self-similar surfaces. Chopp has also constructed a second class of unbounded self-similar surfaces using a slightly different ρ functional. This second class has led to further theoretical results; for example, see Angenent, Chopp, and Ilmanen [11]. These and other such pictures may be found in Chopp [42].

10.4 Motion under the second derivative of curvature: the sintering of materials

The methodology can be extended to another practical problem, which, while still purely geometrical, pushes our approach quite a bit further. Sintering (see [106, 149, 202]) is the process under which a compact consisting of many particles is heated to such a high temperature that the particles becomes a viscous creeping fluid, and the particles begin to coalesce together. One of the oldest technological examples is in production of bricks; other examples include formation of rock strata from sandy sediments, and the motion of thin films of metals in the microfabrication of electronic components.

At issue is the solution of the equations for creeping flow, in which the body forces on the boundary of the materials depends on the tangential derivative in the stress on the boundary. In one component of this model, the speed F of interface in its normal direction depends on the second derivative of the curvature. Thus, in our level set framework, one wants (in two dimensions), to follow a curve propagating with speed F where

$$F = \nabla \cdot \nabla \kappa = \nabla \cdot \nabla \left(\nabla \cdot \frac{\nabla \phi}{|\nabla \phi|} \right). \tag{10.7}$$

This means that the speed depends on the *fourth derivative* of the level set function! As an example, a circle is a stable object, since the curvature is constant; a little examination shows that an ellipse undergoes a restoring force which brings it back into a circle.

What about more complex shapes? The problem is quite subtle; numerical experiments are notoriously unstable when they involve computing fourth derivatives[1]. The numerical instabilities that plague such calculations are eloquently described by Van De Vorst [202]; he uses marker particle schemes together with elaborate remeshing strategies to keep the calculations alive.

A level set approach to this problem was developed by Chopp and Sethian [44]. In that work, the individual derivatives in the above expression are approximated by central difference approximations. Boundary conditions are problematic; instead, a re-initialization strategy is taken in which the level set function ϕ is recomputed periodically. This both avoids artificial errors introduced by the boundary and helps stabilize the calculation around the interface of interest.

Two calculations are shown using this approach. Figure 10.5 shows the evolution of a simple ellipse under this motion. The transformation shows the elliptical initial state on the left, followed by the evolution into a circle which then remains fixed after a large number of calculations. Figure 10.6 shows the evolution of a non-convex initial shape, which again tends to the stable state of a circle. Further shapes and details may be found in [44].

---

[1] For example, computing the solution to the biharmonic equation.

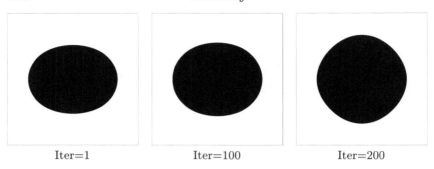

Iter=1   Iter=100   Iter=200

Fig. 10.5. Motion of ellipse under speed $F = \nabla \cdot \nabla \kappa$

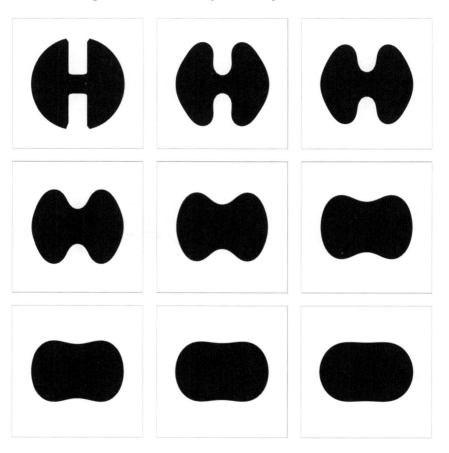

Fig. 10.6. Motion of non-convex curve under speed $F = \nabla \cdot \nabla \kappa$

11

Grid Generation

Outline: *Here, we continue with the "pure" geometry problem of grid generation. The goal is to create a logically rectangular, body-fitted grid, that is, a grid such that each grid point has four (six) neighbors in 2D (3D), and a set of grid lines corresponds to the body. By viewing the body itself as an interface and advancing the interface away from the body, a level set framework provides a natural way of constructing logical rectangular body-fitted grids.*

11.1 Statement of problem

Imagine that one is given a closed body, either as a curve in two space dimensions or a surface in three space dimensions. In many situations, one wishes to generate a logically rectangular, body-fitted grid around or inside this body. By "logically rectangular", we mean that each node of the grid has four neighbors (in two dimensions; in three dimensions, there are six neighbors); by "body-fitted", we mean that the grid aligns itself with the body so that one set of coordinate lines matches the body itself. Such grids are of importance in a variety of areas, for example, in computational fluid dynamics, one might desire a finite difference approximation at each grid point to the Navier–Stokes equations that describe fluid flow around the body. Often, the solution requires that the fluid velocity vanish in the direction both normal and tangential to the solid body. A coordinate system aligned with the body can make the imposition of these boundary conditions considerably easier.

This problem of *grid generation* is difficult in part because of two competing desires: (1) cell uniformity, in which all grid cells are approximately the same area, and (2) mesh orthogonality, which contributes to the accuracy of the finite difference approximation. Only in very special cases can both be obtained; instead, the science and "art" lies in balancing these two goals.

The subject of grid generation is vast, and there are a variety of competing techniques. The reader is referred to the recent books by Knupp and Steinberg [105] and Castillo [38], as well as the work of Eiseman [59] and Thompson et al. [197]. The goal is to produce a body-fitted, logically rectangular grid that balances the competing demands of uniformity in cell sizes and mesh orthogonality. Of course, logically rectangular grids are not the only possibility; so-called "unstructured grids", in which points and their neighbors are less regularly linked, play important roles in a variety of applications. Nonetheless, the focus here will be on logically rectangular, structured grids.

Broadly speaking, techniques for constructing logically rectangular grids include the following:

- *Algebraic/Approximation methods*: In these techniques, a grid of points is placed around the body such that one coordinate line of these points is fitted to the body. The points are then adjusted and fit according to a variety of approximation functions, including polynomial techniques and fitting functions.

- *Elliptic methods*: In these techniques, an elliptic partial differential equation is solved throughout the entire domain, often through iteration or direct techniques. The solution produces the sets of coordinate lines. That is, the grid lines are particular solution values of the equation.

- *Hyperbolic techniques*: Here, a front is advanced away from the body in such a way as to produce an appropriate set of grid lines as the front propagates outwards.

- *Variational methods*: The positions of the grid points are produced through minimizing certain functionals.

Each of the above techniques has virtues and drawbacks. In general, the difficult issues may be summarized as follows:

- Very close to the body, it can be difficult to construct cells that conform to the body landscape and describe a smooth transition into the flow region.

- In the neighborhood of sharp inward corners, grid lines have a tendency to cross over themselves, or create cells with inappropriate aspect ratios.

- In the neighborhood of sharp outward cusps, such as in edges of airfoils, grid lines often yield highly uneven cells, especially in regions where high accuracy is desired.

- Gridding together multiple bodies is, for the most part, difficult and still an art. None of the above techniques easily anticipate other bodies when creating grids, and hence stitching together individual grids for each region into a coherent whole can be problematic.

Level set techniques offer a method for tackling some of these issues. The idea, as presented in Sethian [175], is to exploit the geometric nature of the problem and view the body itself as the initial position of an interface that must be advanced outwards away from the body. The initial position of the interface and its position at later times forms one set of grid lines; its orthogonal set forms the other. This technique roughly falls into the category of a hyperbolic solver. However, by solving the correct evolution equation for an advancing front, the difficulties of shock formation and colliding characteristics that plague most hyperbolic techniques are avoided. User intervention is kept to a minimum; for the most part, grids are generated automatically without the need to adjust parameters.

11.2 Equations of motion

The basic philosophy is to view the body itself as the zero level set of a function, and advance the front away from the body, for either an interior or exterior grid, using a chosen speed function $F(\kappa)$. At discrete chosen time intervals, zero contours of the level set function ϕ are constructed and serve as one set of grid lines. Transverse lines to these grid lines are then constructed. The discussion begins with two-dimensional grids; three-dimensional grids follow later.

11.2.1 Construction of body-fitted lines

First, one must construct an appropriate speed function to generate body-fitted coordinate lines outside a given body. Previous analysis (see [170]) shows that a front propagating with speed $F(\kappa) = 1 - \epsilon\kappa$ evolves towards a circle and hence yields a far-field circular grid. The rate at which the evolving front becomes circular depends on the choice of ϵ; the larger the value of ϵ, the faster the decay in the variation of curvature around the front. In order to ensure that no points of initial high positive curvature move backwards, a minimum positive threshold speed value is chosen. The choice of this threshold value depends on the initial node placement. If a rectangular far-field grid is desired, the developing circular grid can be blended with a distant rectangle; periodic grids are obtained from periodic boundary conditions.

With a different choice of speed function, interior grids may be generated. In the case of a convex initial shape, the front must always remain convex, and hence the speed function $F(\kappa) = -\kappa$ is effective. Once again, in the case of a non-convex initial body, points with high curvature (in this case, high negative curvature) can move against the flow of the grid; again, a remedy is to include a threshold value which ensures that the front always moves inwards, i.e.,

$$F(\kappa) = \min(-\kappa, F_{\text{threshold}}). \tag{11.1}$$

For three-dimensional grids, we have seen that fronts may change topology as they evolve. However, in many examples where an interior grid is desired, the above speed function will yield flow towards a single point.

11.2.2 Construction of transverse lines

Given the above set of body-fitted field lines, transverse lines must be constructed. The goal is to balance the competing desire of orthogonality and equal area/size in the construction of the field lines. This construction of transverse lines produces a grid which may be later adjusted through a variety of elliptic and parabolic smoothers available from more traditional techniques.

The basic technique is to construct field lines by following trajectories normal to evolving outward grid lines; this corresponds to following the gradient of the level function ϕ. Place N nodes at points X_i, $I = 1, N$ on the initial body and solve the N ordinary differential equations

$$\frac{dX_i}{dt} = F(\kappa)\frac{\nabla\phi}{|\nabla\phi|}, \tag{11.2}$$

where $X_i(t)$ is the location of the *ith* grid point at time t; a second order (Heun's) method can be used.

For any choice of ϵ greater than zero, the transverse lines cannot intersect. However, for non-convex initial curves, the constructed transverse lines can come quite close together. The larger the choice of the smoothing parameter ϵ, the more the transverse gradient lines are kept apart, however, at a cost of a large separation of the body-fit field lines. Figure

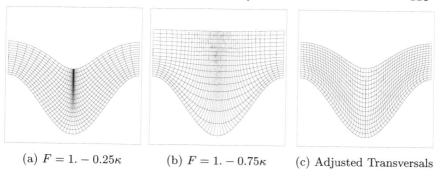

(a) $F = 1. - 0.25\kappa$ (b) $F = 1. - 0.75\kappa$ (c) Adjusted Transversals

Fig. 11.1. Construction of transversals for propagating sine curve

11.1 shows exterior grids generated above a periodic cosine front for various choices of the smoothing parameter. For ϵ small (Figure 11.1(a)), the transverse lines come close together. For ϵ large (Figure 11.1(b)), transverse lines are kept apart, but the rapid motion of the evolving front leaves cells with large aspect ratios.

Judicious choice of the smoothing parameter based on the initial node placement can solve some of these problems.

However, in the case of significant curvature variation in the initial body, some transversal adjustment is desirable. This is accomplished in two ways. First, transverse line trajectories may be readjusted so that their separation distance is proportional to the separation distance along the previous field line. Full use of this technique results in uniform cells, however, gridline orthogonality is not maintained. Second, transverse lines may be readjusted according to the length of the given field line; the total length of the field line is computed, and transverse nodes are readjusted to maintain equal length spacing. Points where the derivative of the curvature vanish, which may be calculated from a suitable difference expression acting on ϕ, act as stable points in this process and are not adjusted. Once again, this technique is linear-weighted against the basic trajectory advection. In addition, a one-dimensional diffusion operator can be applied to the body-fit field lines to separate transverse lines. Figure 11.1(c) shows the use of these techniques applied to the construction of a full set of grid lines above the cosine curve.

Finally, we note several details of the level set grid generation technique:

• Node placement on the boundary and the ensuing interior/exterior grid can be automatically controlled; placement can depend on local

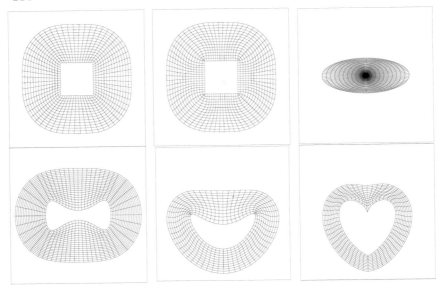

Fig. 11.2. Body-fitted grids generated using level set approach: I

curvature, external functional dependence, or user-controlled specifi-cations.

- In the case of corners and cusps in the initial boundaries, node place-ment may be altered to produce a rarefaction fan of smooth grid lines away from the singularities.
- In some cases, particularly with interior grids, some sort of refinement or coarsening is required; this can be accomplished by hierarchical subdividing or coarsening the grid.

For details, see [175].

11.3 Results, complications, and future work

A variety of grids can be generated using the approach outlined above; the following figures are all taken from Sethian [175]. In Figure 11.2, grids around some relatively straightforward objects are generated to show the idea behind the approach. In Figure 11.3 exterior and interior grids around significantly oscillatory objects are developed; note the ability of the method to resolve deep intrusions and extrusions. In Figure 11.4 grids around sharp objects are constructed, and in Figure 11.5 complex grids are produced.

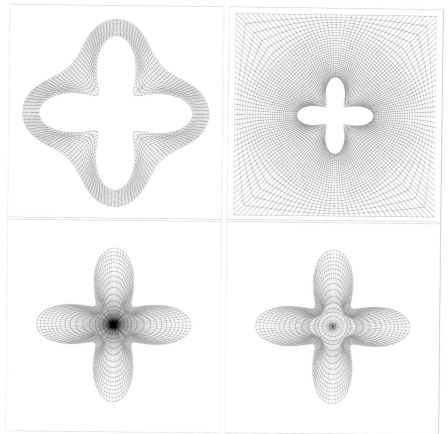

Fig. 11.3. Body-fitted grids generated using level set approach: II

Several improvements to the above techniques are desired. First, in the case of highly non-convex bodies, the above technique will not work; sides of the body will grow together before the front has "time" to escape; in this case, some sort of domain decomposition is required. Second, the use of more standard techniques for modifying the grid, once the basic design is achieved, might prove fruitful. In particular, the grids generated using this approach may make excellent initial grids for variational and algebraic methods. Finally, extension of this work to multiple bodies requires hybrid techniques in which single grids are patched together or allowed to overlap, similar to those commonly used in other schemes. An attractive approach currently under study is the use of these level set techniques for grids near bodies, coupled with a transition to carte-

Grid Generation

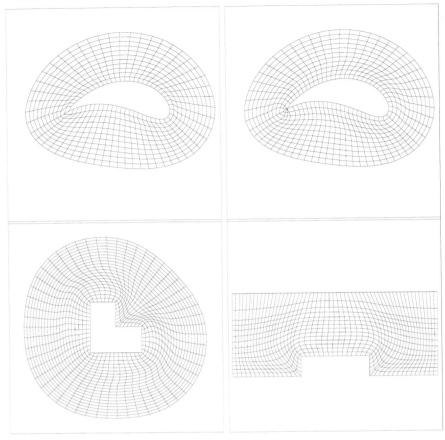

Fig. 11.4. Body-fitted grids generated using level set approach: III

sian grids away from the body; this may be of particular use in fluid dynamics calculations where body-fitted coordinates are attractive to resolve boundary layer calculations, while far-field cartesian grids are appropriate to connect complex geometries.

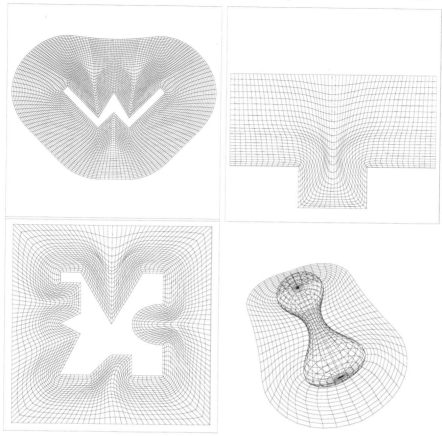

Fig. 11.5. Body-fitted grids generated using level set approach: IV

12

Image Enhancement and Noise Removal

Outline: *The previous two sections concerned geometrical motion of a particular hypersurface of interest. In this chapter, we present schemes for image enhancement and noise removal; in this application, all the level sets have meaning. The central idea is to view an image as a collection of iso-intensity contours, each of which must be evolved. Flow under curvature both removes spikes of noise (since they correspond to high curvature objects) and smooths out oscillations in boundaries; at the same time, sharp boundaries are essentially maintained. Variations on curvature flow lead to effective schemes for variety of image processing applications.*

12.1 Statement of problem

Define an *image* to be an intensity map I given at each point (x, y) of a two-dimensional domain. The range of the function $I(x, y)$ depends on the type of image; for black and white images the range is either 0 or 255 (here we employ the standard convention that 0 corresponds to black and 255 corresponds to white). For grey-scale images $I(x, y)$ is a function mapped between 0 and 255. For color images $I(x, y)$ is a vector-valued function into some color-space; a typical example is either RGB or HSI.

Given such an image, a common wish is to remove noise from the image (see Figure 12.1) without sacrificing useful detail and enhance or highlight certain features. It is important to note that this is a subjective goal; the classification of some information as "noise" and other information as "useful" detail is in the eye of the beholder, and techniques to correspondingly filter images must, at some level, reflect this subjective decision. A natural filter is the idea of scale – we can try to

118

remove information that occupies a small amount of the domain, such as spots of non-matching colors or small oscillations in boundaries of objects.

Fig. 12.1. An image $I(x, y)$ with noise

One of the most straightforward and widely used methods for removing noise is the Gaussian filter, in which both 1-D and 2-D signals are smoothed by convolving them with a Gaussian kernel; the degree of blurring is controlled by the characteristic width of the Gaussian filter. To understand how this works, imagine a grey-scale intensity function $I(x, y)$, and suppose "noise" is added to this image by replacing 10% of the pixels with new values drawn randomly between 0 and 255 (see again Figure 12.1). Viewing the intensity function as a surface plotted above the xy plane, the changed pixels will appear as sharp upwards and downwards spikes on the surface. If this surface is convolved with a Gaussian filter, the spikes will be reduced and will blend into the background values. In this sense, the Gaussian filter removes noise. However, the Gaussian is an isotropic operator; since it smoothes in all directions, sharp boundaries will also be blurred.

Thus, one goal is to improve upon this basic idea and remove noise without being forced into too much blurring. A variety of techniques have been introduced to improve upon this basic idea, including Wiener filters [60], anisotropic diffusion schemes that perform intraregion smoothing in preference to interregion smoothing; see Perona and Malik [148], and more recently wavelet processing (Ruskai et al. [158]). We now discuss some aspects of applying the level set methodology to this problem.

12.2 Equations of motion

12.2.1 Previous techniques

As a starting point, imagine evolving the intensity function $I(x,y)$ under the equation

$$I_t = \nabla^2 I. \tag{12.1}$$

This is just the heat operator applied to the image intensity, and it is easy to believe that the "noise" will be removed, at the cost, however, of smearing out the sharp boundaries in the real image. Equation (12.1) can be rewritten in a slightly odd form, namely,

$$I_t = F|\nabla I| \quad \text{where} \quad F = \frac{\nabla \cdot \nabla I}{|\nabla I|}. \tag{12.2}$$

We note that this is just our level set equation with a bizarre "speed" function and the level set function ϕ replaced by the intensity function. Note, however, that this is a corrupt view, since nothing is propagating normal to the level curves. Instead, smoothing isotropically takes place in all directions. Sharp boundaries are smeared.

Now, consider an alteration to the above, which was introduced by Alvarez, Morel, and Lions [7]. If the gradient is passed *inside* the divergence operator, it yields the evolution equation

$$I_t = F|\nabla I| \quad \text{where} \quad F = \nabla \cdot \frac{\nabla I}{|\nabla I|} = \kappa, \tag{12.3}$$

where here we have noted that $\nabla \cdot \frac{\nabla I}{|\nabla I|} = \kappa$. This is our standard curvature evolution equation. The attractive quality of this approach is that sharp boundaries are preserved; smoothing takes place inside a region, but not across region boundaries. Of course, as shown by Grayson's theorem, eventually all information is removed as each contour shrinks to zero and disappears.

An alternative approach takes a total variation approach to the problem (see Rudin, Osher, and Fatemi [157]), and leads, once again, to a level set methodology and reduces to a very similar curvature-based speed function given by $F(\kappa) = \kappa/|\nabla I|$. Following these works, a variation on these two approaches was produced by Sapiro and Tannenbaum [161]; in that work, a speed function of the form $F(\kappa) = \kappa^{1/3}$ was employed. In each of these schemes, all information is eventually removed through continued application of the scheme. Thus, a "stopping criterion" is required.

A recent level set scheme for noise removal and image enchancement was introduced by Malladi and Sethian [122]. The scheme results from returning to the original ideas of curvature flow, and exploiting a "min/max" function that correctly selects the optimal motion to remove noise. It has two highly desirable features:

(i) There is an intrinsic, adjustable definition of scale within the algorithm, such that all noise below that level is removed, and all features above that level are preserved.

(ii) The algorithm stops automatically once the sub-scale noise is removed; continued application of the scheme produces no change.

These two features are quite powerful, and lead to a series of open questions about the morphology of shape and asymptotics of scale removal. In this next section, we describe this min/max scheme for noise removal and image enhancement; for details, see [124, 122, 125].

12.2.2 The min/max flow

The starting point is the standard speed function $F(\kappa) = -\kappa$. In order for this discussion to make sense, it is important to be careful about signs. Imagine a curve initialized so that the interior of the disk has a negative value for the signed-distance function ϕ and the exterior has a positive value for the signed-distance function ϕ. Then the normal $\nabla\phi/|\nabla\phi|$ points outwards, and the curvature defined as $\nabla \cdot \frac{\nabla\phi}{|\nabla\phi|}$ is always positive on all the convex level contours. Thus, a flow under speed function $F = -\kappa$ corresponds to the collapsing curvature flow, since the boundary moves in the direction of its normal with negative speed, and hence moves inwards.

We need to be further careful about signs, amend a previous definition, and refer to a new speed function $\bar{F}$ in the context of the re-written level set equation

$$\phi_t = \bar{F}|\nabla\phi|; \qquad (12.4)$$

thus, from now on, $\bar{F} = -F$. The reason for doing so is that it produces fewer minus signs in the below discussion. Thus, a curve collapsing under its curvature will correspond to speed $\bar{F} = \kappa$. This will be the convention for the remainder of this chapter.

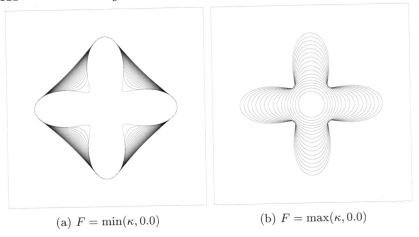

(a) $F = \min(\kappa, 0.0)$ (b) $F = \max(\kappa, 0.0)$

Fig. 12.2. Motion of curve under min/max flow

Now, consider two variations on the basic curvature flow given by

- $\bar{F}(\kappa) = \min(\kappa, 0.0)$
- $\bar{F}(\kappa) = \max(\kappa, 0.0)$

As shown in Figure 12.2, the effect of flow under $\bar{F}(\kappa) = \min(\kappa, 0.0)$ is to allow the inward concave fingers to grow outwards, while suppressing the motion of the outward convex regions. Thus, the motion halts as soon as the convex hull is obtained.[1] Conversely, the effect of flow under $\bar{F}(\kappa) = \max(\kappa, 0.0)$ is to allow the outward regions to grow inwards while suppressing the motion of the inward concave regions. However, once the shape becomes fully convex, the curvature is always positive and the flow becomes the same as regular curvature flow, in which case the shape collapses to a point.

To summarize the above, flow under $\bar{F} = \min(\kappa, 0.0)$ preserves some of the structure of the curve, while flow under $\bar{F} = \max(\kappa, 0.0)$ diffuses away all of the information.

---

[1] We note that the fact that the convex hull is obtained results from our level set embedding perspective. If we just look at a single curve propagating with speed $\min(\kappa, 0.0)$, there are cases in which the curve gets "hung up" and cannot perform the topological change required to produce the convex hull. However, a level set flow under this speed function will change topology and produce the convex hull.

12.2.2.1 Min/max flow on structures of a prescribed scale

The goal is to select the correct choice of flow that both smooths out small oscillations, and maintains the essential properties of the shape. In order to do so, we introduce the idea of the min/max switch.

Consider the following speed function [124, 122]:

$$\bar{F}_{\min/\max}^{\text{Stencil}=k} = \begin{cases} \min(\kappa, 0) & \text{if } Ave_{\phi(x,y)}^{R=kh} < 0 \\ \max(\kappa, 0) & \text{if } Ave_{\phi(x,y)}^{R=kh} \geq 0 \end{cases}. \qquad (12.5)$$

where $Ave_{\phi(x,y)}^{R=kh}$ is defined as the average value of ϕ in a disk of radius $R = kh$ centered around the point (x, y).[2] Here, h is the step size of the grid. Thus, given a "stencil radius" k, the above yields a speed function that depends on the value of ϕ at the point (x, y), the average value of ϕ in neighborhood of a given size, and the value of the curvature of the level curve going through (x, y).

In order to examine this speed function in some detail, consider a black region on a white background, chosen so that the interior has a negative value of ϕ and the exterior a positive value of ϕ.

- Stencil radius $k = 0$

  If the radius $R = 0$ ($k = 0$), then choice of $\min(\kappa, 0)$ or $\max(\kappa, 0)$ depends only on the value of ϕ. All the level curves in the black region will attempt to form their convex hull, when seen from the black side, and all the level curves in the white region will attempt to form *their* convex hull. The net effect will be no motion of the zero level set itself, and the boundary will not move.

- Stencil radius $k = 1$

  If the average is taken over a stencil of radius h, then some movement of the zero level corresponding to the boundary is possible. If there are some oscillations in the front boundary on the order of one or two pixels, then the average value of ϕ at the point (x, y) can have a different sign than the value at (x, y) itself. In this case, the flow will act as if it were selected from the "other side", and some motion will be allowed until these first-order oscillations are removed, and a balance between the two sides is again reached. Once this balance is reached, further motion is suppressed.

- Stencil radius k

  By taking averages over a larger and larger stencil, larger amounts

---

[2] When $k = 0$, we choose the value of ϕ at the grid point itself, rather than the limiting value.

of smoothing are applied to the boundary. In other words, decisions about where features belong are based on larger and larger perspectives. Once features on the order of size k are removed from the boundary, balance is reached and the flow stops automatically. As an example, let $k = \infty$. Since the average will compute to a value close to the background color, on this scale all structures are insignificant, and the max flow will be chosen everywhere, forcing the boundary to disappear.

To show the results of this hierarchical flow, we start with an initial shape in Figure 12.3(a) and first perform the min/max flow until steady-state is reached with stencil size zero in Figure 12.3(b). In this case, the steady-state is achieved right away, and the final state is the same as the initial state. Min/max flow is then performed until steady-state is achieved with stencil size $k = 1$ in Figure 12.3(c), and then min/max flow is again applied with a larger stencil until steady-state is achieved in Figure 12.3(d).

The fact that the curve stops is due to three effects. First, the curve is embedded in a level set framework. Second, the calculation is performed on a grid. And third, the "piling up" of level sets, as discussed in the text, causes a shearing to develop in the level set function. The definition of "stop" here is that the curve motion has essentially gone to zero, and that running the calculation out for an extremely long time is required for any appreciable motion to occur.

These results can be summarized as follows:

- The min/max flow switch selects the correct motion to diffuse the small-scale pixel notches into the boundary.
- The larger, global properties of the shape are maintained.
- Furthermore, and equally importantly, the flow stops once these notches are diffused into the main structure.
- Edge definition is maintained, and, in some global sense, the area inside the boundary is preserved.
- The noise removal capabilities of the min/max flow are scale-dependent, and can be hierarchically adjusted.
- The scheme requires only a nearest neighbor stencil evaluation.

12.2.2.2 Extension of min/max scheme to grey-scale, texture, and color images

The above technique applies to black and white images. An extension to grey-scale images can be easily made by replacing the fixed threshold

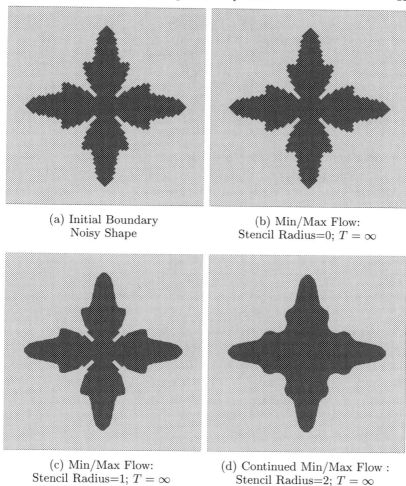

(a) Initial Boundary
Noisy Shape

(b) Min/Max Flow:
Stencil Radius=0; $T = \infty$

(c) Min/Max Flow:
Stencil Radius=1; $T = \infty$

(d) Continued Min/Max Flow :
Stencil Radius=2; $T = \infty$

Fig. 12.3. Motion of star-shaped region with noise under min/max flow at various stencil levels

test value of 0 with a value that depends on the local neighborhood. As designed in [122], let $T_{\text{threshold}}$ be the average value of the intensity obtained in the direction perpendicular to the gradient direction. Note that since the direction perpendicular to the gradient is tangent to the isointensity contour through (x, y), the two points used to compute are either in the same region, or the point (x, y) is an inflection point, in which the curvature is in fact zero and the min/max flow will always yield zero. Here, choosing a larger stencil means computing this tangential average over endpoints located farther apart.

Formally then, a min/max scheme applicable to many types of images, becomes:

$$\bar{F}_{\text{min}/\text{max}} = \begin{cases} \max(\kappa, 0) & \text{if } Ave_{\phi(x,y)}^{R=kh} < T_{\text{threshold}} \\ \min(\kappa, 0) & \text{otherwise.} \end{cases} \qquad (12.6)$$

Further details about this scheme applied to a wide range of images, including salt-and-pepper, multiplicative, and Gaussian noise applied to black and white, grey scale, textured, and color images, may be found in [124].

12.3 Results

First, we show some examples of binary images with grey-scale noise under min/max flow, taken from Malladi and Sethian [124, 122]. The min/max function switch is taken around 128 which is halfway between 0 for black and 255 for white. Figure 12.4 shows a hand-written character with noise is added as follows: 10% noise means that at 10% of the pixels, the given value is replaced with a number chosen with uniform distribution between 0 and 255. The left column gives the original figure with the corresponding percentage of noise; the right column gives reconstructed values. The figures on the right are converged; continued application of the scheme yields no significant change in the results.

Next, salt-and-pepper grey-scale noise is removed from a grey-scale image. Noise is added to the figure by replacing a prescribed percentage of the pixels with a new value, chosen from a uniform random distribution between 0 and 255. The results are obtained as follows. Begin with two levels of noise; 25% noise in Figure 12.5(a) and 50% noise in Figure 12.5(d). First, the min/max flow from equation (12.6) is applied until a steady-state is reached in each case (Figure 12.5(b) and Figure 12.5(e)). This removes most of the noise. Then, the scheme is continued with a larger threshold stencil for the threshold to remove further noise (Figure 12.5(c) and Figure 12.5(f)). For the larger stencil, we compute the average *Ave* over a larger disk, and compute the threshold value $T_{\text{threshold}}$ using a correspondingly longer tangent vector.

Next, the effect of this min/max scheme on multiplicative noise added to a grey-scale image is considered. Figure 12.6 shows the reconstruction of an image with 15% multiplicative noise.

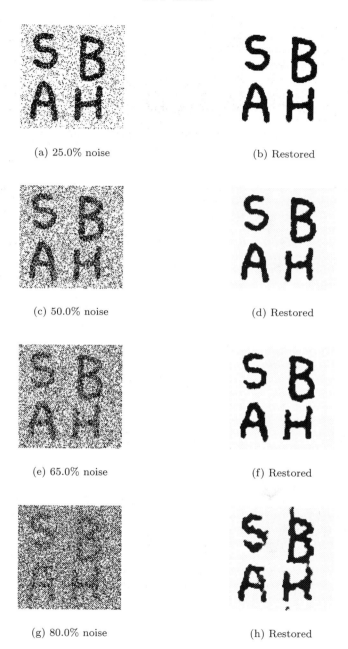

(a) 25.0% noise

(b) Restored

(c) 50.0% noise

(d) Restored

(e) 65.0% noise

(f) Restored

(g) 80.0% noise

(h) Restored

Fig. 12.4. Image restoration of binary images with grey-scale salt-and-pepper noise using min/max flow: Restored shapes are final shape obtained ($T = \infty$)

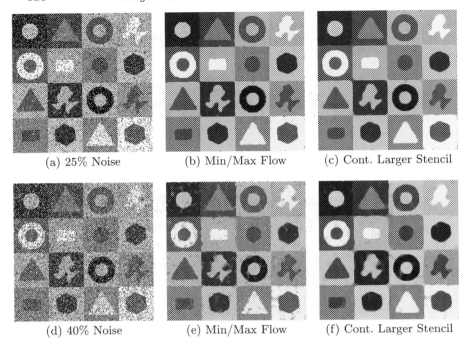

(a) 25% Noise   (b) Min/Max Flow   (c) Cont. Larger Stencil

(d) 40% Noise   (e) Min/Max Flow   (f) Cont. Larger Stencil

Fig. 12.5. Min/max flow. The left column is the original with noise, the center column is the steady-state of min/max flow, the right column is the continuation to steady-state of the min/max flow using a larger stencil

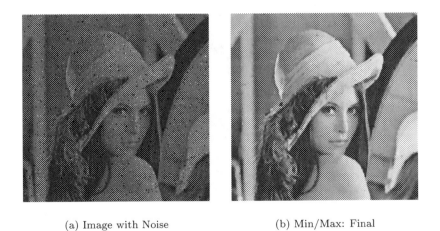

(a) Image with Noise   (b) Min/Max: Final

Fig. 12.6. Min/max flow applied to multiplicative noise

These schemes can also be used to remove noise and accentuate features in medical images. In Figure 12.7 a series of original and reconstructed images are shown. Here, no noise is artificially added; instead the goal is to enhance certain features within the given images for later recovery.

Finally, this min/max algorithm can be applied to an image to which 100% Gaussian grey-scale noise has been superimposed; a random component drawn from a Gaussian distribution with mean zero is added to each (every) pixel. Figure 12.8 shows the "noisy" original together with the reconstructed min/max flow image.

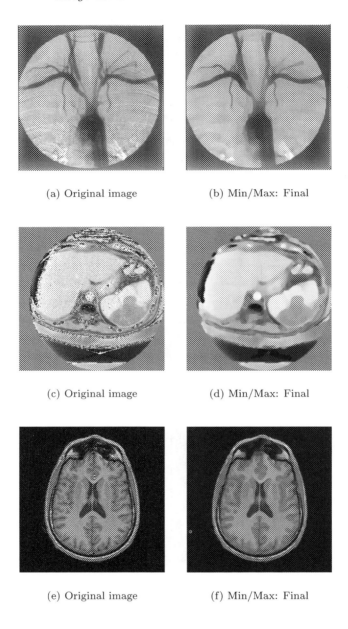

(a) Original image   (b) Min/Max: Final

(c) Original image   (d) Min/Max: Final

(e) Original image   (f) Min/Max: Final

Fig. 12.7. Min/max flow with selective smoothing

(a) Original Image with Gaussian Noise

(b) Reconstructed Min/Max Flow

Fig. 12.8. Continuous Gaussian noise added to image

13

Minimal Surfaces and Surfaces of Prescribed Curvature

Outline: *In this section, we explore problems in which the geometry of the interface is constrained as it evolves, which can be important in the construction of minimal surfaces, surface fitting, and computer-aided design.*

13.1 Minimal surfaces: Background

Consider a closed curve Γ in R^3 with the goal of constructing a membrane with boundary Γ and minimal surface area. In some cases, this can be achieved as follows. Given the bounding wire frame Γ, consider some initial surface $S(t = 0)$ whose boundary is Γ. Let $S(t)$ be the family of surfaces (parameterized by t) obtained by allowing the initial surface $S(t = 0)$ to evolve under mean curvature, with the boundary always given by Γ. Defining the surface S by $S = \lim_{t\to\infty} S(t)$, one expects that the surface S will be a minimal surface for the boundary Γ. Several computational approaches exist to construct such minimal surfaces based on this approach, including K. Brakke's Surface Evolver program [27].

Chopp [41] developed a level set approach to this problem by embedding the motion of the surface towards its minimal energy as the zero level set of a higher dimensional function. Thus, given an initial surface $S(0)$ passing through Γ, construct a family of neighboring surfaces by viewing $S(0)$ as the zero level set of some function ϕ over all of R^3. Using the level set equation (2.5), evolve ϕ according to the speed law $F(\kappa) = -\kappa$. Then a possible minimal surface S will be given by

$$S = \lim_{t\to\infty} \{x | \phi(x, t) = 0\}. \tag{13.1}$$

The difficult challenge with the above approach is to ensure that the

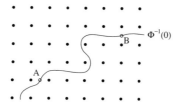

Fig. 13.1. Grid points around the boundary

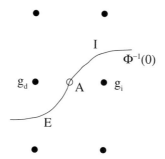

Fig. 13.2. Grid points around the boundary

evolving zero level set always remains attached to the boundary Γ. This is accomplished by creating a set of boundary conditions on those grid points closest to the wire frame that link together the neighboring values of ϕ in order to force the level set $\phi = 0$ through Γ. The underlying idea is most easily explained through a one-dimensional example. Here, we follow the discussion in Chopp [41].

13.2 Equations of motion/algorithm

Consider the warm-up problem of finding the shortest distance between two points A and B in the plane. The goal is to give conditions on the level set function $\phi(x,t) = 0$ defined in R^2 so that $\phi(A,t) = \phi(B,t) = 0$ for all time.

In Figure 13.1, an initial curve is shown which corresponds to the level set $\phi(x,t) = 0$, together with boundary points A and B. Suppose that the point A is located in between two grid points g_i and g_d (Figure 13.2). In order to force $\phi(A,t) = 0$ for all time, we can require that $\phi(g_i,t) = -\phi(g_d,t)$. Chopp's scheme determines the normal direction, and labels points in that direction as "independent"; points on the other side are hence dependent and controlled by the values for the independent points. More precisely, label the subscripts d and i for dependent and independent, and set the dependent point in terms of the independent point. This binds the dependent points to the independent points in a way that forces the zero level set through the points A and B. In general, the boundary conditions will be represented as a vector equation of the form

$$v_{\text{dep}} = A v_{\text{ind}}, \tag{13.2}$$

where

$$v_{\text{dep}} = \left\{ \begin{array}{c} \phi(g_{d,1}) \\ \phi(g_{d,2}) \\ \vdots \\ \phi(g_{d,m}) \end{array} \right\} \qquad v_{\text{ind}} = \left\{ \begin{array}{c} \phi(g_{i,1}) \\ \phi(g_{i,2}) \\ \vdots \\ \phi(g_{i,n}) \end{array} \right\}, \tag{13.3}$$

and A is an $m \times n$ matrix. The matrix A is determined from the chosen mesh and wire frame, and both the classification of dependent and independent points and the matrix A need only be computed once at the beginning of the calculation. This links the set of all dependent points in terms of the set of all independent points in such a way that the level set $\phi = 0$ is forced to pass through the wire frame. Complete details of the automatic technique for generating this list of boundary conditions may be found in [41].

There is one additional issue that comes into play in the evolution of the level set function ϕ towards a minimal surface. By the above set of boundary conditions, only the zero level set $\phi = 0$ is constrained. Thus the other level surfaces are free to move at will, which means that on one side of the level set $\phi = 0$ the surfaces will crowd together, while on the other side they will pull away from the zero level set. This causes numerical difficulties in the evaluation of derivatives over such a steep gradient. A re-initialization procedure is used to remedy this situation[1]; after a given number of time steps, the level set $\phi = 0$ is computed, and the function ϕ is re-initialized by directly computing the signed-distance function. This uniformly redistributes the level sets so that the calculation can proceed.

---

[1] In fact, this was the first such re-initialization procedure developed for level set methods.

Fig. 13.3. Minimal surface: Catenoid

13.3 Results

As a test example, the minimal surface spanning two rings has an exact solution given by the catenoid

$$r(x) = a \cosh(x/a), \tag{13.4}$$

where $r(x)$ is the radius of the catenoid at a point x along the x axis, and a is the radius of the catenoid at the center point $x = 0$. Suppose that the boundary consists of two rings of radius R located at $\pm b$ on the x-axis. Then the parameter a is determined from the expression

$$R = a \cosh(b/a). \tag{13.5}$$

If there is no real value of a that solves this expression, then a catenoid solution between the rings does not exist. Thus, for a given R, if the rings are closer than some minimal distance $2b_{\max}$ apart, then there are two distinct catenoid solutions, one of which is stable and the other is not. For rings exactly $b_{\max}$ apart, there is only one solution. For rings more than $b_{\max}$ apart, there is no catenoid solution.

In Figure 13.3, taken from [41], the minimal surface spanning two rings each of radius 0.5 and at positions $x = \pm.277259$ is computed. A cylinder spanning the two rings is taken as the initial level set $\phi = 0$. A $27 \times 47 \times 47$ mesh with space step 0.025 is used. The final shape is shown in Figure 13.3.

Next, in Figure 13.4 (again taken from [41]), this same problem is computed, but the rings are placed far enough apart so that a catenoid solution cannot exist. Starting with a cylinder as the initial surface, the evolution of this surface is computed as it collapses under mean curvature while remaining attached to the two wire frames. As the surface evolves, the middle pinches off and the surface splits into two surfaces, each of

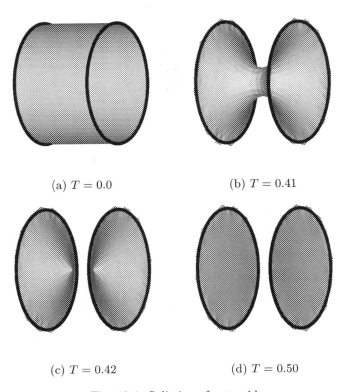

(a) $T = 0.0$ (b) $T = 0.41$

(c) $T = 0.42$ (d) $T = 0.50$

Fig. 13.4. Splitting of catenoid

which quickly collapses into a disk. The final shape of a disk spanning each ring is indeed a minimal surface for this problem. This example illustrates a virtue of a level set approach. No special cutting or *ad hoc* decisions are employed to decide when to break the surface. By viewing the zero level set as but one member of a family of flowing surfaces, a smooth transition occurs.

13.4 Extensions to surfaces of prescribed curvature

The above technique can be extended to produce surfaces of constant but non-zero mean curvature (see Chopp and Sethian [43]). To do so requires further inspection of the suggestive example of a front propagating with speed $F(\kappa) = 1 - \epsilon\kappa$. Suppose that $\epsilon = 1$, and consider the evolution of the partial differential equation

$$\phi_t + (1 - \kappa)|\nabla \phi| = 0, \tag{13.6}$$

where again, the mean curvature is given by equation (5.33), and choose initial data given by

$$\phi(x, y, z, t = 0) = (x^2 + y^2 + z^2)^{1/2} - 1. \tag{13.7}$$

The zero level set is initially the sphere of radius one, which remains fixed under the motion $F(\kappa) = 1 - \kappa$. All level surfaces inside the unit sphere have mean curvature greater than one, and hence propagate inwards, while all level surfaces outside the unit sphere have mean curvature less than one, and hence propagate outwards. Thus, the level sets on either side of the zero level set unit sphere pull apart. If one were to apply the level set algorithm in free space, the gradient $|\nabla \phi|$ would flatten out to zero across the unit sphere surface, causing numerical difficulties. However, the re-initialization process described earlier periodically rescales the labeling of the level sets, and thus $|\nabla \phi|$ is renormalized, producing a final surface of constant mean curvature $\kappa = 1$. Thus, in order to construct a surface of constant curvature κ_0, start with any initial surface passing through the initial wire frame and allow it to propagate with speed

$$F(\kappa) = \kappa_0 - \kappa. \tag{13.8}$$

Here, as before, the "constant advection term" κ_0 is taken as the hyperbolic component F_A and treated using the entropy-satisfying upwind difference solver, while the parabolic term κ is taken as F_B, and is approximated using central differences.

Using the two ring "catenoid" problem as a guide (taken from [43]), in Figure 13.5 this technique is used to compute the surface of constant curvature spanning the two rings. In each case, the initial shape is the cylinder spanned by the rings. The final computed shapes are shown for a variety of different mean curvatures. In Figure 13.5(a) a surface of mean curvature $\kappa = 2.50$ is given: the rings are located a distance .61 apart and have diameter 1.0. The resulting surface bulges out to fit against the two rings. In Figure 13.5(b) a surface of mean curvature $\kappa = 1.0$ is found, which corresponds to the initial surface. The slight bowing is due to the relatively coarse $40 \times 40 \times 40$ mesh. In Figure 13.5(c) the catenoid surface of mean curvature $\kappa = 0.0$ is given. We isolated the value of $\kappa = -0.33$ as a value close to the breaking point (Figure 13.5(d)). In Figure 13.5(e), a mean curvature value of $\kappa = -0.35$

is prescribed, causing the initial bounding cylinder to collapse onto the two rings and bulge out slightly. Finally, in Figure 13.5(f), bowing out disks corresponding to surfaces of mean curvature $\kappa = -1.00$ are shown. These techniques can be extended to the construction of surfaces of non-constant curvature, as well as the construction of geodesics on manifolds. For details, see [41, 43, 42, 100].

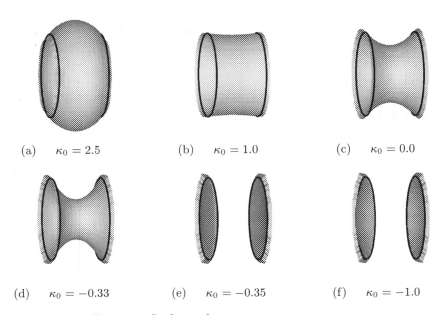

(a) $\kappa_0 = 2.5$ (b) $\kappa_0 = 1.0$ (c) $\kappa_0 = 0.0$

(d) $\kappa_0 = -0.33$ (e) $\kappa_0 = -0.35$ (f) $\kappa_0 = -1.0$

Fig. 13.5. Surfaces of constant mean curvature

14

Combustion, Crystal Growth, and Two-Fluid Flow

Outline: *In this chapter, we briefly consider some applications of the level set methodology to a large and challenging class of interface problems. These problems are characterized by physical phenomena in which the front itself acts as an internal boundary condition to a partial differential equation, and the solution of this equation controls the motion of the front. In combustion problems, the interface is a flame, and both exothermic expansion along the front and flame-induced vorticity drive the underlying fluid mechanics. In crystal growth and dendritic formation, the interface is a solid/liquid boundary, and is driven by a jump condition related to heat release along the interface. In two-fluid problems, the interface represents the boundary between two immiscible fluids of different densities and/or viscosities, and the surface tension along this interface plays a significant role in the motion of the fluids.*

From an algorithmic perspective, a significant and challenging issue in the development of a level set approach is that information about the speed of the front must be somehow transferred to the Eulerian framework that updates the level set function at the fixed grid points. This is a significant challenge for two reasons:

- In many situations, the interface velocity is determined by the interaction of local geometric quantities of the front itself (such as curvature) with global variables on either side of the interface (for example, jumps in velocity, heat, or concentration of species). If these global variables are calculated on a grid, it may be difficult to extend the values to the front itself where they are required to evaluate the speed function F. However, these quantities may have meaning only at grid points, not at the front itself.

139

- Conversely, it may be difficult to extend the interface velocity back to the grid points (that is, to the other level sets). This problem, known as the *extension problem*, see [2, 3], must be solved in order for the level set method to work; some mechanism of updating the grid points in the neighborhood of the zero level set is required.

In this chapter, we discuss three areas where these problems have been addressed. The common link in these sections is the presence of a term in the equation represented by a Dirac delta function along the interface. The emphasis here will be on the algorithmic issues involved in converting the level set formulation to the setting under discussion, rather than a detailed discussion of the relevant physics. The interested reader is referred to the literature cited below for a detailed description of the algorithms and results.

14.1 Turbulent combustion of flames: Vorticity, exothermicity, flame stretch, and wrinkling

14.1.1 Background

In Rhee, Talbot, and Sethian [154], a flame is viewed as an infinitely thin reaction zone, separating two regions of different but constant densities. The hydrodynamic flow field is two-dimensional and inviscid, and the Mach number is vanishingly small. This corresponds to the equations of zero Mach number combustion, introduced in Majda and Sethian [118]. The flame propagates into the unburnt gas at a prescribed flame speed S_u that depends on the local curvature.

The reason for this flame speed dependence on curvature comes from the role of heat conduction. Imagine a slightly perturbed planar flame front. The concave part of the perturbed flame is surrounded by burnt gases, which provides more heating to the reactants than would occur with a purely planar interface. Conversely, the convex part of the perturbed flame is surrounded by unburnt gases, which heats up the reactants less. This model, due to Markstein [128], indicates that the flame speed depends on the local curvature, that is,

$$S_{\text{unburnt}} = S^o_{\text{unburnt}}(1 - L\kappa), \qquad (14.1)$$

where S^o_{unburnt} is the speed of a planar flame and L is a constant. For details on this model, see [154, 169, 74, 168].

As the reactants are converted to products (that is, as the material makes the transition from "unburnt" to "burnt"), the local fluid under-goes a volume increase known as exothermic expansion, associated with the density jump. At the same time, pressure gradients tangential to the flame cause different accelerations in the light and heavy gases. This causes a production of vorticity (known as baroclinic torque) across the flame, since the pressure gradient is not always aligned with the den-sity gradient. Together, the burning of the flame acts as a source of both vorticity and volume for the underlying hydrodynamic field, both of which in turn affect the evolution of the flame interface.

This model presents a significant opportunity for a level set method. The flame is represented as the zero level set whose speed is controlled by local curvature and whose position is advanced according to both burning and hydrodynamic advection under the fluid flow field. At the same time, the position of the interface acts as a source of exothermic volume on the right-hand side of a Poisson's equation for the velocity. In addition, the local stretch of the interface in the tangential direction acts as a source of vorticity that also contributes to the hydrodynamic flow field. We now explain this model in more detail and follow the discussion in [154].

14.1.2 Equations of motion

Following the derivation in Pindera and Talbot [150], the velocity U is decomposed into the three components

$$U = U_s + U_v + U_p, \tag{14.2}$$

where U_s is the incompressible velocity field due to exothermic expansion along the front, U_v is the rotational velocity field due to stretch-induced vorticity, and U_p is the potential velocity of the incident flow. Thus, the individual component fields satisfy

$$\nabla \cdot U_s = m\, \delta(x - x_f); \nabla \times U_s = 0, \tag{14.3}$$

$$\nabla \times U_v = \omega(x); \nabla \cdot U_v = 0, \tag{14.4}$$

$$U_p = \nabla \Phi; \nabla \cdot U_p = 0, \tag{14.5}$$

where m is the volume source strength per unit length associated with the amount of expansion along the flame front, x_f is the location of the flame, $\omega(x)$ is the vorticity field, Φ is the vector potential of the incident flow, and $\delta(x)$ is the two-dimensional Dirac delta function. The volume expansion m is related to the normal velocity S_{unburnt} of the flame on the unburnt side through

$$m = \frac{\rho_{\text{unburnt}} - \rho_{\text{burnt}}}{\rho_{\text{burnt}}} S_{\text{unburnt}}, \tag{14.6}$$

where $\rho_{\text{burnt}}(\rho_{\text{unburnt}})$ is the density in the burnt(unburnt) gases. The vorticity transport equation, obtained by taking the curl of the Navier–Stokes equation (discussed in the next section) is given by

$$\frac{D}{Dt}\left(\frac{\omega}{\rho}\right) = \left(\frac{\omega}{\rho}\right)\nabla \cdot U + \nu\nabla^2\omega + \frac{1}{\rho^2}\nabla\rho \times \nabla P, \tag{14.7}$$

where P is the pressure and ρ is the density.

A formula for the vorticity jump $[\omega]$ was produced by Hayes [84] in the inviscid limit, and is given by

$$
\begin{aligned}
[\omega] &= \left(\frac{1}{\rho_{\text{burnt}}} - \frac{1}{\rho_{\text{unburnt}}}\right)\nabla_\tau\left(\rho_{\text{unburnt}}S_{\text{unburnt}}\right) \\
&\quad - \frac{\rho_{\text{burnt}} - \rho_{\text{unburnt}}}{\rho_{\text{unburnt}}\rho_{\text{unburnt}}}\left[\frac{dU_\tau}{dt} + U_\tau(\nabla_\tau U_\tau - V_n\kappa) - V_n\frac{\partial V_n}{\partial\tau}\right]
\end{aligned} \tag{14.8}
$$

where U_τ is the flow velocity at the flame in the direction tangential to the flame, ∇_τ is its gradient along the flame, and V_n is the absolute normal flame speed. Here, d/dt is the time derivative taken at a point which lies on the front. Defining the flame stretch K as

$$K = \frac{1}{A}\frac{dA}{dt} = \nabla_\tau U_\tau - V_n\kappa, \tag{14.9}$$

where A is an elemental flame front area, we then have

$$
\begin{aligned}
[\omega] &= \left(\frac{1}{\rho_{\text{burnt}}} - \frac{1}{\rho_{\text{unburnt}}}\right)\nabla_\tau(\rho_{\text{unburnt}}S_{\text{unburnt}}) \\
&\quad - \frac{\rho_{\text{burnt}} - \rho_{\text{unburnt}}}{\rho_{\text{unburnt}}S_{\text{unburnt}}}\left[\frac{dU_\tau}{dt} + U_\tau K - V_n\frac{\partial V_n}{\partial\tau}\right].
\end{aligned} \tag{14.10}
$$

This gives the amount of vorticity produced due to flame propagation.

14.1.3 Results

The flame is tracked by identifying the flame interface as the zero level set of the level set function. The curvature is determined using the expression given in equation (5.32). The vortical field U_v is represented by a collection of vortex blobs using Chorin's vortex method [46]; see also [174]. The exothermic field is determined by solving a Poisson's equation

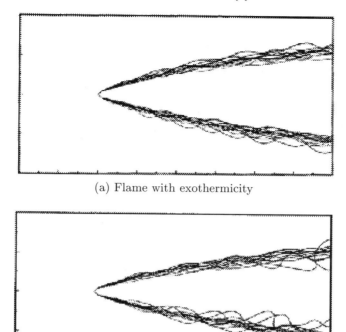

(a) Flame with exothermicity

(b) Flame with exothermicity and vorticity

Fig. 14.1. Comparison of flame brush

on the underlying grid with the right-hand side given by smearing the Dirac delta function to the neighboring grid points. The no-flow boundary is satisfied by the addition of a potential flow that exactly cancels the existing flow field. Finally, the tangential stretch component is evaluated by tracing back the values of U_τ along a normal vector from the given position backwards normal to the front to evaluate the derivative $V_n = \frac{\partial U_\tau}{dt}$.

The algorithm explicitly marches ahead in time as follows. To advance from one time step to the next, imagine that the various fluid velocities U_v, U_s, and U_p are all known at a given time step, as is the level set function ϕ that describes the location of the flame. The algorithm advances from one time step to the next through the following steps:

(i) Given the level set function, the local curvature is evaluated.

(ii) Cells containing the front are located, and volume sources m are extrapolated to nearby grid points. If Δl is an element of flame, then the strength $m = \left(\dfrac{\rho_{\text{unburnt}} - \rho_{\text{burnt}}}{\rho_{\text{burnt}}} \right) S_u \Delta l$, is area-weighted to neighboring grid points.

(iii) The volumetric flow field is determined by solving the Poisson equation $\nabla^2 \Psi = f_{ij}$, where f_{ij} are the volume weights; then $U_s = \nabla \Psi$.

(iv) The flame stretch is computed, and new vortex elements are added to the flow by evaluating the right-hand side of equation (14.11).

(v) The vortical flow U_v is calculated by using a vortex method over the total accumulated vortices.

(vi) The entire velocity field is assembled.

(vii) The potential flow U_p is computed to account for the incident flow field. A suitable Neumann boundary condition is supplied so that the total flow satisfies the no-slip boundary condition.

(viii) The vortex elements are updated and the level set function is advanced under both curvature-controlled burning and hydrodynamic advection.

Figure 14.1, taken from [154], shows two results from this algorithm used to model an anchored flame, with upstream turbulence imposed by a statistical distribution of positive and negative vortices. The goal is to understand the effect of exothermicity and flame-induced vorticity on the flame wrinkling and stability. In Figure 14.1(a), an anchored flame in the oncoming turbulent field under the effects of exothermic expansion due to the density jump across the flame is shown; here, different time snapshots are superimposed upon each other to show the flame "brush". In Figure 14.1(b), the effects of both volume expansion and vorticity generation along the flame front are activated. The resulting flow field generates a significantly wider flame brush, as the vorticity induces flame wrinkling which influences the exothermicity of the surrounding flow field.

In the above application of the level method, the front acted as a source of both volume and vorticity. In the next application, the interface motion is controlled by a complex jump condition.

14.2 Crystal growth and dendritic solidification

Level set techniques for tracking interfaces have also been applied to crystal growth and dendritic solidification in Sethian and Strain [182]. In that work, a different extension approach is employed; information about the speed of the interface is extended to the other level sets by means of a boundary integral along the front that is evaluated everywhere in space.

14.2.1 Background

Imagine a container filled with a liquid such as water, which has been smoothly and uniformly cooled below its freezing point so that the liquid does not freeze. The system is now in a "metastable" state, where a small disturbance such as dropping a tiny seed of the solid phase into the liquid will initiate a rapid and unstable process known as *dendritic solidification*. The solid phase will grow from the seed by sending out branching fingers into the distant cooler liquid nearer the undercooled wall. This growth process is *unstable* in the sense that small perturbations of the initial data can produce large changes in the time-dependent solid–liquid boundary.

Mathematically, this phenomenon can be modeled by a moving boundary problem. The temperature field satisfies a heat equation in each phase, coupled through two boundary conditions on the unknown moving solid–liquid boundary, as well as initial and boundary conditions. The moving boundary conditions explicitly involve geometric properties of the boundary itself, such as the local curvature and the normal direction, as well as the temperature field. For further details, see Cahn and Hilliard [31], Gurtin [82], and Mullins and Sekerka [139].

14.2.2 Equations of motion

Following [182], the model under consideration includes the effects of undercooling, crystalline anisotropy, surface tension, molecular kinetics, and initial conditions. Consider a square container B, filled with the liquid and solid phases of some pure substance. The unknowns are the temperature $u(x, t)$ for x in B, and the solid–liquid boundary $\Gamma(t)$.

The temperature field u is taken to satisfy the heat equation in each phase, together with an initial condition in B and boundary conditions on the container walls.

$$u_t = \nabla^2 u \text{ in } B \text{ off } \Gamma(t), \tag{14.11}$$

$$u(x,t) = u_0(x) \text{ in } B \text{ at } t = 0, \tag{14.12}$$

$$u(x,t) = u_B(x) \text{ for } x \text{ on } \partial B. \tag{14.13}$$

Since the position and velocity of the moving boundary $\Gamma(t)$ are unknown, two boundary conditions on $\Gamma(t)$ are required to determine u and $\Gamma(t)$. Let n be the outward normal to the boundary, pointing from solid to liquid. The first boundary condition is the classical Stefan condition:

$$\left[\frac{\partial u}{\partial n}\right] = -HV \text{ on } \Gamma(t). \tag{14.14}$$

Here $[\partial u/\partial n]$ is the jump in the normal component of heat flux $\partial u/\partial n$ from solid to liquid across $\Gamma(t)$, V is the normal velocity of $\Gamma(t)$, taken positive if the liquid is freezing, and the constant H is the dimensionless latent heat of solidification. The signs of geometric quantities are chosen so that if $\partial u/\partial n < 0$ in the liquid phase and $\partial u/\partial n = 0$ in the solid phase, then $[\partial u/\partial n]$ is negative and $V > 0$, indicating that the solid phase is growing. The speed V of the interface is linked to the jump in heat flux across the boundary, hence physically this means that undercooling drives solid growth. The latent heat of solidification controls the balance between geometry and temperature effects.

The second boundary condition on $\Gamma(t)$ is the classical Gibbs–Thomson relation, modified to include crystalline anisotropy and molecular kinetics as well as the surface tension:

$$u(x,t) = -\epsilon_\kappa(n)\kappa - \epsilon_V(n)V \text{ for } x \text{ on } \Gamma(t). \tag{14.15}$$

This says that the temperature on the interface depends on the surface tension and the velocity V. Here κ is the curvature at x on $\Gamma(t)$, taken positive if the center of the osculating circle lies in the solid. The anisotropy functions are modeled by

$$\epsilon_\kappa(n) = \epsilon_\kappa(1 - A\cos(k_A\theta + \theta_0)) \tag{14.16}$$

$$\epsilon_V(n) = \epsilon_V(1 - A\cos(M_A\theta + \theta_0)), \tag{14.17}$$

where θ is the angle between n and the x-axis, and ϵ_κ, ϵ_V, A, M_A, and θ_0 are constants depending on the material and the experimental arrangement. For example, if $\epsilon_\kappa = 0$ ($\epsilon_V = 0$), there are no surface tension (molecular kinetic) effects. For $A = 0$, the system is isotropic, while if $A > 0$, the solid is M_A-fold symmetric with a symmetry axis at angle θ_0 to the x-axis. Typically $A \leq 1$.

14.2.3 Algorithm/results

A variety of techniques can be used to approximate numerically these equations of motion. One approach is to solve the heat equation numerically in each phase and try to move the boundary so that the two boundary conditions are satisfied; see Chorin [48], Smith [185], Kelly and Ungar [94], Meyer [135], Sullivan, Lynch, and O'Neill [192], and Dzuik and Schmidt [57, 165]. Another approach is to recast the equations of motion as a single integral equation on the moving boundary and solve the integral equation numerically, as is done in Kessler and Levine [95], Langer [108], Meiron [133], and Strain [189].

In [182] a hybrid level set/boundary integral approach was taken. The central idea is to exploit a transformation due to Strain [189] that converts the equations of motion into a single, history-dependent boundary integral equation on the solid–liquid boundary that can be evaluated by a combination of fast techniques. This boundary integral equation is given by

$$\epsilon_\kappa(n)\kappa + \epsilon_V(n)V + U + H \int_0^t \int_{\Gamma(t')} K(x, x', t - t')\, V(x', t')\, dx'\, dt' = 0$$

(14.18)

for all x on the interface $\Gamma(t)$, where K is the heat kernel. Note that the velocity V depends not only on the position of the front but also on its previous history. Thus, as shown in Strain [189], information about the temperature off the front is stored in the previous history of the boundary.

As in other level set applications, the interface is then identified with the zero level set of ϕ. All that remains is to extend the velocity to the grid points so that all of the level sets can be advanced. This is done by evaluating equation (14.18) in *all of space*. An accurate evaluation of the integral then comes from breaking it up into two components: first, a history part that contains information about the past beyond a certain time, and second, a local part that is accurate in a close space/time neighborhood. The advantage to this split is that each part can be evaluated by its own accurate and fast technique (see Strain [188, 189, 190] and Greengard and Strain [81]). In order to evaluate this history integral, the zero level set is found and used to produce a set of quadrature points; these points are then used to evaluate the integral equation and compute the velocity V at each grid point.

Figure 14.2 shows one example from [182] in which the effect of changing the latent heat of solidification H is analyzed. Since the latent heat H controls the balance between the pure geometric effects and the solution of the history-dependent heat integral, increasing H puts more emphasis on the heat equation/jump conditions. Calculations are performed on a unit box, with a constant undercooling on the side walls of $u_B = -1$. The kinetic coefficient is $\epsilon_V = .001$, the surface tension coefficient is $\epsilon_\kappa = .001$, and there is no crystalline anisotropy ($M_A = 0$, $A = 0$). The initial shape was a perturbed circle with average radius $R = .15$ and perturbation size $P = .08$ and $L = 4$ limbs. A 96×96 mesh is used with time step $\Delta t = .00125$. The calculations are all plotted at the same time.

In the calculations shown, H is varied. In Figure 14.2(a), $H = .75$ and the dominance of geometric motion serves to create a rapidly evolving boundary that is mostly smooth. H is increased in each successive figure, ending with $H = 1.0$ in Figure 14.2(d). As the latent heat of solidification is increased, the growing limbs expand outwards less smoothly, and instead develop flat ends.

These flat ends are unstable and serve as precursors to tip splitting. Note that the influence of the heat integral slows down the evolving boundary, as witnessed by the fact that all the plots are given at the same time. Presumably increasing latent heat decreases the most unstable wavelength, as described by linear stability theory. The final shape shows side-branching, tip-splitting, and the strong effects of the side walls.

14.3 Two-phase flow

In this last section, we discuss level set methods applied to problems of two-phase flow.

Two early applications of fluid dynamical problems using level set methods to track the interface are the projection method calculations of compressible gas dynamics of Mulder, Osher, and Sethian [138] and the combustion calculations of Zhu and Sethian [207]. Each viewed the interface as the zero level set, and tracked this interface as a method of separating the two regions.

To begin, in [138] the evolution of rising bubbles in compressible gas

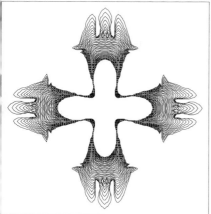 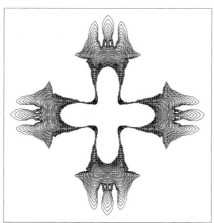

Upper Left: $H = .75$ Upper Right: $H = .833$
Lower Left: $H = .916$ Lower Right: $H = 1.0$

Fig. 14.2. Effect of changing latent heat

dynamics was studied. The level set equation for the evolving interface separating two fluids of differing densities was incorporated inside
the conservation equations for the fluid dynamics. Both the Kelvin–
Helmholtz instability and the Rayleigh–Taylor instability were studied;
the density ratio was about 30 to 4, and both gases were treated as per-
fect gases. Considerable discussion was devoted to using the advantages
and disadvantages of embedding the level set equation as an additional
conservation law.

Next, in the combustion calculations presented in [207], the interface
was a flame propagating from the burnt region into the unburnt region.
Unlike the above calculations concerning flame stability in flame hold-
ers, in these calculations the flame was viewed as a "cold flame"; that
is, the hydrodynamic flow field affected the position of the flame, but
the advancing flame did not in turn affect the hydrodynamic field. In
these calculations, the hydrodynamic field was computed using Chorin's
projection method [45], coupled to the level set approach; in fact, a second order version developed in Bell, Colella, and Glaz [18] was used.
The problem under study was the evolution of a flame inside a swirling
two-dimensional chamber; and the results showed the intermixing that
can occur, the creating of pockets of unburnt fuel surrounded by burnt
pockets, and the relationship between flame speed and mixing levels.

These two works were followed by level set methods applied to the
motion of incompressible, immiscible fluids in which steep gradients in
density and viscosity exist across the interface. In these problems, the
role of surface tension was crucial, and formed an important part of the
algorithm. A series of impressive calculations using a level set approach
were carried out by Sussman, Smereka, and Osher [193] and Chen, Hou,
Merriman, and Osher [39]. As in [207], the hydrodynamic flow field, was
updated using a second order projection method.

We now discuss these ideas in more detail. Begin with the Navier–
Stokes equations, that is,

$$u_t + (u \cdot \nabla)u = F + \frac{1}{\rho}(-\nabla P + \mu \nabla^2 u + ST). \tag{14.19}$$

Here, u is the fluid velocity, F is a forcing term (typically gravity), ρ is
the fluid density, μ is the fluid velocity, P is the pressure, and ST is the
surface tension of the interface. Assume a sharp fluid interface between
two fluids with different densities ρ_1 and ρ_2, and also that the flow is
incompressible, and thus

$$\nabla \cdot u = 0. \tag{14.20}$$

This surface tension term acts normal to the fluid interface, and is proportional to the curvature, due to a balance of force argument between the pressure on each side of the interface, and leads to the relation

$$ST = \sigma\kappa\delta(d)n, \tag{14.21}$$

where σ is the coefficient of surface tension, κ is the curvature, n is the normal to the interface, $\delta(d)$ is the Dirac delta function, and d is the distance to the front. Thus, the effect of surface tension is to act as an additional forcing term in the direction normal to the fluid interface. Once again, similar to the example in combustion given earlier, the goal is to smear this delta function to neighboring grids points.

Using a formulation developed by Brackbill, Kothe, and Zemach [25], Sussman, Smereka, and Osher [193] performed this smearing as follows; see also Chen, Hou, Merriman, and Osher [39]. Begin with the surface tension expression $\sigma\kappa\delta(d)n$. By replacing the normal n by $\nabla\phi/|\nabla\phi|$, and noting that the distance d is approximated by $\phi/|\nabla\phi|$ (this is just the slope formula), we have that

$$\sigma\kappa\delta(d)n = \kappa(\phi)\delta(\phi)\nabla\phi. \tag{14.22}$$

The net effect of this is to recast the surface tension in the level set framework. Then if ϕ is always re-initialized to the distance function, the delta function itself can be smoothed over several grid points, using one of many smoothing operators. Some further details are required, including special care taken in the differencing of this curvature term necessitated by the projection method. For details, see [193].

In Zhu and Sethian [208], the fall of a heavy fluid bubble in a lighter density fluid was performed using these techniques as a test calculation for a fully three-dimensional code under development. Here, a narrow band technique was used, as was a re-initialization based on the time crossing flowing method described earlier. Figure 14.3 shows the results of one such calculation. The initial shape is a circle, and a sequence is shown as the bubble falls. The density ratio between the heavy and light fluid is 2 to 1; in the time evolution, one sees the development of the typical spiral vortical rollups.

Calculations performed using these techniques show a wide range of applications concerning falling drops, colliding drops, and the role of surface tension. We refer the reader to [39, 193, 208] for further details.

$t = 0$ $t = 0.2$

$t = 0.4$ $t = 0.6$

$t = 0.7$ $t = 0.8$

Fig. 14.3. Falling bubble: Density ratio 2:1

15

Computer Vision
Shape Detection and Recognition

Outline: *In this section, we discuss two different aspects of computer vision: shape detection/recovery and shape recognition. Given an image, one goal in* shape detection/recovery *is to extract a particular shape from that image; here, "extract" means to produce a mathematical description of the shape that can be used in a variety of forms. The goal in* shape recognition *is to identify the extracted shape. Both problems can be pursued in the level set framework. Finally, we end with an application of the level set framework coupled to the fast narrow band work to produce an algorithm for performing Boolean operations on shapes, which is applicable in certain situations.*

Suppose one is given a medical scan, with the goal of isolating and identifying tumors. If the tumors are manifested as areas with markedly different contrasts from the background, one might isolate these shapes by propagating a front to "lock on" to the boundary, with a stopping criteria built from the image gradient. Once such a shape is found, it can be compared against a library of images. In this section, we discuss level set techniques for these problems, which rely on the above discussions of methods for image processing, fast level set methods, and front propagation.

15.1 Shape detection/recovery

The idea of using level set methods for shape recovery was proposed by Malladi, here, we follow the discussion in Malladi, Sethian, and Vemuri [120]; further work using the level set scheme in the context of shape recovery may be found in [119, 121, 126, 123] and the work of Caselles,

Catte, Coll, and Dibos [36]. We refer the interested reader to those papers for motivation, details, and a large number of examples.

Given an image with the goal of isolating a shape within the image, the approach is motivated by the active force contour/snake approach to shape recovery given by Kass, Witkin, and Terzopoulos [92]. Consider a speed function of the form $\pm 1 - \epsilon\kappa$ where ϵ is a constant. As seen earlier, the constant acts as an advection term, and is independent of the moving front's geometry. The front uniformly expands (contracts) with speed 1 (-1) depending on the sign, and is analogous to the inflation force defined in Cohen [50]. The diffusive second term $\epsilon\kappa$ smoothes out the high curvature regions, and has the same regularizing effect as the internal deformation energy term in thin-plate-membrane splines [92].

The goal now is to define a speed function from the image data that acts as a halting criterion for this speed function. Multiply the above speed function by the term:

$$k_I(x,y) = \frac{1}{1+\mid \nabla G_\sigma * I(x,y) \mid},\qquad(15.1)$$

where the expression $G_\sigma * I$ denotes the image convolved with a Gaussian smoothing filter whose characteristic width is σ. The term $\nabla G_\sigma * I(x,y)$ is essentially zero except where the image gradient changes rapidly, in which case the value becomes large. Thus, the filter $k_I(x,y)$ is close to unity away from boundaries, and drops to zero near sharp changes in the image gradient, which presumably corresponds to the edge of the desired shape. In other words, the filter function anticipates steep drops in the image gradient, and retards the evolving front from passing out of the desired region.

Thus the algorithm works as follows. A small front (typically a circle) is started inside the desired region, grown outwards, and stopped at the shape boundary as the filter term reduces the speed function F to near zero. There are several desirable aspects of this approach.

- The initial front can consist of many fronts; due to the topological capabilities of the level set method, these fronts will merge into a single front as it grows into the particular shape.
- The front can follow intricate twists and turns in the desired boundary.
- The technique can be used to extract three-dimensional shapes as well by initializing in a ball inside the desired region.
- Small isolated spots of noise where the image gradient changes substantially are ignored; the front propagates *around* these points and closes back in on itself and then disappears.

As a demonstration, the recovery of the structure of an arterial tree is considered, taken from [120]. The real image has been obtained by clipping a portion of a digital subtraction angiogram. This is an example of a shape with extended branches and significant protrusions. The front is initialized in Figure 15.1(a). In subsequent frames the front evolves into the branches and finally in Figure 15.1(f) completely reconstructs the complex tree structure. Thus, a single initialization of the shape model sprouts branches and recovers all the connected components of a given shape. Calculations were carried out on a 64×64 grid with a time step of $\Delta t = 0.001$.

This shape recovery work can be combined with the min/max approach to noise removal and enhancement. By doing so, artificial boundaries in the image, which may slow down or derail the evolving front, can be removed. The following examples are taken from Malladi and Sethian [125].

In Figure 15.2 these combined techniques are applied to the reconstruction of the liver from two-dimensional slices. Results of two different initialization sequences are shown. In Figure 15.2(a), a single contour is used in the initialization. In Figure 15.2(b) the final shape is obtained. Figure 15.2(c) shows an initialization with two separate contours of a different height slice; here, the two fronts merge and in Figure 15.2(d) the final shape is obtained.

Finally, level set shape recovery techniques are applied to the difficult problem of extracting the left and right ventricles of the heart. In these calculations, the problem is initialized by simultaneously tagging both the left and the right ventricles; both are found at the end of Stage One by the evolving fronts. Note that in the evolution of the right ventricle front, the papillary muscle is also found (see Figure 15.3); this results from a single contour that wraps around the papillary muscle and separates into an inner ring and outer ring. After the outer wall of the left and right ventricles are recovered, the outer wall of the right ventricle is extracted; this is done by temporarily relaxing the stopping criteria, and allowing the front to move past the inner wall of the right ventricle. Once this occurs, the stopping criterion is turned back on, and the front expands in Stage Two until the outer wall is found.

This technique for shape detection/recovery can be performed in three dimensions if three-dimensional data are available. In Figure 15.4, a three-dimensional reconstruction of the two femurs and surrounding thighs taken from [123] is shown.

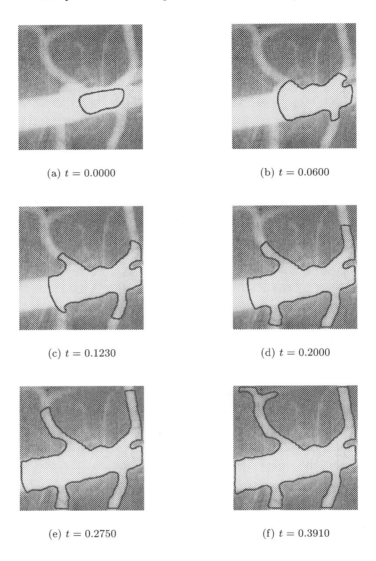

(a) $t = 0.0000$ (b) $t = 0.0600$

(c) $t = 0.1230$ (d) $t = 0.2000$

(e) $t = 0.2750$ (f) $t = 0.3910$

Fig. 15.1. Reconstruction of a shape with significant protrusions: An arterial tree structure

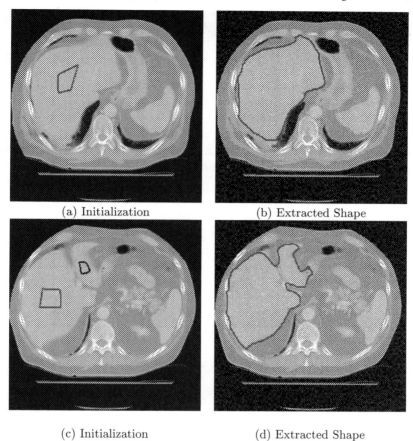

(a) Initialization   (b) Extracted Shape

(c) Initialization   (d) Extracted Shape

Fig. 15.2. Shape extraction of liver data

15.2 Shape recognition: Hand-written character recognition

Given a shape that has been represented in some fashion, an additional
objective is to identify the shape. This is a notoriously hard problem,
touching on psychology, artificial intelligence, and cognitive and computer science. One of the first steps is to find a representation of the
shape boundary that is amenable to comparison with other shapes. Two
common representations are:

- *Boundary-Based Approaches:* Here, the goal is to focus on the boundary of the shape. In these techniques, chain codes, introduced by
  Freeman [71], encode a shape by traversing the shape boundary assuming either a 4 or an 8 connectivity. Polygonal approximations

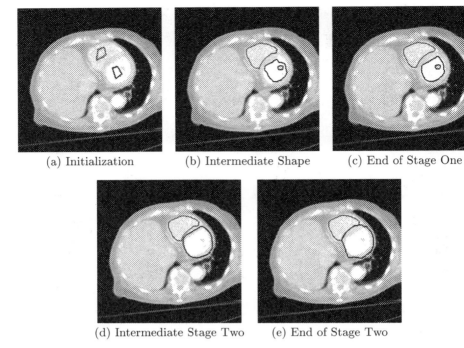

(a) Initialization   (b) Intermediate Shape   (c) End of Stage One

(d) Intermediate Stage Two   (e) End of Stage Two

Fig. 15.3. Shape extraction from heart data

(Pavlidis [146]) describe a complex boundary by a sequence of straight lines. Shape features such as one-dimensional moments (Gonzalez and Wintz [80]) and Fourier descriptors (Pearson and Fu [147]) are computed from the shape boundary. In addition, these features can be made invariant to similarity and affine transformations (Arbter [12] and Crimmins [55]). Such an invariant representation markedly aids in recognition techniques.

- *Region-Based Approaches:* Here, the goal is to focus on the region as a whole. Among the region-based shape representation schemes, one of the most typical is a "skeleton" (Blum [22]) or the medial-axis transform (Lee [110]) approach. There are a large number of skeletonization algorithms (see Leymarie and Levine [114], Mayya and Rajan [130], Olniewicz and Ilg [141], and references therein). Although skeletons provide a compact shape description, they may contain a large number of redundant edges that may minimally contribute to shape information. Efficient edge pruning schemes are discussed in [101, 130, 141].

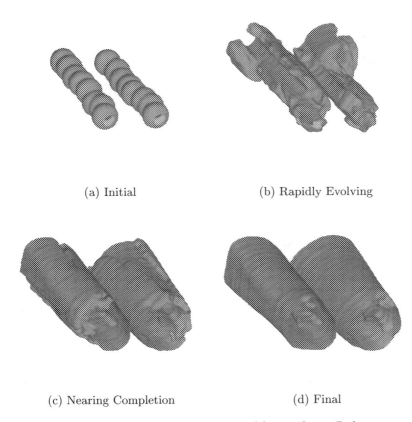

(a) Initial   (b) Rapidly Evolving

(c) Nearing Completion   (d) Final

Fig. 15.4. Stages in reconstruction of femurs from 3D data

A different approach is to use a level set perspective to represent and recognize shapes. Once again, the boundary of the region is represented as the zero level set of the signed-distance function (we note that other distance transforms have been used before for image analysis (see Danielson [56] and Borgefors [23]). There are several advantages to this approach. First, boundary- and region-based representations are implicitly contained in the signed-distance function; the boundary is simply its zero level set. Second, the notion of "holes" in the boundary is seamlessly contained in this representation; unlike a boundary-based representation, a small "hole" in the object does not create an entire new set of features in the object. Third, and most importantly, a level set representation permits the evolution of the shape; such an evolution

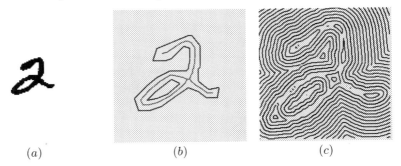

(a) (b) (c)

Fig. 15.5. Representations of the numeral 2

can be used to accentuate certain features of the shape. One possibility is to exploit the level set evolution equation both to classify and to "perturb" boundaries to help find a way to classify them.

As an example, consider the shape of a hand-written numeral "2" in Figure 15.5(a). This shape can be represented by its boundary or by its skeleton as shown in Figure 15.5(b). Alternatively, the shape boundary can be embedded in the signed-distance function ψ defined in a square region enclosing it. Figure 15.5(c) shows the level sets (equal distance contours) of the function ψ. Furthermore, a level set representation can be modified to find an acceptable classification.

This is the approach taken in Malladi and Sethian [119], in which a level set perspective was used to classify hand-written characters (optical character recognition). To be sure, there exists a full gamut of shape features for this problem, and a thorough review on historical development of OCR (optical character recognition) technology may be found in Mori et al. [137]. Such schemes include statistical classification methods with global feature analysis schemes such as moments and mathematical transforms (Fourier, Walsh, wavelet), and syntactical methods used with structural features such as loops, junctions, strokes, convexities, etc. (see Suen et al. [191]). By no means are we suggesting that level set methods offer an optimal way to perform this task. However, they offer an interesting way to explore the notion of shape perturbation, and we now describe this approach in somewhat more detail.

15.2.1 Training the neural network

To begin, a database was built from a large collection of numeral samples extracted from the NIST special databases 3 and 7 of segmented characters. First the signed-distance function was computed on a square grid for a collection of numeral shapes. A back-propagation neural network classifier is then used as a recognition system. The network was trained on a random set of N sample shapes, the network weights are stored, and then tested against N testing samples. The feature vector was the signed-distance function expressed on a 16×16 grid. Briefly, the neural network was a fully-connected architecture consisting of 256 input nodes, 10 internal nodes, and 10 output nodes corresponding to 10 numeral classes.

A series of preprocessing steps are performed prior to training. First, a noise removal step is executed; second, the boundary of each numeral is traced using a chain code procedure. Following this, size normalization is achieved by finding the bounding rectangle of every numeral shape and mapping it into a square region of side 0.5 and centered at the origin. During this processing step, care must be taken not to skew the shape artificially either horizontally or vertically. Next, the signed-distance function is computed in the square region by considering all the contours found by the chain code procedure.

Given the level set signed-distance function description of character shapes, a multiple neural net approach is used to achieve high reliability as follows. The different neural nets correspond to using different underlying grids to evaluate the signed-distance function. This can be thought of as a version of adaptive mesh refinement: a feature vector results from a particular underlying grid. The network is first trained on one feature vector grid using a random set of 3189 numeral samples and upon convergence tested on another set of 3158 samples. Given a testing numeral sample, the trained network classifies it with a confidence value lying in the interval $[0 \ldots 1]$. Reliability is improved by accepting only classifications made with high confidence and discarding the rest. The neural net classification is repeated using a different feature vector obtained by evaluation on a different grid; results are accepted only if both classification networks agree. The best results obtained using this approach yield a rate of 99.56% correct with 12.88% discards on NIST database 3 and 99.18% correct with 38.65% discards on NIST database 7 (database 7 is considerably harder). Here, "discards" are characters that do not fall into acceptance criteria levels, and hence the network does not offer a guess as to their nature.

While the results are encouraging, given the small number of characters used in the training, the idea of using successive sieves of network classifiers means that a relatively large number of discards are generated. It is the discards that are then subjected to "perturbation".

15.2.2 Perturbing the characters: Searching neural net space

The theory is to evolve the signed-distance function under the level set equation to generate perturbations of characters in the discard set. These perturbations are constantly checked against the existing neural net classifiers for acceptance. If one of the perturbations moves within the classification range, it is accepted. The hope is that although a given member of the discard set may not be acceptable for classification, it presumably is closer to its "correct" category than it is to the other categories. Hence, perturbations are performed in neural net space, creating an expanding ball around the given discard, and the first point on that ball that falls into some network's acceptance criteria is accepted.

What remains is to generate a set of flow rules that form the perturbations. Flow rules taken from previous level set applications include:

- *Curvature Flow:* The interface (that is, the boundary between the inside and outside of a character) is moved inward in its normal direction according to its curvature. As shown previously, this flow smoothes out oscillations in the shape boundary.

- *Outward Constant Flow:* The interface propagates outward with constant speed (see [170, 173]); as discussed previously, this flow removes oscillations and closes off holes.

- *Horizontal Anisotropic Flow:* As discussed in [182], anisotropic flow is an integral part of crystal growth and dendritic solidification. The anisotropic symmetry gives preferred directions of growth. Two-fold symmetry in the horizontal direction is taken, which means that shapes move under speed laws that prefer to move them in horizontal directions.

- *Vertical Anisotropic Flow:* The same as the above, except that flow in the vertical direction is preferred.

- *Growing Limbs:* One would like a flow that performs the opposite of the curvature flow, in that limbs (regions of high positive curvature) grow outwards. However, as is clear from [170], this is an ill-posed (and numerically unstable) backwards heat equation. Instead, a scheme was invented which grows limbs for a short time. Begin by flowing under curvature flow for a given number of time steps. Then, using this final shape and the initial shape, interpolate backwards in time

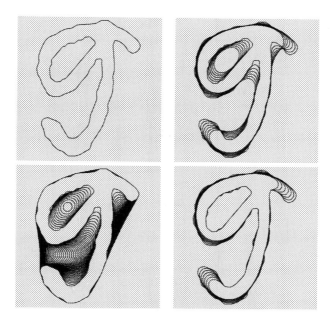

Fig. 15.6. Perturbations of numeral under flow rules

to a previous state, which will have larger "limbs" at places where the initial curvature is positive. Repeat the process of curvature flow to smooth oscillations in the front, plus backwards time interpolation to extend limbs further. This process is unstable, in that refining the time step produces uncontrollable oscillations. However, done on a coarse enough scale, it produces shapes that exaggerate and accentuate limbs and protrusions.

As an example, in Figure 15.6, the perturbation of a sample hand-written numeral "9" is shown under several different flow rules.

Using these flow rules, the discarded characters are perturbed and then compared with the neural net classifiers. Under this strategy, recognition rates of 99.08% with 6% discard are obtained for NIST database 3; for NIST database 7, 98.05% correct is achieved with around 20% discard. This represents a considerable improvement over the static results. As illustration, a sample of the characters that this technique successfully recognizes is shown in Figure 15.7.

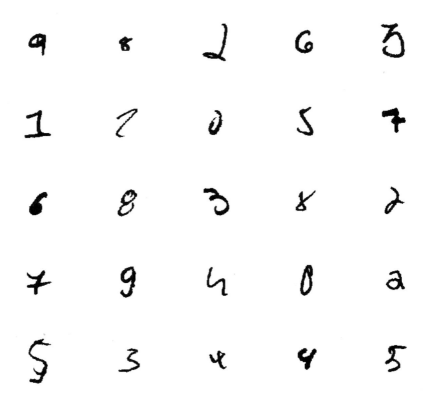

Fig. 15.7. Hand-written NIST characters correctly identified

15.3 Boolean operations on shapes

In this short section, we discuss a different application of the level set approach, and present an algorithm for a well-known problem in computer graphics. The result is a technique for performing Boolean operations on shapes, which can be useful when figures are given implicitly as level set functions.

Suppose one is given a collection of closed, simple curves in the plane. In many applications of computer graphics, animation, and computer-aided design, the goal is to perform the Boolean operations of intersection, union, and subtraction on these shapes. More precisely, given two regions Ω_A and Ω_B, one wants to form $\Omega_A \cup \Omega_B$, $\Omega_A \cap \Omega_B$, and $\Omega_A - \Omega_B$. A variety of algorithms exist to perform such tasks, which are often useful in blending shapes, scene extraction, and shape detection. Of course, the same problem exists in three dimensions where one may want to perform Boolean operations on a collection of closed hypersurfaces. Of particular interest are problems of solid modeling, in which such operations need to be performed many times on complex structures. The work on level set methods applied to multiple interfaces can be jelled into the following relations. Suppose we form the signed-distance function ϕ_A and ϕ_B for the two regions. Then

- $\Omega_A \cup \Omega_B = \min(\phi_A, \phi_B)$
- $\Omega_A \cap \Omega_B = \max(\phi_A, \phi_B)$
- $\Omega_A - \Omega_B = \max(\phi_A, -\phi_B)$

The plan is to devise a fast algorithm for executing these operations.

15.3.1 A slow version

We proceed as follows. Suppose we are given R regions, labelled $k = 1, \ldots, R$, each described by R_k polygons. We can execute Boolean operations on these shapes by first laying down a grid and then computing the signed-distance function ϕ_k on this grid for each region. We can then perform any combination of Boolean operations, for example,

$$[(\phi_1 \cup \phi_3) \cap (\phi_2 \cup \phi_5)] - [(\phi_5 - \phi_2) \cup \phi_1] \qquad (15.2)$$

by parsing from the inside to the outside. Each triple of [level set function, Boolean operation, level set function] is replaced by another level set function using the min and max operations given above.

The above technique can be characterized as follows:

- The level of accuracy is determined by the size of the grid. When these Boolean operations are combined with a level set evolution algorithm, the objects already exist on an underlying grid.
- The signed-distance functions ϕ_k are re-useable. That is, the expense is in the calculation of the signed-distance functions for each region. Once these signed-distance functions are stored, they can be quickly combined under Boolean operations; additionally, new regions then can be added to the operations by calculating their ϕ values and including them in the operations.
- The signed-distance functions are easily translated and rescaled. Thus, a library of ϕ values can be quickly translated or rescaled. Rotation is also straightforward, however some interpolation is required.

- Three-dimensional application is straightforward.

There are two drawbacks to the above algorithm. First, the use of a grid to perform the operations gives an intrinsic resolution scale to the problem. Thus, if the polygon has, for example, long thin spikes, a fine grid may be required to resolve the large aspect ratio. Second, the above algorithm is expensive. As a rough operation count, imagine that we have P polygons, each with S sides, and the calculation is performed on an $N \times N$ grid. Calculating each signed-distance function requires finding the distance from N^2 points to S sides; thus we require $O(N^2 SP)$ operations to find all the values for ϕ_k. Then, if we perform a simple union, for example, this requires P comparisons of N^2 points, producing a total operation count of $O(N^2 PS + PN^2)$. There are faster ways to do this.

15.3.2 *A faster algorithm for Boolean shape operations*

A faster algorithm results from exploiting the work on fast narrow band level set methods. Construct ϕ for each polygon as follows. For each pair of vertices, construct the line segment connecting the two and locate all grid points that lie on the boundaries of cells that are intersected by the line segment; this is done by following the line through the grid and tagging the mesh points. By respecting the orientation of the line segment, the signed-distance function can easily be assigned at the nearby mesh points. This signed-distance function is calculated, and the grid point is tagged as having a value for ϕ for this region. The location of this grid point is added to a list of all tagged grid points. One can proceed through all segments, and then through all remaining polygons.

The above (max/min) functions can be executed to produce the Boolean operations, with one notable exception. We perform the operation only at those tagged grid points that are on the list, and taking as contributions only those values that have been registered. Values that have not been registered do not contribute to the Boolean operations.

A rough operation count can be made on this method. For each side, we tag N points; thus, constructing the signed-distance function requires $O(SN)$ operations. Assuming that a total of PSN points are tagged, then the total operation count to compute the union over all P polygons is $O(PSN + PN)$; a savings of N^3! All that is required to compute the boundary is a contour plotter that looks only for the zero level set in cells

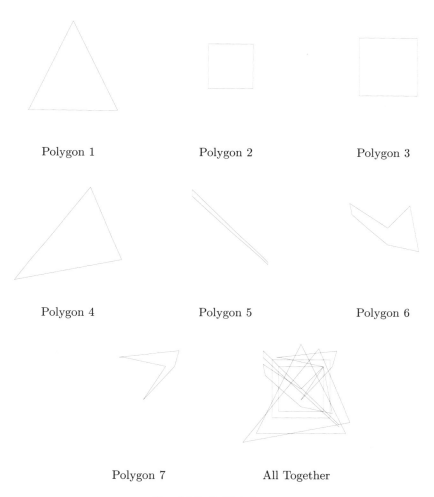

Fig. 15.8. Initial shapes

where all values exist. The same algorithm extends in a straightforward manner to three dimensions.

15.4 Results: Extracting and combining two-dimensional shapes

Figure 15.9 shows the results of applying our algorithm to execute a variety of Boolean operations on these shapes. ϕ values are constructed for

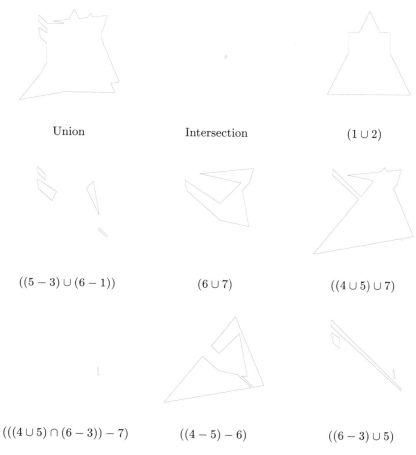

Union   Intersection $(1 \cup 2)$

$((5-3) \cup (6-1))$ $(6 \cup 7)$ $((4 \cup 5) \cup 7)$

$(((4 \cup 5) \cap (6-3)) - 7)$ $((4-5)-6)$ $((6-3) \cup 5)$

Fig. 15.9. Boolean operations

each shape; performing the various Boolean operations is an extremely fast operation.

16

Applications of the Fast Marching Level Set Method

Shape-Offsetting, Shape-from-Shading, Photolithography Development, Geodesic Paths, Robotic Navigation, and Seismic Travel Times

Outline: *As shown previously, the case of a monotonically advancing front whose speed in the normal direction depends only on position can be converted into a stationary time problem. Furthermore, we have developed a fast marching algorithm for solving static Hamilton-Jacobi equations. Here, we give several applications of this fast marching approach, including problems in shape-offsetting, reconstruction of a surface from its reflectance map (the so-called "shape-from-shading" problem), photolithography development, constructing geodesics on surfaces, robotic navigation with constraints, and calculation of first arrivals for seismic travel times.*

The fast marching method for solving static Hamilton–Jacobi equations requires the design of a consistent viscosity scheme that satisfies the upwind requirement given in Chapter 9, namely that the recalculation of any grid value depends only on smaller values. In this chapter, we demonstrate the application of the fast marching methodology to a series of applications, building appropriate schemes as necessary.

16.1 Shape-offsetting

The problem of *shape-offsetting* is straightforward; given a closed shape in two or three dimensions, compute the offset, obtained by propagating the boundary in its normal direction with constant unit speed. All that is required is to compute the distance to the boundary, and plot the level curves. A technique for doing so using a level set approach was given by Kimmel and Bruckstein [99]. Here, a different approach is taken which works directly with the Eikonal equation.

Since the speed is given by $F = 1$, from equation (2.11) we then must

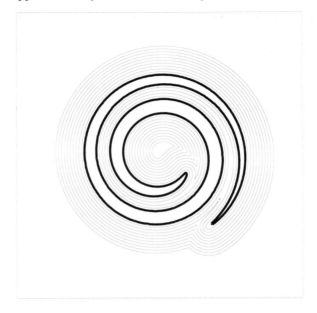

Fig. 16.1. Shape-offsetting of spiral

solve

$$|\nabla T| = 1, \qquad (16.1)$$

where the initial condition is given as $T = 0$ on and inside the given shape. The scheme is the same as that given from Chapter 9, namely,

$$\max(D_{ij}^{-x}T, 0)^2 + \min(D_{ij}^{+x}T, 0)^2 + \max(D_{ij}^{-y}T, 0)^2 + \min(D_{ij}^{+y}T, 0)^2 = F_{ij}^2, \qquad (16.2)$$

where the speed function F_{ij} is one everywhere. In Figure 16.1, given a boundary represented as a dark heavy line, we show the larger shape-offsets, obtained using the fast marching method.

16.2 Shape-from-shading

Imagine a non-self-shadowing surface, illuminated from a single (and far away) point light source. At each point of the surface, one can define the brightness map I which depends on the reflectivity of the surface and the angle between the incoming light ray and the surface normal. Points of the surface where the normal is parallel to the incoming beam are brightest; those where the normal is almost orthogonal are darkest (again, self-shadowing surfaces are prohibited.) The goal of *shape-from-shading* is to reconstruct the surface from its brightness function I; one of the earliest works on this topic is provided by Horn [87].

We point out right away that the problem as posed does not have a unique solution. For example, imagine a beam coming straight down; it is impossible to differentiate a surface from its mirror image from the brightness function. That is, a deep valley could also be a mountain peak. Other ambiguities can exist; we refer the reader to Rouy and Tourin[156] and Kimmel and Bruckstein [98]. Nonetheless, in its simplest form, the shape-from-shading problem provides an example of an Eikonal equation that can be solved using our fast marching level set method.

Begin by considering a surface $T(x, y)$; the surface normal is then given by

$$n = \frac{(-T_x, -T_y, 1)}{(|\nabla T|^2 + 1)^{1/2}}. \tag{16.3}$$

Let (α, β, γ) be the direction from the light source. In the simplest case of a Lambertian surface, the brightness map is given by

$$I(x, y) = (\alpha, \beta, \gamma) \cdot n. \tag{16.4}$$

Thus, the shape-from-shading problem is to reconstruct the surface $T(x, y)$ given the brightness map $I(x, y)$.

Consider the case in which the light comes from straight down. Then the light source vector is $(0, 0, 1)$, and thus

$$I(x, y) = \frac{1.}{(|\nabla T| + 1)^{1/2}}. \tag{16.5}$$

Rearranging terms produces an Eikonal equation for the surface, namely,

$$|\nabla T| = \sqrt{\frac{1}{I^2} - 1}, \tag{16.6}$$

where n is the normal to the surface. As initial conditions for this problem, imagine that at extrema of the surface the values of T are known. Then a viable solution surface can be constructed using the fast marching method.

To demonstrate, we start with a given surface, first compute the brightness map I, and then reconstruct the surface by solving the above Eikonal equation. Figure 16.2 shows a paraboloid surface of the form $T = 3. - 3(x^2 + y^2)$. Figure 16.2(a) shows the original surface, Figure

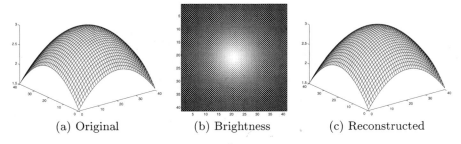

(a) Original   (b) Brightness   (c) Reconstructed

Fig. 16.2. Shape-from-shading reconstruction of paraboloid surface

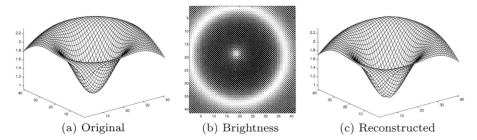

(a) Original   (b) Brightness   (c) Reconstructed

Fig. 16.3. Shape-from-shading reconstruction of double Gaussian surface

16.2(b) shows the brightness map $I(x, y)$, and Figure 16.2(c) shows the reconstructed surface. This surface is "built" by setting $T = 3$ at the point where the maximum is obtained, and then solving the Eikonal equation.

As a more complex example, consider a double Gaussian function of the form

$$T(x, y) = 3e^{-(x^2 + y^2)} - 2e^{-20((x - .05)^2 + (y - .05)^2)}. \qquad (16.7)$$

Figure 16.3 shows the original figure, the brightness map and the reconstructed surface. For further application of the fast marching scheme to shape-from-shading problems, including oblique light sources, see [5].

16.3 Photolithography development

One component process in the manufacturing of microchips is the process of *lithography development* (see Chapter 17). In this process, the resist properties of a material have been altered due to exposure to a beam that has been partially blocked by a pattern mask. The material is then "developed", which means the material with less resistivity is etched away. While the process is discussed in more detail in the next chapter, at this point we note that the problem reduces to that of following an initially plane interface propagating downwards in three dimensions, where the speed in the normal direction is given as a supplied rate function at each point. The speed $F = F(x, y, z)$ depends only on position; however, it may change extremely rapidly. The goal in lithography development is to track this evolving front. In order to develop realistic structures in three-dimensional development profiles, a grid of size $300 \times 300 \times 100$ is not unreasonable; hence a fast algorithm is of considerable value in the development step.

Fig. 16.4. Lithographic development on $50 \times 50 \times 50$ grid

In Sethian [178], this fast marching level set method was applied to lithography development. As a warm-up test example, Figure 16.4 shows the evolution until $T = 10$ of a flat profile at height $z = 1$ in the unit cube centered at $(.5, .5, .5)$ under a model Gaussian rate function given by

$$F(x, y, z) = e^{-64(r^2)}(\cos^2(12z) + .01), \qquad (16.8)$$

where $r = \sqrt{(x - .5)^2 + (y - .5)^2}$. This rate function F corresponds to the effect of standing waves which change the resist properties of the material, and causes sharp undulations and turns in the evolving profile.

Figure 16.5 shows timings for our Gaussian speed function. Note that loading the rate file is a significant proportion of the total compute time.

Grid Size	Time to Load Rate File	Time to Propagate Front	Total Time
50x50x50	0.1 secs	0.5 secs	0.6 secs
100x100x100	1.2 secs	5.1 secs	6.3 secs
150x150x150	3.9 secs	20.0 secs	23.9 secs
200x200x200	9.0 secs	55.0 secs	64 secs

Fig. 16.5. Timings for development to $T = 10$: Sparc 10

In Figure 16.6 accuracy is evaluated using the breakthrough time T_{final} when the profile reaches the bottom center point. The exact answer (computed using fourth order Runge-Kutta) is $T_{final} = 10.36761$.

Grid Size	50^3	100^3	150^3	200^3	Exact
Breakthrough Time T_{final}	9.8090801	10.33976	10.36608	10.36669	10.36761
Relative Error $\left(\dfrac{\lvert\text{Computed} - \text{Exact}\rvert}{\text{Exact}} \right)$	.05387	.00268	.00014	.00008	0.0

Fig. 16.6. Accuracy of calculation of breakthrough time

To show a more realistic example of lithography development, a rate function calculated using the three-dimensional exposure and post-exposure bake modules of TMA's Depict 4.0 [198] is coupled to our fast marching level set method. Figure 16.7(a) shows the top view of a mask placed on the board; the dark areas correspond to areas that are exposed to light. The presence of such factors as standing waves in the etching profile depends on issues such as the reflectivity of the surface. In Figure 16.7(b) a view of the developed profile is shown from underneath; the etching of the holes and the presence of standing waves can easily be seen. For further results, see [179].

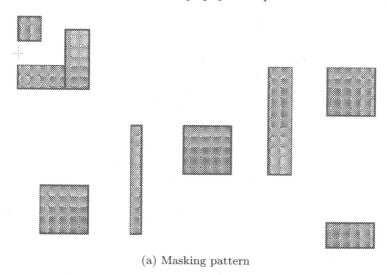

(a) Masking pattern

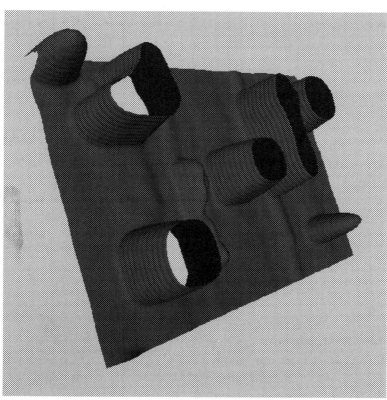

(b) Lithographic development: View from below

Fig. 16.7. Lithographic development using fast marching method

16.4 Paths on networks

The next example comes from paths on networks, and is closely related to Dijkstra's algorithm [166]. Imagine an N-dimensional rectangular grid, and let the value F, $F > 0$, at each grid point be the cost of *entering* that node; we assume no cost for exiting the node. Given an initial set of grid points Ω, the object is to find the minimum cost u required to reach any other grid point from the initial set Ω.

The solution can easily be computed using the fast marching framework. For ease of exposition, we limit the domain to a two-dimensional grid; the goal is to compute the solution to the static problem

$$\max(|u_x|, |u_y|) = \frac{1}{F}, \tag{16.9}$$

where $u = 0$ on the set Ω. A discrete version is given by

$$\max\left(|\max(D_{ij}^{-x}u, -D_{ij}^{+x}, 0)|, |\max(D_{ij}^{-y}u, -D_{ij}^{+y}, 0)|\right) = \frac{1}{F_{ij}}. \tag{16.10}$$

This scheme is based on one given in [156], and satisfies the requirements laid out in Chapter 10. The presence of the space step in the difference operators only serves to scale the cost, and can be factored out.

A simple example is the computation of the surface u, with a constant cost function $F_{ij} = 1$. This simple case boils down to the computation of distance with respect to the L^1 norm (weighted by F in the more general case). In Figure 16.8(a), starting from the center grid point, equal cost contours are plotted on top of the underlying grid. The results are simply diamond shapes which are the unit spheres of the L^1 norm. A slightly more interesting example comes from letting the cost function be one everywhere except in the upper right quadrant where it is four; in Figure 16.8(b), equal cost contours are shown. In the above scheme, there is no need to solve any quadratic equation and the update procedure is simply $u_{ij} = F_{ij} + \min(u_{i-1,j}, u_{i+1,j}, u_{i,j-1}, u_{i,j+1})$, see [5].

16.5 Construction of geodesics on surfaces

A related problem with application to robotics and navigation considers a surface $z(x_1, x_2, .., x_M)$. The objective is to find the shortest path, known as a minimal geodesic, between two points $(A, z(A))$ and $(B, z(B))$ on that surface. Here, the discussion and results of Kimmel and Sethian [103] are presented almost without change.

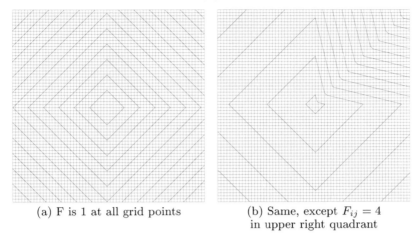

| (a) F is 1 at all grid points | (b) Same, except $F_{ij} = 4$ in upper right quadrant |

Fig. 16.8. Equal cost contours for network paths

Imagine the propagation of the initial surface curve $\Gamma(t)$ along the surface, where $\Gamma(t = 0)$ corresponds to the single point $(A, z(A))$. Furthermore, imagine that this curve propagates with unit speed along the surface. Then the location of the curve at time t will correspond to the set of all points of distance t from the point $(A, z(A))$, and again, the shortest path will correspond to back propagation along the surface vector field orthogonal to the surface curves Γ.

These surface curves may be constructed in a different way as follows. Since the surface $z(x, y)$ is a graph, there exists some speed function $\tilde{F}$ which provides the corresponding motion of the surface curves projected onto the xy plane. The goal is to determine this speed function $\tilde{F}$.

First, note that the evolution on the surface itself before the projection is given by

$$\Gamma_t = N \times T, \tag{16.11}$$

where, using the notation $(p, q) = \nabla z$, the surface normal is $N = (-p, -q, 1)/\sqrt{1 + p^2 + q^2}$, and T is the tangent to the current equal geodesic distance contour Γ. This evolution can be used to compute the geodesic distance map from a given point or a set of points on the surface $z(x, y)$. Thus

$$\frac{1}{\tilde{F}(\nabla z, n)} = (\mathbf{\Pi} \circ N \times T, n), \tag{16.12}$$

where $\mathbf{\Pi} \circ (x, y, z) = (x, y)$ is the projection operation onto the xy coordinate plane.

It can be shown (see [103]), that the tangent T is given by

$$T = \frac{(-u_y, u_x, qu_x - pu_y)}{\sqrt{u_x^2 + u_y^2 + (qu_x - pu_y)^2}}.$$

Since $n = \nabla u / |\nabla u|$, one can solve for $|\nabla u|$ to produce a static Hamilton–Jacobi equation of the surface distance map u, namely

$$|\nabla u|^2 = \tilde{F}(\nabla z, n)^2. \tag{16.13}$$

The result is given by $u = 0$ at A as boundary conditions to the solution of

$$\frac{u_x^2(1 + q^2) + u_y^2(1 + p^2) - 2pqu_x u_y}{1 + p^2 + q^2} = 1. \tag{16.14}$$

This results in the following Hamiltonian

$$H(u_x, u_y) = (1 + q^2)u_x^2 + (1 + p^2)u_y^2 - 2pqu_x u_y - (1 + p^2 + q^2). \tag{16.15}$$

Again, the objective is to find the surface u that solves the static Hamilton–Jacobi equation given by $H(u_x, u_y) = 0$, with the boundary conditions $u = 0$ at A.

Finally, given the solution u to the above static Hamilton–Jacobi equation, we can construct the actual geodesics by back propagating from the point B to the starting point A by solving the ordinary differential equation

$$X_t = -\mathbf{\Pi} \circ (N \times T) \qquad \text{given} \qquad X(0) = B. \tag{16.16}$$

Since N is given as a function of ∇z, and T is obtained by back projecting the level set of u onto z, substitution into the above expression becomes

$$X_t = -\frac{(u_x(1 + q^2) - pqu_y, u_y(1 + p^2) - pqu_x)}{\sqrt{(1 + p^2 + q^2)(u_x^2 + u_y^2 + (qu_x - pu_y)^2)}}. \tag{16.17}$$

A consistent viscosity scheme which satisfies the fast marching upwind definition can be designed from the scheme proposed in [102], i.e., the minmod approximation for $u_x u_y$, and $\max(D_{ij}^{-x}, -D_{ij}^{+x}, 0)^2$ for u_x^2; in part, this is based on the scheme from Rouy and Tourin [156]. Then, select the largest root, and verify that it is larger than those neighboring grid points that took active part in its computation; i.e., the u values at the neighboring points that result from the selected quadratic equation are smaller than the selected root. This produces a scheme that satisfies

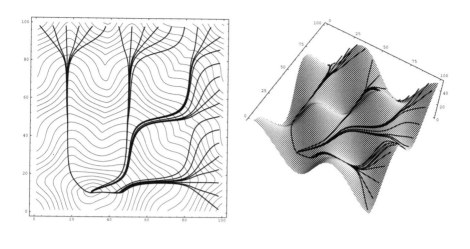

(a) Geodesics on level sets   (b) A perspective view

Fig. 16.9. Construction of geodesics on sinusoidal surface

the fast marching requirements. Once the solution u is obtained, second order Heun's method is used together with bilinear interpolation between grid points to solve the ordinary differential equation given by equation (16.17). For details, see [103].

In Figure 16.9, the geodesics are found on the sinusoidal surface $z(x, y) = 0.25 \sin(2\pi 1.5x) \sin(2\pi 1.5y)$ defined on the unit box $[-0.5, 0.5] \times [-0.5, 0.5]$. In Figure 16.9(a), the geodesics are the thick curves on the level sets of the u geodesic distance map. In Figure 16.9(b), a perspective view over the surface z is shown, together with 28 geodesics connecting to the source point $(30, 10)$.

16.6 Calculating first arrivals: Seismic travel times

Another example of the application of the fast marching method is in computing the solution to the Eikonal equation for calculation of seismic travel times. Here, one objective is to construct the arrival times of waves propagating through a media whose density is given at each point. In a common simplification, see van Trier and Symes [203] and Vidale [204], the Eikonal equation is used to measure first arrival times. As

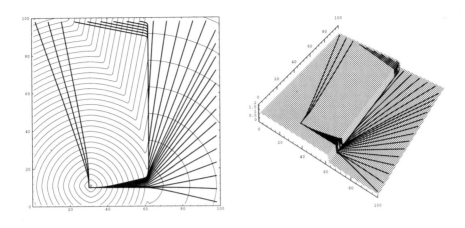

(a) Shortest paths for seismic travel times   (b) A perspective view

Fig. 16.10. Computation of seismic travel times and shortest paths for two-valued media

such, the application is a combination of our earlier examples, including aspects of the lithographic development calculations presented and the back propagation methods to compute geodesics. Starting with an initial disturbance, the goal is to compute the arrival time at every point in the media.

As a simple example, taken from [103], in Figure 16.10, a domain of 100×100 grid points is shown, in which the speed in the light gray region is $F(x, y) = 1$ for $i < 60$, and in the dark gray region the speed is $F(x, y) = 5$ for $i \geq 60$. Thus, there is a speed jump of a factor of five between the left and right sides. A disturbance is started in the slower region at the point $(30, 10)$, and the equi-time contours are computed, together with the geodesic paths from a set of points reaching back to the initial disturbance. Figure 16.10(a) shows these paths drawn on the equi-time contours; note that the two sets of curves are perpendicular to each other as expected. In Figure 16.10(b), we plot the geodesics on a perspective view where the height corresponds to the speed. As can be seen, some of the geodesics in the slow region reach back to the initial disturbance by first moving over to the fast region, tracking back along the boundary between the fast and slow, and then reaching back to the initial disturbance. Of course, the use of an Eikonal equation to compute wave motion in this problem represents a significant simplification; by aiming towards viscosity solutions, one computes first arrival times, and ignores reflected effects, etc. Full techniques which make use of the Eikonal equation for computing first arrival times, plus asymptotic expansions for later arrivals based on solving additional transport equations are possible (see Fatemi, Engquist, and Osher [70]). A variety of such techniques are currently being coupled to fast marching methods, for details, see [181].

16.7 Robotic navigation under constraints

The above ability to compute first arrival times for static Hamilton–Jacobi equations can be used to construct solutions to some problems in robotic navigation. Here, we discuss the problem briefly; for details, see Kimmel and Sethian [104].

As a simple example, imagine a starting point A and a finishing point B in the plane, and a collection of subsets of the plane which represent obstacles Ω_l, $l = 1, \ldots, L$. The shortest path under a speed function $F(x, y)$ from A to B which avoids these obstacles can be found by computing the solution to the Eikonal equation

$$|\nabla T| = \frac{1}{F(x, y)}, \tag{16.18}$$

where $F(x, y)$ is reset to a very small number ϵ at those (x, y) which belong to one of the subsets. Once the solution is found, back propagation from B to A along the gradient constructs the optimal path.

As an illustration, imagine the problem of a robot in the plane with a movable arm of length *Length*. Thus, the state of the robot is defined by the coordinate triple (x, y, θ), where (x, y) is the location and θ is the angle the robot arm makes with the positive x axis. Furthermore, imagine a set of obstacles Ω_l located in the plane which neither the robot nor its arm can penetrate. Finally, assume that one is given a function $F(x, y, \theta)$, which is the "speed" function at each point of the configuration space (x, y, θ). Note that this formulation allows for the possibility that it is easier to turn the robot arm through some angles at different points in the plane than it is at others.

Let a point A be the starting position and arm orientation specified by (x_A, y_A, θ_A), with an end point B similarly described. The goal is to find the optimal path from A to B.

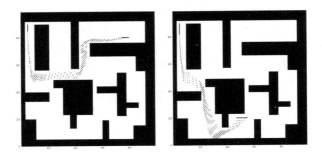

Fig. 16.11. Navigation with constraints

Note that we need to be careful about the obstacles; it is not enough to simply set the speed function F to be a small number whenever (x, y) is inside Ω_i. This is because the orientation of the arm may be such that the robot cannot get within $Length$ of the obstacle. Thus, one approach is to build the appropriate modified speed function $\bar{F}(x, y, \theta)$ as follows. Lay down a grid (i, j, k) in x, y, θ space, and consider the robot as a point in that space. For each discretization angle θ_k between 0 and 2π, extend each obstacle by a length $\pm Length$ in the direction θ_k, and set $\bar{F}(x, y, \theta_k)$ equal to a small number ϵ if (x, y) falls within that extended region. (This extension in some cases may itself be done using the fast marching method.) In other words, we shrink the robot down to size zero and move its size/orientation to the obstacles. Then the Eikonal equation

$$[T_x^2 + T_y^2 + T_\theta^2]^{1/2} = \frac{1}{\bar{F}(x, y, \theta)} \qquad (16.19)$$

is solved, followed by back propagation to compute the optimal trajectory.

Figure 16.11 shows two solutions to the problem of finding the optimal path to move a piano through a narrow corridor. We assume $F = 1$ everywhere, treat the corridor as an obstacle, compute the modified speed function $\bar{F}(x, y, \theta)$, and solve using the fast marching method. For details and further applications, including three-dimensional problems with larger and more complex constraint spaces, see [104].

16.8 Shape recovery using fast marching methods

Finally, we refer the reader to Malladi and Sethian [127], where the fast marching method is combined with the shape recovery techniques discussed in Chapter 15. In Figure 16.12 we show the final snapshot of a full reconstruction of the brain from MRI data; the results are obtained by starting with some spheres as initial data and employing the fast marching method together with suitable stopping criteria.

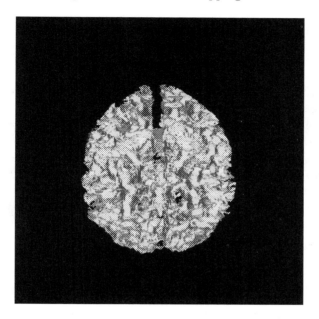

Fig. 16.12. Fast marching reconstruction of brain from initial spheres

17

Etching and Deposition in Microchip Fabrication

Outline: *We end with the application of level set methods to tracking interfaces in the microfabrication of electronic components; the goal is to follow the changing surface topography of a wafer as it is etched, layered, and shaped during the manufacturing process. The problem requires the combination of many of the previously discussed techniques, including narrow band methods, the fast marching technique for the Eikonal equation, masking, discontinuous speed functions, visibility determinations, and algorithms for subtle speed laws. In particular, some aspects of the manufacturing process lead to a non-convex speed function, which can easily be handled with the level set methodology.*

17.1 Physical effects

The goal of numerical simulations in microfabrication is to model the process by which silicon devices are manufactured. Here, we briefly summarize some of the stages involved. First, a single crystal ingot of silicon is extracted from molten pure silicon. This silicon ingot is then sliced into several hundred thin wafers, each of which is then polished to a smooth finish. A thin layer of crystalline is then oxidized, a light-sensitive "photoresist" that is sensitive to light is applied, and then the wafer is covered with a pattern mask that shields part of the photoresist. This pattern mask contains the layout of the circuit itself. Under exposure to a light or an electron beam, the exposed photoresist polymerizes and hardens, leaving an unexposed material that is then etched away in a dry etch process, revealing a bare silicon dioxide layer. Ionized impurity atoms such as boron, phosphorus, and argon are then implanted into the pattern of the exposed silicon water, and silicon dioxide is deposited at reduced pressure in a plasma discharge from gas mixtures at

184

a low temperature. Finally, thin films such as aluminum are deposited by processes such as plasma sputtering, and contacts to the electrical components and component interconnections are established. The result is a device that carries the desired electrical properties.

The above processes produce considerable changes in the surface profile as it undergoes various effects of etching and deposition. This problem is known as the "surface topography problem" in microfabrication, and is controlled by a large collection by physical effects, including the visibility of the etching/deposition source at each point of the evolving profile, surface diffusion along the front, non-convex sputter laws that produce faceting, shocks and rarefactions, material-dependent discontinuous etch rates, and masking profiles.

The underlying physics and chemistry that contributes to the motion of the interface profile is very much an area of active research. Nonetheless, once empirical models are formulated, the problem ultimately becomes the familiar one of tracking an interface moving under a speed function F. This final chapter on level set application reviews some recent work on level set methods for these problems. In particular, they track the evolution of surface evolving under a non-convex speed function that arises during the ion-milling/sputter etch process. Simulations in this chapter are taken from Adalsteinsson and Sethian [2, 3, 4]; complete details may be found therein.

17.2 Background

The underlying physical effects involved in etching, deposition, and lithography are quite complex; excellent overviews can be found in Scheckler [163], Scheckler, Toh, Hoffstetter, and Neureuther [164], Toh [199], and Toh and Neureuther [200]; see also Rey, Cheng, McVittie, and Saraswat [153], McVittie, Rey, Bariya, et al. [132], and Cale and Raupp [32, 33, 34]. The effects may be summarized briefly as follows:

- *Deposition:* Particles are deposited on the surface, which causes build-up in the profile. The particles may either isotropically condense from the surroundings (known as chemical or "wet" deposition), or be deposited from a source. In the latter case, particles leave the source and deposit on the surface; the main advantage of this approach is increased control over the directionality of surface deposition. The rate of deposition, and hence growth of the layer, may depend on source masking, visibility effects between the source and surface point, angle-

dependent flux distribution of source particles, the angle of incidence
of the particles relative to the surface normal direction, reflection of
deposited particles, and surface diffusion effects.

- *Etching:* Particles remove material from the evolving profile boundary.
  The material may be isotropically removed, known again as chemical
  or "wet" etching, or chipped away through reactive ion etching, also
  known as "ion-milling". Similar to deposition, the main advantage
  of reactive ion etching is enhanced directionality, which becomes in-
  creasingly important as device sizes decrease substantially and etching
  must proceed in vertical directions without affecting adjacent features.
  As described in Singh et al. [184], the total etch rate consists of an
  ion-assisted rate and a purely chemical etch rate due to etching by
  neutral radicals, which may still have a directional component. As
  in the above, the total etch rate due to wet and directional milling
  effects can depend on source masking, visibility effects between the
  source and surface point, angle-dependent flux distribution of source
  particles, the angle of incidence of the particles relative to the surface
  normal direction, reflection/re-emission of etching/milling particles,
  and surface diffusion effects.

- *Lithography:* The underlying material is treated by an electromagnetic
  wave that alters the resist property of the material. The aerial image
  is found, which then determines the amount of crosslinking at each
  point in the material, which then produces the etch/resist rate at each
  point of the material. A profile is then etched into the material, where
  the speed of the profile in its normal direction at any point is given
  by the underlying etch rate.

In the rest of this section, we formalize the above. Define the coordinate system with the x- and y-axes lying in the plane and z being the
vertical axis. Consider a periodic initial profile $h(x, y)$, where h gives
the height of the initial surface above the x, y plane, as well as a source
Z given as a surface above the initial profile, and write $Z(x, y)$ referring
to the height of the source at the point (x, y).

For both etching and deposition, define the source ray to be the ray
leaving the source and aimed towards the surface profile. Let ψ be
the angle variation in the source ray away from the negative z axis; ψ
runs from 0 to π, though it is physically unreasonable to have ϕ values
between $\pi/2$ and π. Let γ be the angle between the projection of the
source ray in the x, y plane and the positive x-axis. Let n be the normal

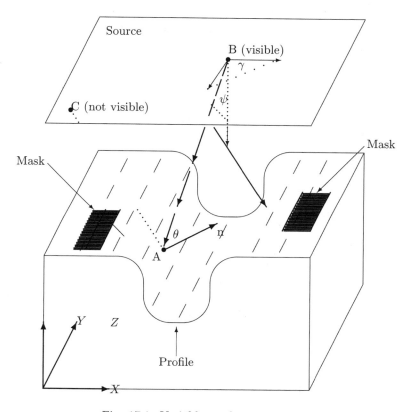

Fig. 17.1. Variables and setup

vector at a point x on the surface profile, and θ the angle between the normal and the source ray.

In Figure 17.1, these variables are indicated. Masks, which force flux rates to be zero, are indicated by heavy dark patches on the initial profile. At each point of the profile, a visibility indicator function $M_\Upsilon(\vec{x}, \vec{x}')$ is assigned which indicates whether the point $\vec{x}$ on the initial profile can be seen by the source point $\vec{x}'$.

17.3 Equations of motion for etching/deposition

The goal is to write the effects of deposition and etching on the speed F at a point $\vec{x}$ on the front. (We shall treat lithography separately, although it is amenable to the same unified level set approach). We refer the interested reader to a large collection of previous work on this topic, including [32, 33, 34, 85, 93, 111, 132, 153, 163, 164, 183, 184, 199, 200].

17.3.1 Individual terms

17.3.1.1 Etching

We consider two separate types of etching:

- $F_{\text{Iso}}^{\text{Etch}}$: *Isotropic etching.* Uniform etching, also known as chemical or wet etching.
- $F_{\text{Dir}}^{\text{Etch}}$: *Direct etching.* Etching from an external source; this can be either a collection of point sources, or from an external stream coming from a particular direction. Visibility effects are included; and the flux strength can depend on both the solid angle from the emitting source and the angle between the profile normal and the incoming source. Etching can include highly sensitive dependence on angle such as in ion-milling.

17.3.1.2 Deposition

We consider four separate types of deposition:

- $F_{\text{Iso}}^{\text{Dep}}$: *Isotropic deposition.* Uniform deposition, also known as chemical or wet deposition.
- $F_{\text{Dir}}^{\text{Dep}}$: *Direct deposition.* Deposition from an external source; this can be either a collection of point sources, or from an external stream coming from a particular direction. Visibility effects are included; and the flux strength can depend on both the solid angle from the emitting source and the angle between the profile normal and the incoming source.
- $F_{\text{Re-Dep}}^{\text{Dep}}$: *Re-deposition.* Particles that are expelled during the etching process. These particles then attach themselves to the profile at other locations; the strength and distribution of the re-deposition flux function can depend on such factors as the local angle. A re-deposition coefficient, $\beta_{\text{re-deposition}}$ can range from zero to unity to reflect the fraction of re-deposition that results from the etching process.

- $F_{\text{Re-Em}}^{\text{Dep}}$: *Re-emission deposition.* Particles that are deposited from direct deposition may in fact not stick and are then re-emitted into the domain. The amount of particles re-emitted depends on a sticking coefficient $\beta_{\text{re-emission}}$.

We generalize all of these effects as the "source". Thus, the line source may consist of locations which emit either unidirectional deposition or point source deposition.

17.3.2 Assembling the terms

We may, somewhat abstractly, assemble the above terms into the single expression

$$F = F_{\text{Iso}}^{\text{Etch}} + F_{\text{Dir}}^{\text{Etch}} + F_{\text{Iso}}^{\text{Dep}} + F_{\text{Dir}}^{\text{Dep}} + F_{\text{Re-Dep}}^{\text{Dep}} + F_{\text{Re-Em}}^{\text{Dep}}. \qquad (17.1)$$

The two isotropic terms are evaluated at a point x by simply evaluating the strengths at that point. The two direct terms are evaluated at a point x on the profile by first computing the visibility to each point of the source, and then evaluating the flux function; thus these terms require computing an integral over the entire source. To compute the fifth term, $F_{\text{Re-Dep}}$ at a point x, the contributions of every point on the profile are checked for re-deposition particles arising from the etching process, thus this term requires computing an integral over the profile itself. The sixth term, $F_{\text{Re-Em}}$ is more problematic; since every point on the front can act as a deposition source of re-emitted particles that do not stick, the total flux function deposition function comes from evaluating an integral equation along the entire profile.

In more detail, let Ω be the set of points on the evolving profile at time t, and let So be the external source. Given two points $\vec{x}$ and $\vec{x}'$, let $M_{\Upsilon}(\vec{x}, \vec{x}')$ be one if the points are visible from one another and zero otherwise. Let r be the distance from x to x', $\vec{n}$ be the unit normal vector at the point x, and finally, let $\vec{\alpha}$ be the unit vector at the point $\vec{x}'$ on the source pointing towards the point x on the profile. Then we may refine the above terms for the flux FL as:

$$
F = \left[
\begin{array}{c}
\mathrm{FL}^{\mathrm{Etch}}_{\mathrm{Iso}} \\[2mm]
+ \\[2mm]
\int_{So} \mathrm{FL}^{\mathrm{Etch}}_{\mathrm{Dir}}(r,\psi,\gamma,\theta,\vec{x}) M_{\Upsilon(\vec{x},\vec{x}')}(\vec{n}\cdot\vec{\alpha}) d\vec{x}' \\[2mm]
+ \\[2mm]
\mathrm{FL}^{\mathrm{Dep}}_{\mathrm{Iso}} \\[2mm]
+ \\[2mm]
\int_{So} \mathrm{FL}^{\mathrm{Dep}}_{\mathrm{Dir}}(r,\psi,\gamma,\theta,\vec{x}) M_{\Upsilon(\vec{x},\vec{x}')}(\vec{n}\cdot\vec{\alpha}) d\vec{x}' \\[2mm]
+ \\[2mm]
\int_{\Omega} \beta_{re-dep} \mathrm{FL}^{\mathrm{Dep}}_{\mathrm{Re\text{-}dep}}(r,\psi,\gamma,\theta,\vec{x}) M_{\Upsilon(\vec{x},\vec{x}')}(\vec{n}\cdot\vec{\alpha}) d\vec{x}' \\[2mm]
+ \\[2mm]
\int_{\Omega} \beta_{re-em} \mathrm{FL}^{\mathrm{Dep}}_{\mathrm{Re\text{-}em}}(r,\psi,\gamma,\theta,\vec{x}) M_{\Upsilon(\vec{x},\vec{x}')}(\vec{n}\cdot\vec{\alpha}) d\vec{x}'
\end{array}
\right]
$$

$$(17.2)$$

The integrals are performed in a straightforward manner. The front is located by constructing the zero level set of ϕ; in two dimensions it is represented by a collection of line segments, in three dimensions by a collection of voxel elements, see [2, 3]. The centroid of each element is taken as the control point, and the individual flux terms are evaluated at each control point. In the case of the two isotropic terms, the flux is immediately found. In the case of the two integrals over sources, the source is suitably discretized and the contributions summed. In the fifth term, corresponding to re-deposition, the integral over the entire profile is calculated by computing the visibility to all other control points and the corresponding re-deposition term produced by the effect of direct deposition. Thus, as presented, this last term requires N^2 evaluations, where N is the number of control points which approximate the front.

17.3.3 Evaluation of the re-emission term

The last term is somewhat more time-consuming to evaluate, since the integral requires evaluation of the flux contribution from each point of the interface, each of which depends on the contribution from all other points. Thus, this is an integral equation which must be solved to produce the total deposition flux at any point. In order to evaluate this term, it is somewhat easier to group all the direction deposition effects

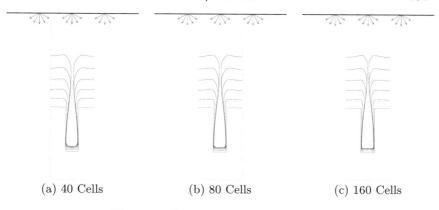

(a) 40 Cells   (b) 80 Cells   (c) 160 Cells

Fig. 17.2. Source deposition into trench

as the flux $FL_{\text{Direct}}^{\text{Deposition}}$. Thus, this term is meant to contain all deposition effects coming directly from the source itself.[1] This resulting matrix M is full and non-symmetric, and hence can be quite substantial if the front is complex. Details about the construction of this integral equation may be found in [4].

17.4 Results

17.4.1 Two-dimensional results

17.4.1.1 Etching/deposition

Figure 17.2 shows a deposition source above a trench, with deposition material emitted from a line source from the solid line above the trench. In this experiment, the deposition rate is the same in all directions. The effects of shadowing are considered. Figure 17.2(a) shows results for 40 computational cells across the width of the computational region (between the two vertical dashed lines); Figure 17.2(b) has 80 cells; and Figure 17.2(c) has 160 cells. The time step for all three calculations is $\Delta t = .00625$. The calculations are performed with a narrow band tube width of 6 cells on either side of the front. There is little change between the calculation with 80 cells and the one with 160 cells, indicating that the solution converged.

As the walls pinch toward each other, the seen visible angle decreases and the speed diminishes. Next, consider directional etching into a

---

[1] If it is desired to include ion-induced re-deposition particles as possible candidates for re-emission, this can be incorporated into this term as well.

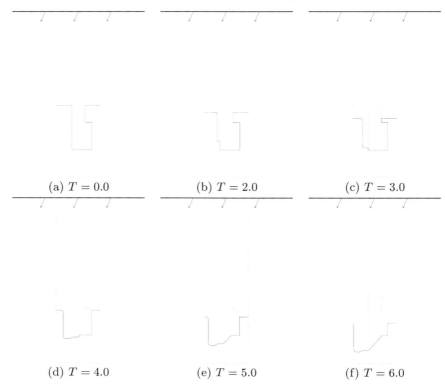

(a) $T = 0.0$ (b) $T = 2.0$ (c) $T = 3.0$

(d) $T = 4.0$ (e) $T = 5.0$ (f) $T = 6.0$

Fig. 17.3. Directional etching into cavity

trench/cavity. Material emits from the line source at an angle of 30 degrees from the vertical. Figure 17.3 shows results at various times, starting with the initial state. Again, there is no yield variation in the etch rate due to angle of incidence with the normal; in other words, the speed of the profile in the normal direction is just the projection of the directional etch rate in that normal direction. Due to the effects of shadowing, as the profile evolves it aligns itself along the incoming unidirectional etching stream.

17.4.1.2 Masking

The effect of masking is studied using a square with masks covering segments of the boundary. Imagine the square surrounded by an etching substance. In Figure 17.4 the etch eats into the non-masked walls, and the resulting front moves into the region and reconnects with other parts of the advancing front.

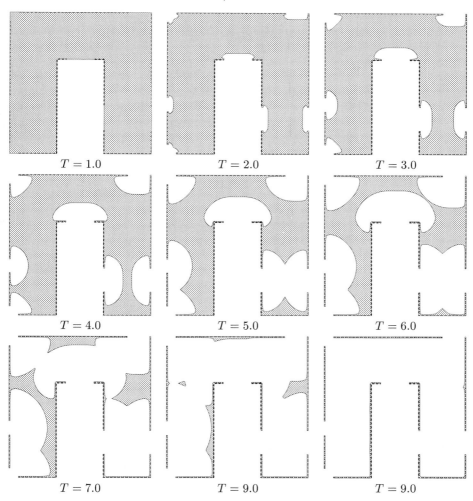

Fig. 17.4. Chemical etching into multiply-masked region

17.4.1.3 Ion-milling: Non-convex sputter laws

A more sophisticated set of examples arises in simulations (for example, of ion-milling) in which the normal speed of the profile depends on the angle of incidence between the surface normal and the incoming beam. This yield function is often empirically fit from experiment, and has been observed to cause such effects as faceting at corners (see Leon et al. [111] and Katardjiev, Carter, and Nobes [93]). As shown in [2, 3], such yield functions can often give rise to non-convex Hamiltonians, in which case alternative schemes must be used.

As an example, consider an etching beam coming down in the vertical direction. In the cases under study here, the angle θ shown in Figure 17.1 refers to the angle between the surface normal and the positive vertical. For this set of calculations, in order to focus on the geometry of sputter effects on shocks/rarefaction fan development, visibility effects are ignored. Following our usual notation, let $F(\theta)$ be the speed of the front in direction normal to the surface, and consider three different speed functions:

- $F(\theta) = 1$
- $F(\theta) = \cos(\theta)$
- $F(\theta) = [1. + 4\sin^2(\theta)]\cos(\theta)$

The first case corresponds to isotropic etching. We shall now show that the third case leads to a non-convex Hamiltonian. We have

$$\phi_t + F|\nabla\phi| = \phi_t + [(1 + A)\cos\theta - A\cos^3\theta]|\nabla\phi|. \qquad (17.3)$$

Noting that $\cos\theta = \frac{\phi_y}{|\nabla\phi|}$, some manipulation produces

$$\phi_t + H(\phi_x, \phi_y) = 0, \qquad (17.4)$$

where the Hamiltonian H is now $H = (1 + A)\phi_y - A\frac{\phi_y^3}{|\nabla\phi|^2}$. This Hamiltonian is in fact non-convex for $A > 0$.

Thus, in the case of this non-convex Hamiltonian, appropriate non-convex schemes of the sort given earlier are required. Figure 17.5 shows the results of applying both the convex and the non-convex schemes. In column A, the effects of purely isotropic motion are shown, thus the yield function is $F = 1$. Located above the yield graph are the motions of a downwards square wave under etching. The top row is calculated using the convex scheme, and the second row using the non-convex scheme. In column B, the effects of directional motion are shown, thus the yield function is $F = \cos(\theta)$. In this case, the horizontal components on the profile do not move, and vertical components move with unit speed. In column C, the effects of a yield function of the form $F = [1 + 4\sin^2(\theta)]\cos(\theta)$ are shown.

The results of these calculations are given in Figure 17.5. The results show that the effects of angle dependent yield functions are pronounced. In Column A the isotropic rate produces smooth corners, correctly building the necessary rarefaction fans in outward corners and

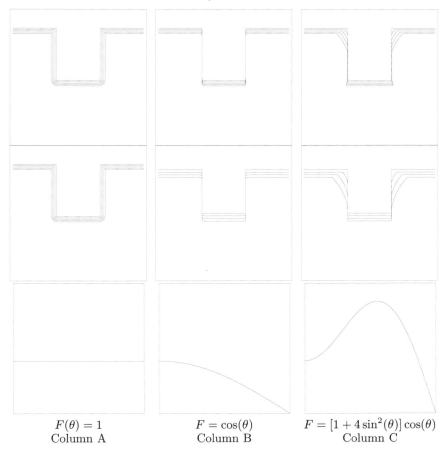

$F(\theta) = 1$
Column A

$F = \cos(\theta)$
Column B

$F = [1 + 4\sin^2(\theta)]\cos(\theta)$
Column C

Fig. 17.5. Ion-milling under various yield functions. Top row: Convex scheme; Middle row: Non-convex scheme; Bottom row: Yield curves

entropy-satisfying shocks in inward corners as discussed and analyzed in [167, 170]. In Column B, the directional rate causes the front to be essentially translated upwards, with minimal rounding of the corners. In Column C, the yield function results in faceting of inward corners where shocks form together with smooth regions. We note that the application of the convex scheme to the non-convex Hamiltonian in Column C leads to incorrect results, whereas application of the non-convex scheme produces the expected answer.

17.4.1.4 Discontinuous etch rates

Next, the effects of etching through different materials are studied. In this example, the etch rates are discontinuous, and hence sharp corners develop in the propagating profile. The results of these calculations are shown in Figure 17.6. A top material masks a lower material, and the profile etches through the lower material first and underneath the upper material. The profile depends on the ratio of the etch rates. In Figure 17.6(a), the two materials have the same etch rate, and hence the front simply propagates in its normal direction with unit speed, regardless of which material it is passing through. In Figure 17.6(b), the bottom material etches four times faster than the top; in Figure 17.6(c), the ratio is 10 to 1. Finally, in Figure 17.6(d), the ratio is 40 to 1, in which case the top material almost acts like a mask.

17.4.1.5 Simultaneous etching and deposition

Next, a parameter study of simultaneous etching and deposition is taken from [4], using speed function

$$F = (1 - \alpha)F_{\text{etch}} + \alpha F_{\text{deposition}} \tag{17.5}$$

where

$$F_{\text{etch}} = (5.2249 \cos \theta - 5.5914 \cos^2 \theta + 1.3665 \cos^4 \theta) \tag{17.6}$$

$$F_{\text{deposition}} = \beta F_{\text{isotropic}} + (1 - \beta)F_{\text{source}}. \tag{17.7}$$

Visibility effects are considered in all terms except isotropic deposition. Figure 17.7 shows the results of varying α and β between 0 and 1.

17.4.1.6 Re-deposition and re-emission

Next, we show a combination of effects. Figure 17.8, taken from [4], includes a combination of ion-milling (using a non-convex sputter law), and ion-induced sputtered re-deposition, together with conformal deposition and direct deposition. In both calculations, the direct deposition term includes the effect of visibility, and the conformal deposition is isotropic. In Figure 17.8(a), the ion-induced sputter re-deposition co-efficient is set to zero. In Figure 17.8(b), which requires the solution of the matrix integral equation, re-deposition occurs during the etching process, resulting in considerable rounding of the sharp corners.

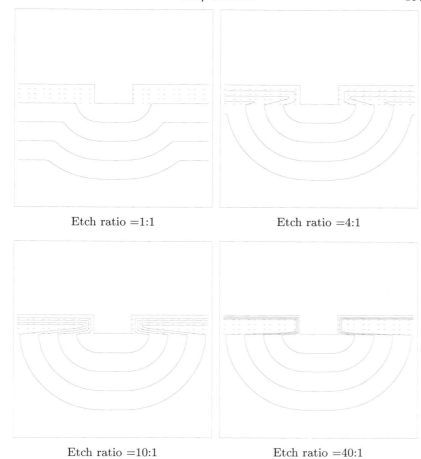

Etch ratio =1:1   Etch ratio =4:1

Etch ratio =10:1   Etch ratio =40:1

Fig. 17.6. Etch ratio = Bottom material rate to top material rate

17.4.2 Three-dimensional simulations

A lithographic development profile is shown in Figure 17.9, using a rate function obtained from other numerical simulations; see [205]. A second order method is employed with a grid size of $50 \times 50 \times 47$; this was computed using the time-dependent narrow band level set method rather than the fast marching Eikonal method described earlier.

Next, Figure 17.10 shows the effects of unidirectional etching under a bridge structure. The bridge initially has a thin curtain stretched underneath it; the thickness of the curtain is smallest at the middle. Here, the pillars shadow the profile, and their effect can be seen on

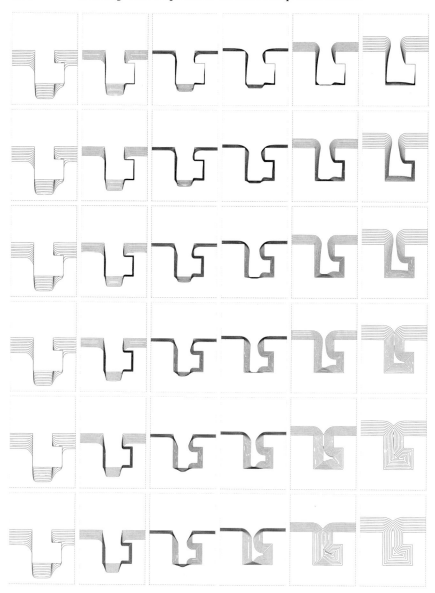

$$F = (1 - \alpha)F_{\text{etch}} + \alpha F_{\text{deposition}}$$

$$F_{\text{etch}} = (5.2249 \cos \theta - 5.5914 \cos^2 \theta + 1.3665 \cos^4 \theta) \cos \theta$$

$$F_{\text{deposition}} = \beta F_{\text{isotropic}} + (1 - \beta)F_{\text{source}}$$

α Increases from left to right
β Increases from top to bottom

Fig. 17.7. Simultaneous etching and deposition

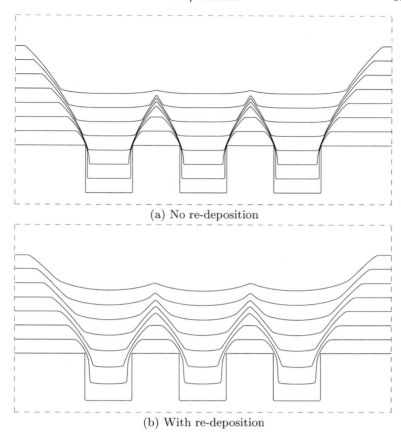

(a) No re-deposition

(b) With re-deposition

Fig. 17.8. Combination of ion-milling, direct deposition and conformal deposition

the flat part of the surface as the bridge is etched away. Finally, a three-dimensional example of a non-convex sputter yield law is applied to an indented saddle, which gives rise to faceting as shown in Figure 17.11. Complete details of the above and a large variety of simulations of etching, deposition, and lithography development may be found in [2, 3, 4].

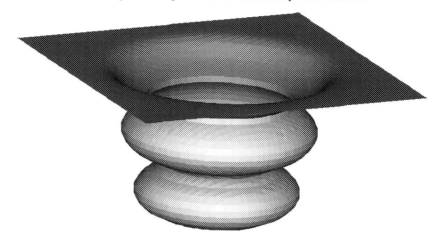

Fig. 17.9. Lithography: 2nd order; Grid size=50 × 50 × 47

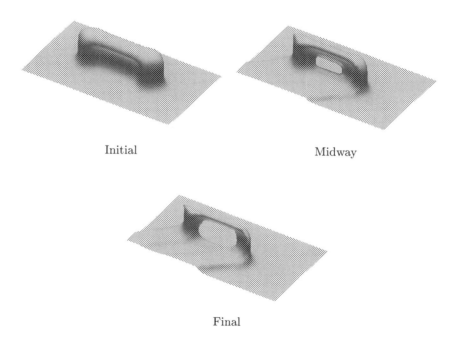

Initial   Midway

Final

Fig. 17.10. Unidirectional etching of bridge

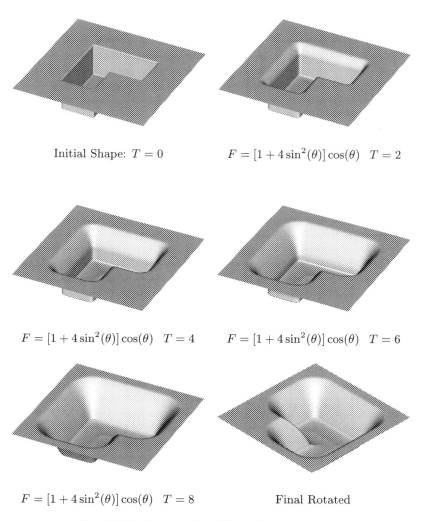

Initial Shape: $T = 0$

$F = [1 + 4\sin^2(\theta)]\cos(\theta)$ $T = 2$

$F = [1 + 4\sin^2(\theta)]\cos(\theta)$ $T = 4$

$F = [1 + 4\sin^2(\theta)]\cos(\theta)$ $T = 6$

$F = [1 + 4\sin^2(\theta)]\cos(\theta)$ $T = 8$

Final Rotated

Fig. 17.11. Downward saddle under sputter etch

18

New Areas

18.1 Other work

The range of level set techniques extends far beyond the work covered here. Here, we point the reader to some additional topics.

On the theoretical side, considerable analysis of level set methods has been performed in recent years; see, for example, Brakke [26], Ecker and Huisken [58], Evans and Spruck [64, 65, 66, 67], Chen, Giga, Goto, and Ishii [40, 75, 76], and Ambrosio and Soner [9]. These works have concentrated on many aspects, including questions of existence and uniqueness, pathological cases, extensions of these ideas to fronts of co-dimension greater than one (such as evolving curves in three dimensions), coupling with diffusion equations, links between the level set technique, and Brakke's groundbreaking original varifold approach.

On the theoretical/numerical analysis side, level set techniques exploit the considerable technology developed in the area of viscous solutions to Hamilton–Jacobi equations; see the work in Barles [16] and in Crandall, Evans, Ishii, and Lions [52, 53, 54, 116].

A wide range of applications relate to level set methods, including work on minimal arrival times by Falcone [68], flame propagation work by Zhu and Ronney [206], gradient flows applied to geometric active contour models in Caselles, Kimmel, and Sapiro [37] and Kichenassamy, Kumar, Olver, Tannenbaum and Yezzi [96], and affine invariant scale space in Sapiro and Tannenbaum [160]. We also refer the reader to a study of various interface techniques in [155] and the collection of papers from the International Conference on Mean Curvature Flow [30].

18.2 Guide to new problems

As a general guideline, how can one transform new interface problems into the level set framework? As we have seen, considerable work is required to transform a particular interface problem into a level set framework. The reason is that the extension of information from the front, where variables have a natural meaning, to grid points where the level set function is defined, can be a delicate issue. First, the information may not have any reasonable meaning away from the front, in which case an artificial velocity field must be constructed that updates the level set function, and defaults to the correct value on the front. Second, if the physics/chemistry of the problem requires the solution of some set of equations on either side of the interface, carrying this information back to the front itself has an additional error; it is for this reason that many people choose instead to work with a moving body-fitted grid, in which the coordinate system lies along the interface. Level set methods require considerable care in order to build correct derivative operators at the appropriate grid points.

Given a moving interface, what is the most reasonable approach? The answer probably lies in a combination of the various techniques. Geometric terms, such as curvature, can be evaluated for each level set; that is, at each grid point. Terms that depend on the entire front (such as visibility in the etching/deposition work) are probably best handled by extrapolating values from the front itself. And terms arising from the solution of differential equations across the interface, for example, surface tension in two-phase flow, are probably best handled by viewing them as right-hand sides to discrete, grid-based operators. Some of the most promising ways of computing solutions to differential equations with profound jumps conditions due to interfaces may come from immersed interface methods, see [113]; in these techniques, coefficients in the partial differential equation are adjusted through one-sided Taylor series expansions to account for the presence of the interface. The associated physics are then solved on a full grid, and the solution can then be carried back to the interface. Coupling this approach to the level set methodology is promising.

Level set methods require, in many cases, careful attention to the underlying physics, and a delicate linking of the dynamics of the interface motion with the driving equations. The payoff is robust, accurate, and versatile algorithms for highly complex problems.

Acknowledgements

All calculations were performed at the University of California at Berkeley and the Lawrence Berkeley Laboratory. The detailed applications of the level set schemes discussed in this work are joint with D. Adalsteinsson, D. Chopp, R. Kimmel, R. Malladi, B. Milne. C. Rhee, J, Strain, L. Talbot, and J. Zhu. E-mail may be sent to the author at sethian@math.berkeley.edu; a level set web page may be found at http://math.berkeley.edu/~sethian/level_set.html.

Bibliography

[1]   Adalsteinsson, D., and Sethian, J.A., *A Fast Level Set Method for Propagating Interfaces*, J. Comp. Phys., 118, 2, pp. 269–277, 1995.

[2]   Adalsteinsson, D., and Sethian, J.A., *A Unified Level Set Approach to Etching, Deposition and Lithography I: Algorithms and Two-dimensional Simulations*, 120, 1, pp. 128–144, 1995.

[3]   Adalsteinsson, D., and Sethian, J.A., *A Unified Level Set Approach to Etching, Deposition and Lithography II: Three-dimensional Simulations*, 122, 2, pp. 348–366, 1995.

[4]   Adalsteinsson, D., and Sethian, J.A., *A Unified Level Set Approach to Etching, Deposition and Lithography III: Complex Simulations and Multiple Effects*, to be submitted, J. Comp. Phys., 1996.

[5]   Adalsteinsson, D., Kimmel, R., Malladi, R., and Sethian, J.A., *Fast Marching Methods for Computing the Solutions to Static Hamilton–Jacobi Equations*, CPAM Report 667, Univ. of California, Berkeley, submitted for publication, SIAM J. Num. Anal., Feb., 1996.

[6]   Altshuler, S., Angenent, S.B., and Giga, Y., *Mean Curvature Flow through Singularities for Surfaces of Rotation*, in press, J. Geom. Anal., 1995.

[7]   Alvarez, L., Lions, P.L., and Morel, M., *Image Selective Smoothing and Edge Detection by Nonlinear Diffusion. II,* SIAM J. Num. Anal. 29, 3, pp. 845–866, 1992.

[8]   Alvarez, L., and Mazorra, L., *Signal and Image Restoration using Shock Filters and Anisotropic Diffusion*, SIAM J. Num. Anal., 31, 2, pp. 590–605, 1994.

[9]   Ambrosio, L., and Soner, H.M., *Level Set Approach to Mean Curvature Flow in Arbitrary Co-dimension*, in press, J. Diff. Geom, 1995.

[10]   Angenent, S., *Shrinking Doughnuts*, in "Proceedings of Nonlinear Diffusion Equations and Their Equilibrium States", 3, Eds. N.G. Lloyd et al., Birkhauser, Boston, MA, 1992.

[11]   Angenent, S., Chopp., D.L., and Ilmanen, T., *On the Singularities of Cones Evolving by Mean Curvature*, Comm. Partial Diff. Eqns., to appear, 1995.

[12]   Arbter, K., Snyder, W.E., Burkhardt, H., and Hirzinger, G., *Application of Affine-invariant Fourier Descriptors to Recognition of 3-D*

Objects, IEEE Trans. on Patt. Anal. and Mach. Intell., 12, 7, pp. 640–647, 1990.

[13]   Bajcsy, R., and Solina, F., *Three-Dimensional Object Representation Revisited*, in "Proceedings of First International Conference on Computer Vision", pp. 231–240, London, England, 1987.

[14]   Bardi, M., and Falcone, M., *An Approximation Scheme for the Minimum Time Function*, SIAM J. Control Optim, 28, pp. 950–965, (1990),

[15]   Barles, G., *Remarks on a Flame Propagation Model*, INRIA Report 464, 1985.

[16]   Barles, G., *Discontinuous Viscosity Solutions of First Order Hamilton–Jacobi Equations: A Guided Visit*, Non-linear Analysis: Theory, Methods, and Applications, 20, 9, pp. 1123–1134, 1993.

[17]   Barles, G., and Souganidis, P.E., *Convergence of Approximation Schemes for Fully Non-linear Second Order Equations*, Asymptotic Anal., 4, pp. 271–283, 1991.

[18]   Bell, J.B., Colella, P., and Glaz, H.M., *A Second-Order Projection Method for the IncompressibleNavier-Stokes Equations*, J. Comp. Phys., 85, pp. 257–283, 1989.

[19]   Berger, M., and Colella, P., *Local Adaptive Mesh Refinement for Shock Hydrodynamics*, J. Comp. Phys., 1, 82, pp. 62–84, 1989.

[20]   Binford, T.O., *Visual Perception by Computer*, invited talk, IEEE Systems and Control Conference, Miami, FL.

[21]   Blake, A., and Zisserman, A., *Visual Reconstruction*, MIT Press, Cambridge, MA, 1987.

[22]   Blum, H., *A Transformation for Extracting New Descriptors of Shape*, in "Models for the Perception of Speech and Visual Form", Ed. W. Wathen-Dunn, MIT Press, Cambridge, MA, 1967.

[23]   Borgefors, G., *Distance Transformations in Digital Images*, Computer Vision, Graphics, and Image Processing, 34, pp. 344–371, 1986.

[24]   Bourlioux, A., *A Coupled Level-Set Volume of Fluid Algorithm for Tracking Material Interfaces*, Sixth International Symposium on Computational Fluid Dynamics, Sept. 4-8, 1995, Lake Tahoe, NV.

[25]   Brackbill, J.U., Kothe, D.B., and Zemach, C., *A Continuum Method for Modeling Surface Tension*, J. Comp. Phys., 100, pp. 335–353, 1992.

[26]   Brakke, K.A., *The Motion of a Surface by Its Mean Curvature*, Princeton University Press, Princeton, NJ, 1978.

[27]   Brakke , K.A., Surface Evolver Program, Research Report GCC 17, the Geometry Supercomputer Project, University of Minnesota, Minneapolis, MN, 55455, 1990.

[28]   Bronsard, L., and Kohn, R.V., *Motion By Mean Curvature as the Singular Limit of Ginzburg-Landau Dynamics*, J. Diff. Eqns., 90, 2, pp. 211–237, 1991.

[29]   Bronsard, L., and Wetton, B., *A Numerical Method for Tracking Curve Networks Moving with Curvature Motion*, J. Comp. Phys., 120, 1, pp. 66–87, 1995.

[30]   Buttazzo, G., and Visitin, A., *Motion by Mean Curvature and Related Topics*, Proceedings of the International Conference at Trento, 1992, Walter de Gruyter, New York, 1994.

[31]   Cahn, J.E., and Hilliard, J.E., *Free energy of a nonuniform system. 1. Interfacial free energy*, Jour. Chem. Phys. 28, pp. 358–367, 1958.

[32] Cale, T.S., and Raupp, G.B., *Free Molecular Transport and Deposition in Cylindrical Features*, J. Vac. Sci. Tech., B, 8, 4, pp. 649–655, 1990.

[33] Cale, T.S., and Raupp, G.B., *Free Molecular Transport and Deposition in Long Rectangular Trenches*, J. Appl. Phys., 68, 7, pp. 3645–3652, 1990.

[34] Cale, T.S., and Raupp, G.B., *A Unified Line-of-Sight Model of Deposition in Rectangular Trenches*, J. Vac. Sci. Tech., B, 8, 6, pp. 1242–1248, 1990.

[35] Canny, J., *A Computational Approach to Edge Detection*, IEEE Trans. on Patt. Anal. and Mach. Intell., 8, pp. 679–698, 1986.

[36] Caselles, V., Catte, F., Coll, T., and Dibos, F., *A Geometric Model for Active Contours in Image Processing*, Internal Report No. 9210, CEREMADE, Université de Paris-Dauphine, France.

[37] Caselles, V., Kimmel, R., Sapiro, G., *Geodesic active contours*, Proc. Fifth IEEE International Conference on Computer Vision, ICCV '95, pages 694–699, Cambridge, USA, June 1995.

[38] Castillo, J.E., *Mathematical Aspects of Grid Generation*, Frontiers in Applied Mathematics, 8, SIAM Publications, Philadelphia, PA, 1991.

[39] Chang, Y.C., Hou, T.Y., Merriman, B., and Osher, S.J., *A Level Set Formulation of Eulerian Interface Capturing Methods for Incompressible Fluid Flows*, Jour. Comp. Phys., 124, pp. 449–464, 1996.

[40] Chen, Y., Giga, Y., and Goto, S., *Uniqueness and Existence of Viscosity Solutions of Generalized Mean Curvature Flow Equations*, J. Diff. Geom, 33, 749, 1991.

[41] Chopp, D.L., *Computing Minimal Surfaces via Level Set Curvature Flow*, Jour. of Comp. Phys., 106, pp. 77–91, 1993.

[42] Chopp, D.L., *Numerical Computation of Self-Similar Solutions for Mean Curvature Flow* J. Exper. Math., 3, 1, pp. 1–15, 1994.

[43] Chopp, D.L., and Sethian, J.A., *Flow Under Curvature: Singularity Formation, Minimal Surfaces, and Geodesics*, Jour. Exper. Math., 2, 4, pp. 235–255, 1993.

[44] Chopp, D.L., and Sethian, J.A., *A Level Set Approach to the Numerical Simulation of Viscous Sintering*, work in progress, 1996.

[45] Chorin, A.J., *Numerical Solution of the Navier-Stokes Equations*, Math. Comp., 22, pp. 745, 1968.

[46] Chorin, A.J., *Numerical Study of Slightly Viscous Flow*, J. Fluid Mech., 57, pp. 785–796, 1973.

[47] Chorin, A.J., *Flame Advection and Propagation Algorithms*, J. Comp. Phys., 35, pp. 1–11, 1980.

[48] Chorin, A.J., *Curvature and Solidification*, J. Comp. Phys., 57, pp. 472–490, 1985.

[49] Chorin, A.J., and Marsden, J.E., *A Mathematical Introduction to Fluid Mechanics*, Springer-Verlag, New York, NY, 1980.

[50] Cohen, L.D., *On Active Contour Models and Balloons*, Computer Vision, Graphics, and Image Processing, 53, 2, pp. 211–218, 1991.

[51] Colella, P., and Puckett, E.G., *Modern Numerical Methods for Fluid Flow*, Lecture Notes, Department of Mechanical Engineering, University of California, Berkeley, CA, 1994.

[52] Crandall, M.G., Evans, L.C., and Lions, P-L., *Some Properties of Viscosity Solutions of Hamilton–Jacobi Equations*, Tran. AMS, 282, pp. 487–502, 1984.

[53] Crandall, M.G., Ishii, H., and Lions, P-L., *User's Guide to Viscosity*

Solutions of Second Order Partial Differential Equations, Bull. AMS, 27/1, pp. 1–67, 1992.

[54] Crandall, M.G., and Lions, P-L., *Viscosity Solutions of Hamilton–Jacobi Equations*, Tran. AMS, 277, pp. 1–43, 1983.

[55] Crimmins, T., *A Complete Set of Fourier Descriptors for Two-dimensional Shapes*, IEEE Trans. on Syst. Man, and Cyber., 12, 6, 1982.

[56] Danielson, P.E., *Euclidean distance mapping*, Computer Graphics and Image Processing, 14, pp. 227–248, 1980.

[57] Dziuk, Gerhard, *An Algorithm for Evolutionary Surfaces*, Num. Math. 58, pp. 603–611, 1991.

[58] Ecker, K., Huisman, G., *Interior Estimates for Hypersurfaces Moving by Mean Curvature*, Inventiones Mathematica, 105, 3, pp. 547–569, 1991.

[59] Eiseman, P.R., *Grid Generation for Fluid Mechanics Computations*, Ann. Rev. Fluid Mech., 17, pp. 487–522, 1985.

[60] Elliot, D.F. and Rao, K.R., *Fast Transforms: Algorithms, Analyses, Applications*, Academic Press, New York, NY, 1982.

[61] Engquist, B., and Osher, S.J., *Stable and Entropy-Satisfying Approximations for Transonic Flow Calculations*, Math. Comp., 34, 45, 1980.

[62] Evans, L.C., *Partial Differential Equations*, Berkeley Mathematics Lecture Notes Series, Vol. 3A, 3B, Center for Pure and Applied Mathematics, University of California, Berkeley, CA, 1994.

[63] Evans, L.C., Soner, H.M., and Souganidis, P.E., *Phase Transitions and Generalized Motion by Mean Curvature*, Communications on Pure and Applied Mathematics, 45, pp. 1097–1123, 1992.

[64] Evans, L.C., and Spruck, J., *Motion of Level Sets by Mean Curvature I*, J. Diff. Geom, 33, 635, 1991.

[65] Evans, L.C., and Spruck, J., *Motion of Level Sets by Mean Curvature II*, Transactions of the American Mathematical Society, 330, 1, pp. 321–332, 1992.

[66] Evans, L.C., and Spruck, J., *Motion of Level Sets by Mean Curvature III*, J. Geom. Anal. 2, pp. 121–150, 1992.

[67] Evans, L.C., and Spruck, J., *Motion of Level Sets by Mean Curvature IV*, J. Geom. Anal., 5, 1, pp. 77–114, 1995.

[68] Falcone, M., *The Minimum Time Problem and Its Applications to Front Propagation*, in "Motion by Mean Curvature and Related Topics", Proceedings of the International Conference at Trento, 1992, Walter de Gruyter, New York, 1994.

[69] Falcone, M., Giorgi, T., and Loretti, P., *Level Sets of Viscosity Solutions: Some Applications to Fronts and Rendez-Vous Problems*, SIAMJ. Appl. Math., 54, 5, pp. 1335–1354, 1994.

[70] Fatemi, E., Engquist, B., and Osher, S.J., *Numerical Solution of the High Frequency Asymptotic Wave Equation for the Scalar Wave Equation*, J. Comp. Phys,. 120, pp. 145–155, 1995.

[71] H. Freeman, *On the Encoding of Arbitrary Geometric Configurations*, IEEE Trans. on Electronic Computers, EC-10, pp. 260–268, 1961.

[72] Gage, M., *Curve Shortening Makes Convex Curves Circular*, Inventiones Mathematica, 76, pp. 357, 1984.

[73] Gage, M., and Hamilton, R., *The Equation Shrinking Convex Planes Curves*, J. Diff. Geom, 23, pp. 69, 1986.

[74]   Ghoniem, A.F., Chorin, A.J., and Oppenheim, A.K., *Numerical Modeling of Turbulent Flow in a Combustion Tunnel*, Philos. Trans. Roy. Soc. Lond. A., 304, pp. 303–325, 1982.

[75]   Giga, Y., and Goto, S., *Motion of Hypersurfaces and Geometric Equations*, Journal of the Mathematical Society of Japan, 44, pp. 99, 1992.

[76]   Giga, Y., Goto, S., Ishii, H., *Global Existence of Weak Solutions for Interface Equations Coupled with Diffusion Equations*, SIAM J. Math. Anal., 23, N4, pp. 821–835, 1992.

[77]   Girao P.M., Kohn, R.V., *Convergence of a Crystalline Algorithm for the Heat Equation in One Dimension and for the Motion of a Graph by Weighted Curvature*, Num. Math., 67, 1, pp. 41–70. 1994.

[78]   Grayson, M., *The Heat Equation Shrinks Embedded Plane Curves to Round Points*, J. Diff. Geom., 26, pp. 285, 1987.

[79]   Grayson, M., *A Short Note on the Evolution of Surfaces Via Mean Curvatures*, J. Diff. Geom., 58, pp. 555, 1989.

[80]   Gonzalez, R. C., and Wintz, P., *Digital Image Processing (2nd Ed.)*, Addison-Wesley, Reading, MA, 1987.

[81]   Greengard, L., and Strain, J., *A Fast Algorithm for Evaluating Heat Potentials*, Comm. Pure Appl. Math., XLIII, pp. 949–963, 1990.

[82]   Gurtin, M.E., *On the Two-Phase Stefan Problem with Interfacial, Energy and Entropy*, Arch. Rat. Mech. Anal., 96, pp. 199–241, 1986.

[83]   Harten, A., Engquist, B., Osher, S., and Chakravarthy, S., *Uniformly High Order Accurate Essentially Non-oscillatory Schemes. III*, J. Comp. Phys., 71, 2, pp. 231–303, 1987.

[84]   Hayes, W.D., *The Vorticity Jump Across a Gasdynamic Discontinuity*, J. Fluid Mech., 2, pp. 595–600, 1959.

[85]   Helmsen, J.J., *A Comparison of Three-Dimensional Photolithography Development Methods,* Ph.D. Dissertation, EECS, University of California, Berkeley, CA, 1994.

[86]   Hirt, C.W., and Nicholls, B.D., *Volume of Fluid (VOF) Method for Dynamics of Free Boundaries*, J. Comp. Phys., 39, pp. 201–225, 1981.

[87]   Horn, B.K.P., and Brooks, Eds., Shape from Shading, MIT Press, Cambridge, MA, 1989.

[88]   Huisken, G., *Flow by Mean Curvature of Convex Surfaces into Spheres*, J. Diff. Geom., 20, pp. 237, 1984.

[89]   Huisken, G., *Asymptotic Behavior for Singularities of the Mean Curvature Flow*, J. Diff. Geom., 31, pp. 285–299, 1991.

[90]   Ilmanen, T., *Generalized Flow of Sets by Mean Curvature on a Manifold*, Indiana University Mathematics Journal, 41, 3, pp. 671–705, 1992.

[91]   Ilmanen, T., *Elliptic Regularization and Partial Regularity for Motion by Mean Curvature*, Memoirs of the American Mathematical Society, 108, 520, 1994.

[92]   Kass, M., Witkin, A., and Terzopoulos, D., *Snakes: Active Contour Models*, International Journal of Computer Vision, pp. 321–331, 1988.

[93]   Katardjiev, I.V., Carter, G., Nobes, M.J., *Precision Modeling of the Mask-Substrate Evolution During Ion Etching*, J. Vac. Science Technology, A 6, 4, pp. 2443–2450, 1988.

[94]   Kelly, F.X., and Ungar, L.H., *Steady and Oscillatory Cellular Morphologies in Rapid Solidification*, Phys. Rev. B, 34, pp. 1746–1753, 1986.

[95]   Kessler, D.A., and Levine, H., *Stability of Dendritic Crystals*, Phys. Rev. Lett., 57, pp. 3069–3072, 1986.

[96]   Kichenassamy, S., Kumar, A., Olver, P., Tannenbaum, A., and Yezzi, A., *Gradient Flows and Geometric Active Contours*, Proc. Fifth IEEE International Conference on Computer Vision, ICCV '95, pages 810–815, Cambridge, USA, June 1995.

[97]   Kimmel, R., *Curve Evolution on Surfaces*, Ph.D. Thesis, Dept. of Electrical Engineering, Technion, Israel, 1995.

[98]   Kimmel, R., and Bruckstein, A., *Shape from Shading via Level Sets*, Center for Intelligent Systems Report No. 9209, Technion-Israel Institute of Technology, June 1992.

[99]   Kimmel, R., and Bruckstein, A., *Shape Offsets via Level Sets*, Computer-Aided Design, 25, 3, pp. 154–161, 1993.

[100] Kimmel, R., and Sapiro, G., *Shortening Three-Dimensional Curves via Two-Dimensional Flows*, Compter. Math. Applic, 29, 3, pp. 49–62, 1995.

[101] Kimmel, R., Shaked, D., Kiryati, N., and Bruckstein, A.M., *Skeletonization via Distance Maps and Level Sets*, Computer Vision and Image Understanding (CVIU) 62, 4, pp. 382–391, 1995.

[102] Kimmel, R., Amir, A., and Bruckstein, A.M., *Finding Shortest Paths on Surfaces Using Level Sets Propagation*, IEEE Trans. Patt. Anal. Machine Intell., 17, 6, pp. 635–640, 1995.

[103] Kimmel, R., and Sethian, J.A., *Fast Marching Methods for Computing Distance Maps and Shortest Paths*, CPAM Report 669, Univ. of California, Berkeley, submitted for publication, IEEE Trans. Patt. Anal. Machine Intell., February 1996.

[104] Kimmel, R., and Sethian, J.A., *Fast Marching Methods for Robotic Navigation with Constraints*, Center for Pure and Applied Mathematics Report, Univ. of California, Berkeley, May 1996, submitted for publication.

[105] Knupp, P.M., and Steinberg, S., *The Fundamentals of Grid Generation*, preprint 1993.

[106] Kuiken, H.K., *Viscous Sintering: the Surface-tension-driven Flow of a Liquid Form under the Influence of Curvature Gradients at its Surface* J. Fluid Mech., 214, pp. 503–515, 1990.

[107] Lafaurie, B., Nardone, C., Scardovelli, R., Zaleski, S., and Zanetti, G., *Modelling Merging and Fragmentation in Multiphase Flows with SURFER*, J. Comp. Phys, 113, 1, pp. 134–47, 1994.

[108] Langer, J.S., *Instabilities and Pattern Formation in Crystal Growth*, Rev. Mod. Phys., 52, pp. 1–28, 1980.

[109] Lax, P.D., *Hyperbolic Systems of Conservation Laws and the Mathematical Theory of Shock Waves*, SIAM Reg. Conf. Series, Lectures in Applied Math, 11, pp. 1–47, 1970.

[110] Lee, D.T., *Medial Axis Transformation of a Planar Shape*, IEEE Trans. Patt. Anal. Machine Intell., 4, pp. 363–369, 1982.

[111] Leon, F.A., Tazawa, S., Saito, K., Yoshi, A., and Scharfetter, D.L., *Numerical Algorithms for Precise Calculation of Surface Movement in 3-D Topography Simulation*, 1993 International Workshop on VLSI Process and Device Modeling: VPAD.

[112] LeVeque, R.J., *Numerical Methods for Conservation Laws*, Birkhauser, Basel, 1992.

[113] LeVeque, R.J., and Li, Z., *The Immersed Interface Method for Elliptic*

Equations with Discontinuous Coefficients and Singular Sources, SIAM J. Num. Anal., 13, pp. 1019–1044, 1994.

[114]   Leymarie, F., and Levine, M.D., *Simulating the Grassfire Transform using an Active Contour Model*, IEEE Trans. Patt. Anal. Machine Intell., 14, 1, pp. 56–75, 1992.

[115]   Li, X.L., *Study of Three-Dimensional Rayleigh-Taylor Instability in Compressible Fluids Through Level Set Method and Parallel Computation*, Phys. Fluids A, 5, 1, pp. 1904–1913, 1993.

[116]   Lions, P.L., *Generalized Solution of Hamilton–Jacobi Equations*, Pittman, London, 1982.

[117]   Lorenson, W.E., and Cline, H.E., *Marching Cubes: A High Resolution 3D Surface Construction Algorithm*, Computer Graphics, 21, 4, 1987.

[118]   Majda, A., and Sethian, J.A., *Derivation and Numerical Solution of the Equations of Low Mach Number Combustion*, Combustion Science and Technology, 42, pp. 185–205, 1984.

[119]   Malladi, R., and Sethian, J.A., *A Unified Approach for Shape Segmentation, Representation, and Recognition*, Report LBL-36069, Lawrence Berkeley Laboratory, University of California, Berkeley, CA, August 1994.

[120]   Malladi, R., Sethian, J.A., and Vemuri, B.C., *Evolutionary Fronts for Topology-independent Shape Modeling and Recovery*, in Proceedings of Third European Conference on Computer Vision, Stockholm, Sweden, Lecture Notes in Computer Science, 800, pp. 3–13, 1994.

[121]   Malladi, R., Sethian, J.A., and Vemuri, B.C., *Shape Modeling with Front Propagation: A Level Set Approach*, IEEE Trans. on Pattern Analysis and Machine Intelligence, 17, 2, pp. 158–175, 1995.

[122]   Malladi, R., and Sethian, J.A., *Image Processing via Level Set Curvature Flow*, Proc. Natl. Acad. of Sci., 92, 15, pp. 7046–7050, 1995.

[123]   Malladi, R., and Sethian, J.A., *Level Set Methods for Curvature Flow, Image Enhancement, and Shape Recovery in Medical Images*, to appear, Proc. of Conf. on Visualization and Mathematics, June, 1995, Berlin, Germany, Springer-Verlag, Heidelberg, Germany, in press.

[124]   Malladi, R., and Sethian, J.A., *Image Processing: Flows under Min/Max Curvature and Mean Curvature*, Graphical Models and Image Processing, 58,2, pp. 127–141, 1996.

[125]   Malladi, R., and Sethian, J.A., *A Unified Approach to Noise Removal, Image Enhancement, and Shape Recovery*, accepted for publication, Jan. 1996, IEEE Trans. on Image Processing, in press.

[126]   Malladi, R., Sethian, J.A., and Vemuri, B.C., *A Fast Level Set based Algorithm for Topology-Independent Shape Modeling* J. Math. Imaging and Vision, 6, 2/3, pp. 269–290, 1996.

[127]   Malladi, R., and Sethian, J.A., *An $O(N \log N)$ Algorithm for Shape Modeling*, accepted, to appear, Proc. Nat. Acad. Sci., 1996.

[128]   Markstein, G.H., *Nonsteady Flame Propagation*, Pergamon Press, 1964.

[129]   Marr, D., and Hildreth, E., *A Theory of Edge Detection*, Proc. of Royal Soc. (London), B207, pp. 187–217, 1980.

[130]   Mayya, N., and Rajan, V.T., "Voronoi Diagrams of Polygons: A Framework for Shape Representation," IBM Research Report, RC 19282, Nov. 1993 (to appear in the *Journal of Mathematical Imaging and Vision*).

[131]   McVittie, J.P., Rey, J.C., Cheng, L.Y., and IslamRaja, M.M, *LPCVD*

Profile Simulation Using a Re-emission Model, IEEE International Electron Devices Meeting 1990. Technical Digest, New York, NY, pp. 917–20, 1990.

[132] McVittie, J.P., Rey, J.C., Bariya, A.J., et al., *SPEEDIE: A Profile Simulator for Etching and Deposition*, Proceedings of the SPIE - The International Society for Optical Engineering, 1392, pp. 126–38, 1991.

[133] Meiron, D.I., *Boundary Integral Formulation Of The Two-Dimensional, Symmetric Model Of Dendritic Growth*, Physica D, 23, pp. 329–339, 1986.

[134] Merriman, B., Bence, J., and Osher, S.J., *Motion of Multiple Junctions: A Level Set Approach*, Jour. Comp. Phys., 112, 2, pp. 334–363, 1994.

[135] Meyer, G. H., *Multidimensional Stefan Problems*, SIAM J. Num. Anal., 10, pp. 552–538, 1973.

[136] Milne, B. *Adaptive Level Set Methods Interfaces*, PhD. Thesis, Dept. of Mathematics, University of California, Berkeley, CA., 1995.

[137] Mori, S., Suen, C.Y., and Yamamoto, K., *Historical review of OCR research and development*, Proc. of the IEEE, 80, 7, pp. 1029–1057, 1992.

[138] Mulder, W., Osher, S.J., Sethian, J.A., *Computing Interface Motion in Compressible Gas Dynamics*, Jour. Comp. Phys., 100, pp. 209–228, 1992.

[139] Mullins, W.W., and Sekerka, R.F., *Morphological Stability of a Particle Growing by Diffusion or Heat Flow*, Jour. Appl. Phys., 34, pp.323–329, 1963

[140] Noh, W., and Woodward, P., *A Simple Line Interface Calculation*. Proceedings, Fifth International Conference on Fluid Dynamics, Eds. A.I. vn de Vooran and P.J. Zandberger, Springer-Verlag, 1976.

[141] Ogniewicz, R., and Ilg, M., *Voronoi Skeletons: Theory and Application*, Proc. of Conf. on Comp. Vis. and Patt. Recog., Champaign, IL, pp. 63–69, 1992.

[142] Oliker, V., *Evolution of Non-parametric Surfaces with Speed Depending on Curvature: I, The Gauss Curvature Case*, Indiana Univ. Math. Journal, 40, 1, pp. 237–258, 1991.

[143] Osher, S., and Rudin, L.I., *Feature-oriented Image Enhancement Using Shock Filters*, SIAM J. Num. Anal., 27, pp. 919–940, 1990.

[144] Osher, S., and Sethian, J.A., *Fronts Propagating with Curvature-Dependent Speed: Algorithms Based on Hamilton–Jacobi Formulation*, Journal of Computational Physics, 79, pp. 12–49, 1988.

[145] Osher, S., and Shu, C., *High-Order Nonoscillatory Schemes for Hamilton–Jacobi Equations*, Jour. Comp. Phys., 28, pp. 907–922, 1991.

[146] Pavlidis, T., *Polygonal Approximations by Newton's Method*, IEEE Trans. on Computers, C-26, 8, pp. 800–807, 1977.

[147] Pearson, E., and Fu, K.S., *Shape Discrimination Using Fourier Descriptors*, IEEE Trans. System, Man, and Cyber., SMC-7, 3, pp. 170–179, 1977.

[148] Perona, P., and Malik, J., *Scale-space and Edge Detection Using Anisotropic Diffusion*, IEEE Trans. Pattern Analysis and Machine Intelligence, 12, 7, pp. 629–639, 1990.

[149] Pimienta, P.J.P., Garboczi, E. J., and Carter, W. C., *Cellular Automaton Algorithm for Surface Mass Transport due to Curvature Gradients: Simulations of Sintering* Comp. Materials Science, 1, pp.

63–77, 1992.

[150] Pindera, M.Z., and Talbot, L., *Flame-Induced Vorticity: The Effects of Stretch*, Twenty-First Symposium (Int'l) on Combustion, The Combustion Institute, Pittsburgh, PA, pp. 1357–1366, 1986.

[151] Press, W.H., Teukolsky, S.A., Vetterling, W.T., and Flannery, B.P., *Numerical Recipes*, Cambridge University Press, New York, 1988.

[152] Puckett, E.G., *A Volume-of-Fluid Interface Tracking Algorithm with Applications to Computing Shock Wave Refraction*, Proceedings of the 4th International Symposium on Computational Computational Fluid Dynamics, Davis, California, 1991.

[153] Rey, J.C., Lie-Yea Cheng, McVittie, J.P., and Saraswat, K.C., *Monte Carlo Low Pressure Deposition Profile Simulations*, Journal of Vacuum Science and Technology A (Vacuum, Surfaces, and Films), May-June 1991, 9, 3, 1, pp. 1083–1087.

[154] Rhee, C., Talbot, L., and Sethian, J.A., *Dynamical Study of a Premixed V flame*, Jour. Fluid Mech., 300, pp. 87–115, 1995.

[155] Rider, W.J., and Kothe, D.B., *Stretching and Tearing Interface Tracking Methods*, 12th AIAA CFD Conference, AIAA-95-1717, San Diego, CA., June 20, 1995

[156] Rouy, E. and Tourin, A., *A Viscosity Solutions Approach to Shape-From-Shading*, SIAM J. Num. Anal, 29, 3, pp. 867–884, 1992.

[157] Rudin, L., Osher, S., and Fatemi, E., *Nonlinear Total Variation-Based Noise Removal Algorithms*, Modelisations Matematiques pour le traitement d'images, INRIA, pp. 149–179, 1992.

[158] W. B. Ruskai et al., *Wavelets and their Applications*, Jones and Barlett Publishers, Boston, MA 1992.

[159] Ruuth, S.J., *An algorithm for Generating Motion by Mean Curvature* preprint, Dept. of Mathematics, Univ. of British Columbia, Vancouver, CA, 1996.

[160] Sapiro, G., and Tannenbaum, A., *Affine Invariant Scale-Space*, Int. Jour. Comp. Vision, 11, 1, pp. 25–44, 1993.

[161] Sapiro, G., and Tannenbaum, A., *Image Smoothing Based on Affine Invariant Flow*, Proc. of the Conference on Information Sciences and Systems, Johns Hopkins University, March 1993.

[162] Sapiro, G., and Tannenbaum, A., *Area and Length Preserving Geometric Invariant Scale-spaces*, Proc. of Third European Conference on Computer Vision, Stockholm, Sweden, Lecture Notes on Computer Science, 801, pp. 449–458, 1994.

[163] Scheckler, E.W., Ph.D. Dissertation, EECS, University of California, Berkeley, CA, 1991.

[164] Scheckler, E.W., Toh, K.K.H., Hoffstetter, D.M., and Neureuther, A.R., *3D Lithography, Etching and Deposition Simulation*, Symposium on VLSI Technology, Oiso, Japan, pp. 97–98, 1991.

[165] Schmidt, Alfred, *Computation of Three-dimensional Dendrites with Finite Elements*, to appear, J. Comp. Phys., 1995.

[166] Sedgewick, R., *Algorithms*, Addison-Wesley, Reading, MA, 1988.

[167] Sethian, J.A., *An Analysis of Flame Propagation*, Ph.D. Dissertation, Dept. of Mathematics, University of California, Berkeley, CA, 1982.

[168] Sethian, J.A., *The Wrinkling of a Flame Due to Viscosity*, Fire Dynamics and Heat Transfer, Eds. J.G. Quintiere, R.A. Alpert and R.A. Altenkirch, HTD, ASME, New York, NY, 25, pp. 29–32, 1983.

[169]   Sethian, J.A., *Turbulent Combustion in Open and Closed Vessels*, J. Comp. Phys., 54, pp. 425–456, 1984.

[170]   Sethian, J.A., *Curvature and the Evolution of Fronts*, Comm. in Math. Phys., 101, pp. 487–499, 1985.

[171]   Sethian, J.A., *Numerical Methods for Propagating Fronts*, in Variational Methods for Free Surface Interfaces, Eds. P. Concus and R. Finn, Springer-Verlag, NY, 1987.

[172]   Sethian, J.A., *Parallel Level Set Methods for Propagating Interfaces on the Connection Machine*, Unpublished manuscript, 1989.

[173]   Sethian, J.A., *Numerical Algorithms for Propagating Interfaces: Hamilton–Jacobi Equations and Conservation Laws*, Journal of Differential Geometry, 31, pp. 131–161, 1990.

[174]   Sethian, J.A., *A Brief Overview of Vortex Methods*, in Vortex Methods and Vortex Motion, Eds. K. Gustafson and J.A. Sethian, SIAM Publications, Philadelphia, PA, 1991.

[175]   Sethian, J.A., *Curvature Flow and Entropy Conditions Applied to Grid Generation*, J. Comp. Phys., 115, pp. 440–454, 1994.

[176]   Sethian, J.A., *Algorithms for Tracking Interfaces in CFD and Material Science*, Annual Review of Computational Fluid Mechanics, 1995.

[177]   Sethian, J.A., *Level Set Techniques for Tracking Interfaces: Fast Algorithms, Multiple Regions, Grid Generation and Shape/Character Recognition*, Proceedings of the International Conference on Curvature Flows and Related Topics, Trento, Italy, 1994, Eds. A. Damlamian, J. Spruck, and A. Visintin, Gakuto Intern. Series, Tokyo, Japan, 5, pp. 215–231, 1995.

[178]   Sethian, J.A., *A Fast Marching Level Set Method for Monotonically Advancing Fronts*, Proc. Nat. Acad. Sci., 93, 4, pp.1591–1595, 1996.

[179]   Sethian, J.A., *Fast Marching Level Set Methods for Three-Dimensional Photolithography Development*, Proceedings, SPIE 1996 International Symposium on Microlithography, Santa Clara, California, March, 1996.

[180]   Sethian, J.A., *A Review of the Theory, Algorithms, and Applications of Level Set Methods for Propagating Interfaces*, Acta Numerica, Cambridge University Press, 1996.

[181]   Sethian, J.A., *Fast Marching Methods for Computing Seismic Travel Times*, in progress.

[182]   Sethian, J.A. and Strain, J.D., *Crystal Growth and Dendritic Solidification* J. Comp. Phys., 98, pp. 231–253, 1992.

[183]   Sherwin, W., Karniadakis, G.E., and Orszag, S.A,. *Numerical Simulation of the Ion Etching Process*, J. Comp. Phys., 110, 2, pp. 373–398, 1994.

[184]   Singh, V.K., Shaqfeh, S.G., and McVittie, J.P., *Simulation of Profile Evolution in Silicon Reactive Ion Etching with Re-emission and Surface Diffusion*, J. Vac. Sci. Tech., B. 10, 3, pp. 1091–1104, 1993.

[185]   Smith, J. B., *Shape Instabilities and Pattern Formation in Solidification: A New Method for Numerical Solution of the Moving Boundary Problem*, Jour. Comp. Phys., 39, pp. 112–127, 1981.

[186]   Sod, G.A., *Numerical Methods in Fluid Dynamics*, Cambridge University Press, 1985.

[187]   Souganidis, P.E., *Approximation Schemes for Viscosity Solutions of Hamilton–Jacobi Equations*, J. Diff. Eqns., 59, pp. 1–43, 1985.

[188]   Strain, J., *Linear Stability of Planar Solidification Fronts*, Physica D, 30, pp. 297–320, 1988

[189]   Strain, J., *A Boundary Integral Approach to Unstable Solidification*, J. Comp. Phys., 85, pp. 342–389, 1989.

[190]   Strain, J., *Velocity Effects in Unstable Solidification.* SIAM Jour. Appl. Math., 50, pp. 1–15, 1990.

[191]   Suen, C.Y., Nadal, C., Legault, R., Mai, T.A., and Lam, L., *Computer Recognition of Unconstrained Handwritten Numerals*, Proc. of the IEEE, 80, 7, pp. 1162–1180, 1992.

[192]   Sullivan, J. M., Lynch, D. R., and O'Neill, K. O, *Finite Element Simulation of Planar Instabilities during Solidification of an Undercooled Melt*, Jour. Comp. Phys., 69, pp. 81–111, 1987.

[193]   Sussman, M., Smereka, P. and Osher, S.J., *A Level Set Method for Computing Solutions to Incompressible Two-Phase Flow*, J. Comp. Phys. 114, pp. 146–159, 1994.

[194]   Taylor, J.E., Cahn, J.W., Handwerker, C.A., *Geometric models of crystal growth.*, Acta Metallurgica et Materialia, 40, 7, pp. 1443–1474, 1992.

[195]   Terzopoulos, D., *Regularization of Inverse Visual Problems Involving Discontinuities*, IEEE Trans. on Patt. Anal. and Mach. Intell., 8, 2, pp. 413–424, 1986.

[196]   Terzopoulos, D., Witkin, A., and Kass, M., *Constraints on Deformable Models: Recovering 3D Shape and Nonrigid Motion*, Artificial Intelligence, 36, pp. 91–123, 1988.

[197]   Thompson, J., Warsi, Z.U.A., and Mastin, C.W., *Numerical Grid Generation, Foundations and Applications*, North-Holland, Amsterdam, 1985.

[198]   Technology Modeling Associates, Three-Dimensional Photolithography Simulation with Depict 4.0", Technology Modeling Associates, Internal Documentation, January 1996.

[199]   Toh, K.K.H., Ph.D. Dissertation, EECS, University of California, Berkeley, CA, 1990.

[200]   Toh, K.K.H., and Neureuther, A.R., *Three-Dimensional Simulation of Optical Lithography*, Proceedings SPIE, Optical/Laser Microlithography IV, 1463, pp. 356–367, 1991.

[201]   Vemuri, B.C., and Malladi, R., *Constructing Intrinsic Parameters with Active Models for Invariant Surface Reconstruction*, IEEE Trans. on Patt. Anal. and Mach. Intell., 15, 7, pp. 668–681, 1993.

[202]   Van de Vorst, G.A.L., *Modeling and Numerical Simulation of Viscous Sintering*, PhD. Thesis, Eindhoven University of Technology, Febodruk-Enschede, The Netherlands, 1994.

[203]   van Trier, J., and Symes, W.W., *Upwind Finite-difference Calculations of Traveltimes*, Geophysics, 56, 6, pp. 812–821, 1991.

[204]   Vidale, J., *Finite-Difference Calculation of Travel Times*, Bull. of Seism. Soc. of Amer., 78, 6, pp. 2062–2076, 1988.

[205]   Young, M.S., Lee, D., Lee., R., and Neureuther, A.R., *Extension of the Hopkins Theory of Partially Coherent Imaging to Include Thin-Film Interference Effects* SPIE Optical/Laser Microlithography VI, 1927, pp. 452–463, 1993.

[206]   Zhu, J., and Ronney, P.D., *Simulation of Front Propagation at Large Non-dimensional Flow Disturbance Intensities*, Comb. Sci. Tech., 100, pp.

183–201, 1995.

[207]   Zhu, J., and Sethian, J.A., *Projection Methods Coupled to Level Set Interface Techniques*, J. Comp. Phys., 102, pp. 128–138, 1992.

[208]   Zhu, J., and Sethian, J.A., *Tracking Two-Phase Flow Problems in Two and Three Dimensions*, in progress, 1996.

Index

Adaptive mesh refinement, 63
Artificial viscosity, 46

Boolean operations on shapes, 164

Cell methods, 29
Characteristics, 37, 41
Chopp surfaces, 102
Combustion, 140
Computer vision, 153
  shape recognition, 157
Conservation form, 47
Convex
  functions, 48, 54
  schemes, 55
Crystal growth, 145
Curvature, 5
  equation of motion, 6, 11
  level set calculation of, 17, 58
  motion under, 99
  singularity in, 8
  smoothing effects of, 10

De-noising, 119
Delta function, 140, 143, 151
Dendritic solidification, 145
Deposition, 185, 188
Discontinuous speed functions, 196
Domain of dependence, 37, 41
Domain of influence, 37

Eikonal equation, 21, 169, 171
  fast marching methods for, 88
Enquist–Osher, 49
Entropy
  entropy solution, 43
  entropy-satisfying schemes, 21
Entropy condition, 9, 11
Etching, 185, 188
Eulerian formulation, 15, 17, 29

Extension velocities, 79, 140

Fast level set methods, 62
  adaptive mesh refinement, 63
  narrow band methods, 65
  parallel algorithms, 62
Fast marching methods, 88, 169, 173
  algorithms, 88
  convergence proof, 90
  cost, 92
  for general static H-J eqns., 93
  heap sort technique, 91
Finite difference approximations, 38
Flame stability, 140
Flux function, 45
  numerical flux function, 47, 52

Gaussian curvature, 58
Gaussian filter, 119, 154
Geodesics on surfaces, 176
Godunov, 48
Grayson's theorem, 100, 101
Grid generation, 109

Hamilton–Jacobi equation, 20, 84
  eikonal equation, 21, 87
  fast marching methods for, 93
  static, 87, 178
Hamiltonian, 52, 54, 84, 194
Huyghen's principle, 9, 34
Hyperbolic conservation law, 13, 36, 83

Image, 118
Image processing, 118
  de-noising, 119
  Alvarez-Morel-Lions scheme, 120
  grey scale, textured, color images, 124
  min/max flow, 123
  stopping criteria, 120, 124
Immersed interface method, 203

217